SEVERED

SEVERED

THE TRUE STORY OF THE BLACK DAHLIA MURDER

John Gilmore

LOS ANGELES

Amok Books edition, January 1999
Second Printing

Cover Design: Tom Dolan

Bibliographic Information for Library of Congress Cataloging-in-Publication Data

Gilmore, John, 1935-
Severed : the true story of the Black Dahlia murder / John Gilmore
Los Angeles: Amok Books, 1998
p. cm.
Short, Elizabeth, 1924-1947.
Murder—California—Los Angeles—Case Studies
Murder—California—Los Angeles—Investigation—Case Studies

ISBN 1-878923-10-2
LC CARD 94-75755

Amok Books are available to bookstores through our primary distributor: The Subterranean Company, Box 168 265 South 5th Street, Monroe, Oregon 97456. Phone: (800) 274-7826. FAX: (503) 847-6018.

UK Distributors: Turnaround Distribution, Unit 3 Olympia Trading Estate, Coburg Road, Wood Green, London N22 6TZ. Phone: 0181 829 3000. FAX: 0181 881 5088.

For personal orders and to request a complete Amok Books catalog, please write to Amok Books, 1764 N. Vermont Avenue, Los Angeles, California 90027. Phone: (213) 663-8618. FAX: (213) 666-8105.

The author expresses his indebtedness to the many members of law enforcement, to newspaper reporters and editors for their assistance and courageous candidness; and to the forensic specialists that have unselfishly aided over the years in the completion of this book. Most notably, my thanks to Capt. Hugh Brown, LAPD Homicide, Detectives Danny Galindo, Finis Brown, William Herrmann, Floyd Phillips, John St. John, Kirk Mellecker, Mervin Enquist, Sam Flowers; and special thanks to Los Angeles County Sheriff's Detective, Joel Lesnick.

To those who have survived to see this book published, and have requested their names be changed—the author has obliged accordingly. Exclusive, childhood materials of Mary Pacios have been used with her permission. My sincere thanks also go to my friend Tony Mostrom, and to Russell Miller for valuable input, to Natalie Nichols for her additional editing of the afterword, to Karen Davis for her thorough proofreading, to Mary Kay Stam for her map design, and to the staffs of UCLA Research Library Special Collections Department, the Delmar Watson Los Angeles Historical Archives, and the Museum of Death, San Diego, California for their assistance with the photographs.

John Gilmore
Los Angeles, 1998

Also by John Gilmore

The Tucson Murders

Cold-Blooded
The Saga of Charles Schmid, "The Pied Piper of Tucson"

The Garbage People
The Trip to Helter Skelter and Beyond with Charlie Manson and the Family

Live Fast, Die Young
Remembering the Short Life of James Dean

Laid Bare
A Memoir of Wrecked Lives and the Hollywood Death Trip

Forthcoming:

Fetish Blonde

You Can't Sleep in a Car in Hollywood

This book is for my father, Robert T. Gilmore, Jr., with love and a heartfelt salute to his long and outstanding career as a policeman with the Los Angeles Police Department: 1942-1973.

PUBLISHER'S PREFACE TO THE REVISED EDITION

"Crime is a fact of the human species, a fact of that species alone, but it is above all the secret aspect, impenetrable and hidden. Crime hides, and by far the most terrifying things are those which elude us."

—Georges Bataille, *The Trial of Gilles de Rais*

The grisly 1947 murder of aspiring starlet and nightclub habitué Elizabeth Short, known even before her death as the "Black Dahlia," has over the decades transmogrified from L.A.'s "crime of the century" into an almost mythical symbol of unfathomable *Hollywood Babylon*/film noir glamour-cum-sordidness. It is somehow fitting that author John Gilmore should be the one to unravel the multilayered mystery of this archetypal Los Angeles slaying as it begins to take its place in the collective memory, somewhere next to Bluebeard and Jack the Ripper, a cautionary tale about the pretty girl who came to Hollywood to be a movie star and wound up in a dirt lot, hacked in two.

Gilmore's father was an LAPD officer at the time of the Dahlia's murder and was involved in the citywide dragnet that immediately followed the discovery of her corpse. His mother was once a would-be starlet under contract with MGM Studios; and Gilmore himself was a rebel-type young actor in the '50s, carousing Screenland with the likes of James Dean, Dennis Hopper, and Vampira. In the '60s and early '70s, Gilmore wrote two true-crime classics: *The Tucson Murders*, about the Speedway Pied Piper Charles Schmid, and one of the finest books ever about the Manson Family, *The Garbage People*.

In *Severed*'s hard-boiled yet haunting prose, Gilmore tells several previously unrevealed stories at once, each filled with its own bizarre elements through which the book transcends the true-crime genre and becomes literature. One is the tale of victim Elizabeth Short, small-town beauty queen with big hopes who seemed to float through her tragically futile life as an alluring yet doom-laden enigma. *Severed* also unfolds the tangled inside story of the police investigation and the remorseless Hearst-stoked press hoopla that paralleled it. Furthermore, Gilmore reveals the twisted psychology and down-and-out life story of the murder suspect—as well as the startling circumstances and gruesome details of the suspect's "indirect confession" wherein he fingers his female-impersonator pal as the purported killer.

The Black Dahlia murder—unlike such earlier headline-grabbing cases as the St. Valentine's Day Massacre and the Lindbergh kidnapping—was the first case to command the attention of post-war America with its stark carnality. One can see the origins of the blood-fueled media feeding-frenzy rituals surrounding subsequent high-profile victims, such as Sharon Tate and Nicole Brown Simpson, in the hypocritical newspaper flogging of the deceased Elizabeth Short.

Growing up in WWII L.A., the impressionable young Gilmore's mind was strongly shaped by emanations from the subterranean American pop-cultural matrix of *Black Mask*, pulp, tabloid, *True Detective*, pin-up, and B-movie, which has come to be known by the French appellation *noir*. He has developed a complex personal relationship with his legendary subject, the seductive cipher we know as the Black Dahlia. "She was my light in this shadow world," he reflects. As Gilmore recounts in his memoirs, *Laid Bare*, she would continue to haunt him for the duration of his work as a screenwriter, as well as through his then-unfashionable fascination with the vanished Hollywood of his youth and its denizens, like actors Franchot Tone, Barbara Payton, and Tom Neal, who were linked in some personal way to the fatal trajectory of the ill-fated beauty.

Having begun his painstaking investigations into the case more than thirty-five years ago, John Gilmore—handsome ex-actor, back then a pulp novelist and aspiring screenwriter—now appears to have been the only one with enough grit and determination to doggedly run down every lead through the bureaucratic miasma, like real detective work entails. Meanwhile, LAPD detectives were holding back evidence and grandstanding to the press to promote their upcoming movie deals.

"You catch them with their pants down," Gilmore says. "I've sought some people out almost as they were breathing their last, choking on blood, in order to get corroboration on something or other. And then what have I got? Words—a jumble of ideas and tapes and transcripts in my head." In the kaleidoscopic blurring of Hollywood fact, fiction, and fantasy so prevalent in the lives of both Elizabeth Short and John Gilmore, it was TV cop Jack Webb of *Dragnet* fame who became the deadpan coach egging Gilmore on in his unflagging pursuit of "the facts."

Severed is the first non-fiction book to offer a documented solution to the Black Dahlia case as endorsed by law enforcement and forensic science experts. In the just over 50 years since the murder, the terms *serial killer* and *behavioral profiling* have moved from FBI jargon to essential archetypes of the American cultural landscape, crossing the nebulous bounds of newspaper, TV, book, and blockbuster movie. The psychosexual nexus of violence and control that impels the serial killer was psychological terra incognita, barely comprehended even by law enforcement, at the midpoint of the twentieth century. Now, through the once-controversial efforts of FBI behavioral sciences unit experts like Robert Ressler and John Douglas, Elizabeth Short's infamous murder can be seen in context as the handiwork of a sexual psychopath who stalked and struck down at least one young woman, and possibly multiple others in various states, with a very similar modus operandi.

John Gilmore is the first writer to bring to light the hushed-up murder of wild young "Sunset Strip socialite" Georgette Bauerdorf, found defiled and slaughtered in her Hollywood bathtub only months before the murder of Elizabeth Short. Bauerdorf's car, stolen by her fugitive murderer, was recovered afterward, a short distance away from the building in which Short is believed to have been murdered and not far from where her mutilated corpse was found. Using the now-accepted methodology of behavioral profiling, Gilmore is able to show how the two murders bear the same psychopathic "signature" of a serial killer—brutal bathtub slayings of beautiful, flirtatious USO hostesses, who both moved in the same Hollywood nightlife démi-monde as the suspect.

For the Amok Books edition of *Severed*, Gilmore has penned an afterword that recounts for the first time his personal involvement with the alleged murderer. "I soon found that this elusive bum was watching me—the watcher being watched. For over 13 years, I'd be intermittently contacted by this limping stranger, a man who'd hobble up and down the more soused he'd get, an almost nameless character who possessed knowledge of a deed so overwhelmingly notorious, and yet no one knew but him. He wanted to tell someone, he said, 'because death was breathing on his neck.' He wanted to tell someone who would understand—who could appreciate," Gilmore recalls.

Now that the reader can put a face to Elizabeth Short's killer through Gilmore's relentless spade work, the spectral luster of this most spectacular "unsolved" murder in American crime history seems not diminished but enhanced. Ultimately, John Gilmore boils down its undying allure to this haiku-like equation: "The pale white body severed in two and left for the world to view, and her name: Black Dahlia."

Stuart Swezey
Amok Books

January 15, 1947

1

Smudge pots burned for the first night that winter to keep the frost from killing the citrus. The cold had settled in from a cloudless sky that by dawn shone like dull gray metal that revealed no shadows.

Shortly after six o'clock that morning, a boy walked his bicycle through the weeds of a stretch of vacant lots south of Hollywood. His trouser cuffs grew wet from the cold dew as he crossed the empty field. He'd later tell the police that crossing through the lots was his usual shortcut to a paper route along Crenshaw Boulevard. The graded land along Norton Avenue between 39th Street and Coliseum, bordered on the west by Crenshaw, was called the Leimert Park section of Los Angeles. Sidewalks, driveways, and fire hydrants were there, but the war had stopped development and the lots were overgrown with weeds.

The boy slowed down to glance back at the sound of a car, an older black sedan, possibly a Ford. The early morning light reflected on the windshield, and he couldn't see anyone behind the wheel. But he would remember mud spattered on one front fender and dents along the passenger side. Cars heading north and south along Crenshaw still had their headlights on, but the one creeping onto the driveway of the vacant lot had the lights turned off. It stopped partly against the curb and sat idling, the exhaust smoke rising in the air.

It was not unusual for couples to park on those streets after dark, but rarely did anyone stop there during the daylight. The boy had watched some men from the fire department working on one of the hydrants the week before, but he couldn't remember having seen anyone else stop there.

Almost late for his paper route, the boy gave no further thought to that lone car on Norton. But soon he would find out that someone—whoever had been in that car—had left something so terrible in the vacant lot that for the rest of his life the boy would remember that windshield. He would try to picture a face behind the glass, but he never could see one.

It wasn't until after ten o'clock that morning, when the dew was evaporating, that someone noticed what had been placed a few feet from where the boy had seen the car come to a stop.

Betty Bersinger, an attractive young housewife, was walking south on Norton pushing her three-year-old daughter in a baby stroller. She was heading to a shoe repair shop two blocks south of 39th. Suddenly she stopped and looked at something white just ahead, close to the edge of the sidewalk.

It looked like somebody was lying on the ground. She took a few more steps and then stopped again, puzzled by the waxy whiteness of the form—a kind of reflection like white paper or cardboard with the light shining on it. She turned the stroller around, protecting the child from something she instinctively felt was awful. It had to be a dummy, she thought—the undressed bottom half of a store window mannequin. It must have fallen out of a truck and broken apart at the middle, and someone picked it up out of the street and put it near the sidewalk. There were legs and a section of hip that seemed disconnected from the dummy's waist, like a mannequin in a department store window when displays were changed and the clothing was removed. The top torso was close to the bottom section, both facing up.

The young woman noticed something like dark red lines on the surface of the form, then a sort of red bubble on one side of the chest. It was part of a breast, and there was a breast on the other side. The arms were raised up above the head, with the face turned toward the street. She wouldn't remember for sure if the eyes were open or closed. She would recall that possibly the eyes had been open, and that the face was a waxy white. Only a moment passed as she stood there with the little girl. The buzzing of flies filled the air, swarming noisily over the form in the weeds.

Quickly she pushed the baby stroller to the nearest house, another long block south. She rapped on the door, told the woman who answered that there was someone lying in the weeds up the street and she had to call the police. "It has to be attended to!" she said. She used the neighbor's telephone and told the policeman on the complaint board that the person on the ground wasn't wearing any clothes. She said, "There are flies all around it and someone better do something—" She hung up without giving her name.

Within minutes a radio call was dispatched from University Station as a code 390, "man down" at 39th and Norton. Officers Will Fitzgerald and Frank Perkins, heading west along Exposition Boulevard, responded to the call and turned immediately onto Coliseum. They drove west for eight blocks, then south on Norton.

Halfway down the block they observed a tall, thin boy standing near a fire hydrant, waving his arm at the approaching patrol car. When the policemen pulled to the curb, the boy pointed into the weeds as he walked toward the car.

"He was in his mid-teens," recalls Frank Perkins, "and was sort of shocked-looking or stunned in appearance."

The two policemen got out of the car, putting on their uniform caps. Fitzgerald asked the boy if he had made a call about a drunk or someone sleeping in the lot.

"That's a dead woman," the boy said. "Looks like it to me. . . ."

"Jeezus!" Perkins said, and Fitzgerald turned to his partner at the edge of the sidewalk. "Someone's cut this girl right in half!" Fitzgerald stooped down, staring at the body. "Get on the radio,"

Perkins told him, "and put straight through to the watch commander. Get them over here fast."

For a moment Fitzgerald seemed to sway a little, then he quickly climbed back into the car and grabbed the microphone wand from the dash cradle. He reported "a dead body at the 390 location." It appeared to be a homicide, he said, and requested a direct line to Lieutenant Paul Freestone, the watch commander.

Perkins asked the teenager how long he'd been there. The boy replied he had just crossed the street and saw the dead woman, then noticed the police car heading toward him. It had all taken no more than a few minutes. Perkins wanted to know if he'd seen anyone else—any cars or pedestrians—anyone in the vacant lots or in the area. The boy said he hadn't seen anyone. He'd been alone out there.

"The kid looked like he was going into shock," Perkins recalls. He took the boy's name and address and told him to wait across the street until the detectives arrived. The boy said some friends were waiting for him, but Perkins told him not to worry about that. The boy nodded, relieved to get away from the corpse. But even as he walked away, he kept staring back.

It was difficult not to look at it, Perkins thought, the way it lay right on the edge of the sidewalk in plain view from anywhere on the street. Anyone could see it, even from across the street where the boy had sat down on the curb.

Without disturbing the weeds or the immediate area, Perkins observed the dead girl's slashed face and breasts, and made notes on the knife marks to the lower torso. Because there was very little pubic hair, he believed she couldn't have been much older than the teenage boy who had been standing there. He thought, too, that what hair she had in the crotch area might have been cut off because a lot of the lines appeared to be marks made by a knife. The foot of her left leg was inches from the sidewalk, while the upper part of the body angled into the lot. Both sections had been more or less aligned, though she'd been severed at the waist. The cut went straight through the narrowest part between the bottom of her ribs and navel. The two parts had been placed on the ground with a space of approximately ten inches between them. Her legs were spread wide apart, and her arms were bent at right angles and raised above the shoulders. Perkins observed that both cheeks had been cut from the corners of her lips almost to the earlobes.

He noted the victim's age somewhere between fifteen and seventeen. She was completely naked and "her skin was as white as a lily." The only discoloration seemed to be from the knife wounds and in the exposed internal areas of the body. The liver was hanging out, and a large wedge-shaped piece of skin in the left thigh had apparently been gouged out almost to the leg bone. Apart from the telltale bruises of a severe beating, there were rope marks on the wrists, her neck, and around the ankles.

She had jet black hair, wet and reddish in places. It wasn't blood. There wasn't any blood on the body—no signs of coagulated blood around the wounds, and no blood surrounding the body. There was no internal fluid or blood on the ground between the two body sections. There was no way of observing what was *underneath* the body until the detectives arrived and the body was removed by the coroner.

Perkins could make out the grayish white of the girl's spine where it was severed through the vertebrae and past the organs. There was an apparent cavity where it appeared that organs had been removed from the body. The way she'd been bisected reminded him of the belly of a shark he'd seen cut open recently at the Santa Monica Pier—the white, thick outer layer of skin and the exposed inside parts.

Watch Commander Paul Freestone had requested Fitzgerald and Perkins to stand by for Detective Lieutenant Jess Haskins, en route to the scene. Shortly after Fitzgerald finished the report to University, another radio unit arrived, then backed up almost to Fitzgerald's bumper. A police sergeant out of Inglewood joined the two officers on the sidewalk staring at the body. The sergeant, who knew Perkins from the police academy, said he'd been cruising Slauson when the 390 went on the air and had picked up Fitzgerald's call about the dead body. The sergeant's mouth hung open for a moment and he shook his head saying, "Man, oh, man . . ." A third car, a coupe with a press sticker on the windshield, parked in the middle of the street alongside the Inglewood unit. The policemen turned around and watched a short red-headed woman in a raincoat get out of the car, followed from the driver's side by a photographer loading a Speed Graphix camera.

The Inglewood policeman said, "Just wait a minute—" but the woman pushed past him and Fitzgerald and looked up at Perkins.

"I know you," she said, "and you know me. I'm Underwood of the *Herald Express*. My photographer's shot you half a dozen times—twice on fires and a couple of fatalities when you worked traffic. What've you got here?" She stepped forward, looked down and then stopped in her tracks, one foot on the sidewalk and the other almost stepping on the left leg of the body.

Perkins would recall her standing there for just a couple of seconds. "You could see the color drain right out of her like you'd opened a spigot on her bottom side."

"God almighty!" she said. "This kid's been cut in two! Where the hell did somebody do something like this?"

Hotshot crime reporter Aggie Underwood had the reputation of being tough as nails. Perkins had never heard of Underwood getting queasy over a corpse. "It sort of tickled us standing there," he says, "and watching her back up—walking backwards almost right off the edge of the curb—almost down on her keester."

For the moment, Perkins told Underwood, he could tell her nothing more than what she could see for herself.

"I'd like to get some shots," she said. "Is it okay?"

"Go ahead," Perkins said. "You're going to do it anyway, but thanks for asking, Aggie."

The photographer's flashbulbs popped in quick succession until Lieutenant Jess Haskins arrived and asked the uniformed officers to keep everyone temporarily off the sidewalk. He told Fitzgerald and Perkins the lab crew was on the way and that he'd called in two other detectives. "Nobody in town is going to print any pictures of this one," Underwood said to Haskins. "This is the worst one I've ever seen, Jess. They didn't leave much to anyone's imagination this time."

The detective said, "I don't know if it's a *they* or a *he* or a *she*, but I'll let you know as soon as I do." Haskins looked at her as she leaned against the right door of the coupe with the squad car blocking her view of the lot. She then stood very stiffly with her back against the car, clutching her purse and notebook pad against her stomach, and gave Haskins a sad kind of smile as if to say, "What the hell kind of business are we in anyway?"

Haskins had been unable to trace the original complaint made to the station. He only knew that an unidentified female had placed the call. He observed the dead body and the immediate surroundings and told Fitzgerald and Perkins to begin a search without disturbing the area around the corpse. He asked the Inglewood sergeant where the nearest land line was and warned the officers to stay off the radio. "Any personnel going back and forth on the radio are going to have us jammed up with bystanders," he said, adding, "and more cops than we need."

The only possible evidence that was quickly apparent to Haskins was a cement sack bearing spots of watery blood; another blood spot on the sidewalk, found by Fitzgerald; and a heel print in the driveway. The print was apparently made by a heel having stepped in a small spot of blood, but the print was partly obscured by the track of the automobile tire.

The body was cold, and from the marks on her neck the immediate cause of death seemed to be strangulation—not manually, but by rope. It seemed to him that the body may have been soaked in water and washed off so that latent prints or other evidence would have been removed. The body had probably been drained of blood.

Apart from the blood spots, the heel print and cement sack, nothing else was found. It was the kind of homicide that could get the department and the press in a wrangle, Haskins believed. The naked body told him that a sex crime had been committed, not just a dismemberment or ax murder—those were rough enough—but there was something here that went *beyond* unnatural and peculiar.

He felt that the law was facing a "*defiance* killing"— a sex crime, but with other dimensions. The killer had set his handiwork on their doorstep in a manner that not only challenged them, but was an act of defiance against everything that was human. If they weren't on their toes and didn't nab this guy pronto, they'd be in one hell of a tussle with the papers and the radio—"a mess like a pressure cooker that's going to blow up."

The body had a cleanliness or a "fresh" look that Haskins noted, but it was arranged and spread out in what he described as "someone's idea of a dirty post card that suddenly materializes into real life."

It was not unusual—the "*display* idea" as part of a sex crime—but Aggie Underwood's comment that they hadn't tried to hide very much kept coming back to Haskins. *Hiding* it had been the least of the perpetrator's concerns. Something didn't gel—something was cockeyed. It was only surprising to Haskins that the body hadn't been discovered sooner. Anyone passing the location should have noticed it like a billboard. He felt it would take the police psychiatrist to figure out this murder.

Compiling the reports from Perkins and Fitzgerald with his own appraisal of the scene, Haskins drove to the nearest pay phone on Crenshaw and called Captain Jack Donahoe at Central Homicide. The detective had no way of anticipating the police rivalries and problems that would soon arise, but he'd confess at first a reluctance to hand the case over to Central. Stressing the need for a maximum canvassing of the surrounding neighborhood, he told Donahoe it was unlikely that the bisection had occurred far from where the body was found.

"There's some kind of deliberate arrangement of all this," Haskins told Donahoe, "and with all these peculiar cuts, carefully done—she hasn't been hacked up—and even the cut straight through the middle had been done with some sort of skill. The guy could be a doctor or someone with medical knowledge. . . . Hard to tell how much of this was done to her while she was still alive because the body's been so cleaned off, and from what I can tell until the coroner gets here, there's no blood in her to give us any lividity.

"Looks like strangulation, but seems she was trussed up by ropes or maybe wire from some of the marks, maybe spread-eagle or bound upside down the way you'd hang a carcass—that would've drained the blood out. . . . It's almost the worst I've seen, Jack, and I think this nut's probably lining up another one right now."

Jack Donahoe put through a call to Detective Sergeant Harry Hansen, the senior officer supervising most murder investigations in metropolitan Los Angeles. Hansen had been with the police force since 1926, and after assignment to the homicide division, wrote a police handbook on the preservation of evidence and protection of crime scenes.

He was closing another case, with his partner, Finis Brown, in southwest L.A. where the coroner was also needed. Over the radio Donahoe told Hansen, "University's got a bad one, Harry. A girl cut in half around the middle, in a vacant lot. Stark naked and there's already photographs on it. It looks like there might be problems. Get a uniformed officer to stand by where you are, and you and Brown get over to 39th and Norton." Again Donahoe said, "It looks like a bad one, Harry."

By the time Hansen and Brown reached the new location, reporters from L.A.'s newspapers had converged upon the area, littering the street and sidewalk with cigarette butts and the blackened flashbulbs from cameras. Several more police and onlookers had found their way to the site—some were driving around the block while others parked and stood on the roofs of their cars for a better view.

Hansen was bothered from the start.

A murder scene had its own special kind of life for the detective, its own signature. Even though the girl had been murdered elsewhere and the body brought to the lot, the spot where she was found was a "sacred setting," as Hansen called it. Time and circumstances could be read from even the most seemingly insignificant piece of evidence—elements that could shed light not only on the victim but on the murderer. The success of closing a case could be jeopardized from the start by a bunch of curiosity seekers hungry for the gory details.

"Homicide is a union that never dies," Hansen would say. "A bond is formed that finds the two subjects in a set of circumstances that're tighter than a marriage wedding—tied together into infinity. Nobody needs it being busted up from the outside.

"That's why I say it's 'sacred,' because it's ground that's been walked on only once and it's never crossed again. You can get married three times to the same individual, but you can only kill them once, and it's an irreversible act. It can never be changed, or the circumstances altered. And where it's taken place or where you find the body is damn near the same thing because they both were there—the one that's dead and the one that's alive. Even when we catch the living one and hopefully put them to death, there is *still* that union that tied them together. And it's still as irreversible as the very second it happened. . . ."

None of the clues could be separated from the scene as a whole without disrupting the total picture, Hansen said. Every shred of evidence bore a signature, especially in the placement of the corpse. In facsimile, the scene would unfold for a true detective as a kind of work of art, a reflection of a mind and personality, the *traits* of the killer as well as those of the victim—lives peculiar to certain circumstances that could be mirrored in even the most remote clue. The evidence had to be protected as a whole, or the signature would become diffused, then fade and be gone.

Several plainclothes and uniformed officers were stepping carefully through the weeds farther into the field. "We're going over the ground now," Haskins told Hansen. "If anything turns up, we'll have it for the lab crew—they're on the way."

Hansen said it looked as though "everyone" had gone over the ground, and perhaps there wouldn't be much *left* for the lab. "Call Ray Pinker," Hansen said. "Get him over here." Squatting down at the edge of the sidewalk, he stared at the dead girl's face for just a moment. His usual stone-solid objectivity from twenty years of police work seemed to slip a little, according to Brown.

One had to know Hansen well to have observed that. Brown believed few people knew Hansen at all, and understood him even less. He lived in his own world, did things the way he saw fit for them to be done. He left little room for contradiction.

"Someone spent some time on this one," Hansen said. "I can't remember seeing a face cut up like this. It looks cut clean through to the inside of the cheeks."

Haskins, Brown, and Hansen speculated on the cause of death while waiting for the coroner. Had the body been severed by a knife with a serrated edge? "There appear to be no serrated edges to the wounds," Brown said. "What you'd use is something like a bread knife, cutting straight through like you cut through a loaf of bread. She's been so washed off there's no coagulation or evidence to show just what the hell went on." The large wound to the front of the head suggested concussion, and Brown pointed to the ligature marks around her neck, but Hansen didn't think they proved strangulation.

"We'll have to have an immediate postmortem just to see what we're dealing with," Hansen said.

Each of the men, detectives, reporters, and crime lab crews, sensed a strangeness they would carry away with them. It formed an uncomfortable bond between the men. No one seemed to look the other in the eye and the talk became strained or evasive. Without really voicing it, each policeman on the scene knew that this was the worst murder in the city's history. Something was hanging in the air that wanted them to understand the crime as a spectacular act.

The sun was breaking from behind the overcast sky and Hansen wanted the body covered until the coroner arrived. He was concerned with a discoloration of the skin that could be caused by the sun. Several newspapers were taken apart and laid over the body, forming a series of overlapping peaks like roofing, shielding whatever evidence remained with the victim. Only the bare feet with the red-painted toenails protruded from beneath the newspaper pages.

Ray Pinker, head of the crime lab, said she had been placed in the lot sometime before early dawn, after the dew had settled. He determined that the upper torso had been placed face down first, then turned over, face up. Then the lower torso was carried from a vehicle on the cement sack, and positioned where it was found. The sack had been left in the weeds. Pinker couldn't immediately guess at the exact weapon used, but suggested—as Harry had guessed—that contusions to the head, possibly from blows with some blunt object, and lacerations to the face had caused her death.

"Without rectal temperatures," Pinker said, "I can't be sure, Harry, but I'd estimate ten hours dead." He took some small bits of bristle-like fragments from the skin, which appeared to be broken pieces of broom straw or brush bristles, not necessarily pig hairs—maybe car matting. From what he observed, he told Hansen and Brown it appeared that Haskins was right—the girl's hair had been washed or shampooed after she was dead. "Most of what we're dealing with in the way of wounds," Pinker said, "were done following death."

"That's good enough for me," Harry said.

Looking Hansen straight in the face, Pinker said, "This is the worst crime I've ever seen committed upon a woman."

Hansen figured whoever left the body in the lot had stopped in the driveway, then backed up for some reason. The girl's body hadn't been dragged there, and she hadn't been carried in that position, with her legs wide apart. The lower part had been set down and then arranged that way. Whoever left her like that then climbed back into the car and drove away.

When the California Hearse Service panel truck arrived, two attendants placed the sections of the body into a single conveyance casket. Dark grass, damp and bent over, formed two depressions where the body had lain. The surrounding grass was dry and a lighter green. Hansen knew she had been placed there before dawn, when the grass was still wet with dew.

While detectives continued to comb through the vacant lots for evidence, newspaper reporters knocked on doors in the neighborhood, badgering anyone they met for a clue to the victim's identity and possibly for a lead on where the murder had been committed. Several reporters had been ordered to follow the hearse to the morgue, which was located in the downtown Hall of Justice basement. There the body was received by the coroner's deputies, unloaded, and tagged "Jane Doe Number 1" on the PERSONAL DESCRIPTION OF UNKNOWN DEAD line. The call memorandum was completed at the Los Angeles County morgue at 2:45 p.m. by Deputy Coroner Sears. The victim's weight, as read off the morgue scale, was listed as 115 pounds, her complexion light, nose small, chin round, eyebrows brown, build small, teeth poor, eyes green-gray, and age estimated between fifteen and thirty. Her height of five feet, five inches was determined by measuring from the top of her forehead to the edge of the bisected torso, then from the heel of one foot to the severed edge between the second and third vertebrae.

The two body sections were aligned on a steel table, with the head elevated onto a metal brace for a number of black and white photographs. These were followed by several experimental color shots. The lacerations to her face were stitched to align her jaw, and as her fingerprints were rolled, Brown waited in a glass-partitioned area next to the examination room. He was told that the postmortem would be performed the following day by the chief surgeon, but an assistant said she had possibly been kept on ice because her fingerprint ridges appeared shrunken, and the skin of the fingers puckered into grooves. But the deputy coroner rolling the prints believed that a set could be processed to enable a classification—and if she had any sort of record at all, they'd have the identification.

A touched-up rendering of how the girl might have appeared in life was prepared from a head-shot photograph, and on the phone with Captain Donahoe, Brown said, "You can't tell much from the original—her face is bruised and puffed out of shape. We're figuring she was killed quite a while before she wound up in the lot, and maybe she's been in water, so identification is difficult without the artist working up her likeness hopefully into a shape recognizable by someone."

Two hundred photographs were hastily printed and the detectives planned to work around the clock until they came up with her identity—and maybe a lead to her killer.

When the first extra edition hit the street with the rendering of Jane Doe, the police lines jammed with calls about runaways and missing daughters and wives. Missing persons reports were checked and rechecked, and Georgia Street Juvenile had reporters in every doorway and window waiting for a break to Jane Doe's identity.

In the *Examiner*'s city room at 11th and Broadway, Assistant Managing Editor Warden Woolard was pushing for a second extra when he thought of the Soundphoto machine. The rewrite men were putting together stories as fast as the phones were answered, the regular crews were being summoned, and reporters were calling in tips every thirty minutes.

The victim's prints had been airmailed special delivery to the FBI in Washington, but the night editor had complained that the prints might not even get to the FBI because of storms and airplanes being grounded. "It could take a week before there's any word," he said.

Woolard said, "We could send the prints over the wire, on the Soundphoto. It's never been done, but I can't see any reason why it wouldn't work."

The wires were closed for the night, but International News Photowire would open at four o'clock in the morning. "It's not going to take any longer to send one print sheet than any other photograph," Woolard said. He suggested calling Donahoe for a copy of the prints. "They can be wired first thing in the morning," Woolard said. "We can have an FBI agent standing by at the Hearst Bureau to hand carry it straight to their files. If the feds have got a name to match those prints, then the *Examiner*'s got a jump on every paper in the country."

Donahoe agreed to wiring the prints to Washington, for a possible acceleration of the process, though Hansen felt it wasn't the right protocol. He knew Donahoe was in "cahoots" with the *Examiner*'s editor. Hansen wanted no part of that—he only wanted to know who the dead girl was.

At 4:02 the following morning, the sheet of prints went over the wire. With the time difference it was a little after seven o'clock in Washington, D.C. The bureau chief and an FBI agent standing by received the wirephoto, but the agent immediately detected problems to do with the prints. "They're too blurred to yield a classification," he said. "There's defects and blanks in the swirls." He suggested the *Examiner* enlarge and build up the prints in a way that would magnify the defects into a readable presentation.

The *Examiner*'s photo department immediately made separate 8 x 10-inch enlargements of each print, a tedious, time-consuming process. They then leased a special Soundphoto wire to Washington, and each of the separate prints was transmitted over the wire.

Within minutes the FBI was able to identify Jane Doe Number 1. Her fingerprints were on file from a civilian job application taken at an army base located north of Santa Barbara, California. Though it had been four years earlier, the girl was described as five feet five inches in height, with her weight at 115 pounds, brunette, blue eyes, light complexion. Her place of birth was Hyde Park, Massachusetts—July 29, 1924. She was only twenty-two at the time of her death. Her name was Elizabeth Short. She did not have a middle name.

Within days, though, the detectives would learn that in Hollywood she was called the "Black Dahlia."

2

Elizabeth Short's father abandoned his car on the Charlestown Bridge in Massachusetts, and seemed to vanish—to disappear. This was just after he lost his business during the Depression. Everyone said he'd drowned in the deep cold water rushing beneath the bridge.

A neighbor of Cleo Alvin Short says it wouldn't have been so unusual for a man in Cleo's position to have jumped off that famous suicide bridge—at least during that particular time in American history.

"Cleo had been hit with a real bad loss," the neighbor says. "And like many, the pressure was more than the man could take. Imagine the burden of living in a place where you couldn't raise the money for just plain *eating* unless you robbed a bank, and Cleo couldn't have done that. He was a proud *working* man with disaster staring him straight in the face."

It would be a long time before the neighbors in Medford, a few miles north of Charlestown and the forbidding bridge, were able to figure out what had happened to Cleo Short.

Things hadn't always been that way. He'd returned from

World War I a skilled mechanic, and opened an automotive garage in the small town of Wolfboro, New Hampshire. His wife, Phoebe, pregnant with their second child, wanted more for their children than what Wolfboro had to offer. Their first daughter, Virginia—called "Ginnie"—was a talented child, and by the time the second daughter, Dorothea, was born, the garage business was prospering.

It was 1922, and apart from keeping house and caring for the children, Phoebe assisted Cleo with the accounts, billing, and bookkeeping. She suggested selling the business at a profit, and starting a new one in Boston. Phoebe had close relatives in Medford, a small city five miles from Boston, and she believed they'd help with the growing family while she worked with Cleo to build up their new business.

Muriel, the youngest and last of Cleo's and Phoebe's five daughters, would later come to believe that if it hadn't been for raising the girls almost single-handedly, her mother might have made a success in business. Phoebe was ambitious, and not satisfied with the same things in life that seemed to content Cleo. She could see that people who owned amusement arcades and miniature golf courses, very popular then, were making a lot of money. Cleo had often talked of wanting to build something, and Phoebe believed that the profits from the garage would offer the opportunity of installing miniature golf courses.

But Cleo believed in the "tried and true," and was reluctant to change. Medford, he believed, seemed far too expensive a place to live. Rents were more affordable in Hyde Park, a working class section of Boston, but he promised Phoebe that when things got better, when the golf courses proved profitable, the family would move to Medford.

Elizabeth—they called her "Betty"—was born in Hyde Park, and was not yet two years of age when the Shorts finally rented a handsome two-story house on Sheridan Avenue in Medford. The new home had four bedrooms, a spacious den, and sat proudly on a tree-lined street.

Medford was a fair-sized city with a penchant for its historical past, Colonial homes, and old rum distilleries—and for the great clipper ships that had been built there and sailed down the

Mystic River to Boston Harbor and out into the Atlantic Ocean. The river ran through the city, as did cobblestone streets, winding past a variety of neighborhoods, churches, schools, bootmakers, and ice cream parlors.

The two youngest daughters, Eleanora and Muriel, were born in Medford and grew up loving the city as much as their mother did. The miniature golf course Cleo installed near Howard Johnson's Circle was considered one of the best ever built and brought him further work. The family bought new furniture, a new car, a piano, and singing lessons for Ginnie and Dottie. Muriel says, "Mama wanted nothing but the best for us, and she prided herself on etiquette and good manners."

But there was no way for the Shorts to escape the encroaching hard times the Depression would swiftly bring across the country. In the wake of 1929, a game of miniature golf could take one's mind off troubles; but when bread was needed more than amusement, Cleo's construction business began to collapse. Muriel recalls that at first her father did not believe the money crunch was going to last. "He kept repeating to Mama that things were going to get better any day," she says. "He would say the unemployment was going to stop. He would tell Mama people would soon be back to work."

When he was unable to put together a payroll, Cleo quickly realized that the "money crunch" was lasting longer than he expected. The "fine life" with Phoebe and the children was being pulled from under them. With the foreclosure of the business, their dreams merged with thousands of others that were becoming debris washed against a beach.

When Cleo's abandoned car was found in Charlestown, Medford police looked for him; but they believed he'd jumped, and the tide had pulled him down into the currents.

Muriel was only two. "I didn't have a way of really missing him," she says. "But my sisters did, especially Ginnie and Betty. Nobody knew what happened." He had left Phoebe with the bad business—with desperate creditors whose demands she was unable to meet. He'd left her to deal with the bankruptcy, the courts, and with keeping a roof over the girls' heads and food on the table. When Cleo vanished there was food in the house for less than a week. It meant welfare, and standing in long lines to go on the dole, and doing everything a proud, Yankee woman "who'd never taken a dime from anybody" found it almost impossible to do.

But Phoebe did it. She couldn't pay the $35 a month rent, so they moved from the large pleasant house on Sheridan into a smaller place on Evans Street. And a few months later, when that landlord hiked that rent, she was forced to move again. She took the family into the downstairs flat of a two-family house on Magoun Avenue. There were only two small bedrooms, so Phoebe converted the sun porch into a third bedroom that Muriel would share with Betty and Eleanora. The house was cramped, but the neighborhood was good and that was very important to Phoebe. Her worst fear was falling into a bad neighborhood.

To escape from her worries, Phoebe sought solace in the movie houses. She would get passes at W.T. Grant's, and two or three times a week she'd take Muriel and Betty to the movies. "My other sisters weren't interested in the movies unless they were on dates. Ginnie had a boyfriend and Dottie would rather stay home with Nonie (we called Eleanora 'Nonie'). . . . I don't know why Betty and I were like Mama. . . . We loved the movies!"

To Muriel, her sister Betty always made the trip to the movies something special. They would dress up and leave early in order to window shop on the way. The Shorts couldn't afford the things they saw in the store displays, but as Phoebe would tell the two girls, it cost them nothing to look and to plan and dream. "When times were a little better," Muriel says, "we'd stop for ice cream or a sundae at the United Farmers ice cream parlor."

Phoebe worked as a bookkeeper whenever she could find employment, but for the next four years the family mostly depended on Mother's Aid and government handouts. Muriel remembers her mother being upset with the welfare clinic. "Maybe we weren't upset for the same reasons," she says, "but when I started school, the doctor put my vaccination on my arm where it would show, not hidden on my left leg like our own doctor had done with Betty and my other sisters. . . . So everybody was looking at my vaccination. . . . It was like I had something wrong with me."

Twice a week Betty walked Muriel to the firehouse for free milk. They would leave early and only a few people would be in line. But by ten o'clock when the truck arrived with the milk, and the firemen were handing out the bottles, the line would be around the block and doubled back. Muriel recalls a sense of shame whenever their old neighbors would see them with the free milk. "Even as kids," Muriel says, "we seemed to have that Yankee pride of Mama's that you were supposed to stand on your own two feet."

But what *really* bothered Muriel were the welfare shoes. The Swan School is where she would go to pick up the shoes and the nightgowns that were made out of flower sacks. "They had tiny flowers on them," she says. "The shoes were sturdy with thick laces and thick soles, but everyone knew they were the welfare shoes. I didn't feel so bad when I learned there were kids that didn't have *any* shoes."

Muriel was in grammar school when the landlord increased the rent for the flat on Magoun Avenue. Again the family had to move, unable to meet the increase. Phoebe luckily found a walk-up apartment on Salem Street. It was too late in the school year for Muriel to change schools, so for the next few weeks she walked back to the old school—their neighborhood was no longer one of the best in Medford.

Then Betty began to get sick. She became so ill that year she missed 36 days of school and required serious medical treatment several times. Says Muriel, "She had asthma like me and Ginnie, but sometimes she had it worse than we did. Sometimes the three of us would be sitting up all night struggling to breathe. We'd take turns sitting in the rocking chair, but when it got really bad Mama would have to call the doctor. He'd come even in the middle of the night, and give us a shot of adrenaline." They didn't understand about allergies, and at one time the Shorts had two dogs and two cats. Whenever Betty was away from the house, her asthma seemed to get better, but toward the end of spring she became so sick she had to be put in the hospital. It was necessary for her to have an operation to clear one of her lungs. After surgery she went to stay with her grandmother in Maine to recuperate.

The move to the apartment on Salem Street was another step down for Phoebe. But it brought her closer to a new job—six days a week as a full-time clerk at the Mystic Bakery in Medford Square. Muriel remembers her mother working hard, "standing all day dealing with people. On her way home she'd buy groceries and then she'd make supper for all of us." The girls took turns setting the table and washing the dishes. There was a spirit of cooperation, all trying to help out as best they could with chores. Frequently, the three older girls would talk about their father, wondering what happened. Muriel remembers them whispering as though they didn't want to be overheard by Nonie and Muriel.

Saturday nights the faint sound of the radio would drift into the girls' bedrooms as their mother washed and ironed clothes for church, laying out ribbons and polished shoes. "Mama was very particular how we looked," Muriel says, "and we would look so pretty. We'd feel proud as we walked the three blocks to the First Baptist Church on Oakland Street.

"We used to go to the band concerts over at the Commons every Friday night. And when the fife and drum corps practiced, we'd go over, sit on the grass, and watch." There was a boy who would blush when he saw Betty and she would tease him in a friendly way, not mean.

Betty and her oldest sister, Ginnie, *always* fought over the radio. "Especially when Texaco was broadcasting the Metropolitan Opera. Ginnie wanted to listen to the opera, and since Ginnie was the oldest, that's what we listened to. But Betty would quarrel with Ginnie over the music. She didn't want to *always* hear the long-haired stuff—neither did I. Betty liked popular music and show tunes. 'Another Deanna Durbin,' is what people said about her. She wanted to *dance*—she wanted to Lindy. Betty didn't want to stand around caterwauling, as she called it . . . even though Ginnie had been studying opera and had started singing professionally, concerts at Jordan Hall."

During the winter of 1940 when Betty was sixteen, she made her first trip away from home. Phoebe arranged for her to stay with friends in Miami Beach for the winter, hoping that the mild weather would improve her health. And since Betty had her work permit, it was possible she could get a part-time job at one of the beach resorts.

The letters Betty wrote home, sometimes several in a week, were addressed to Phoebe, but intended for all her sisters as well. She often sent funny postcards to Muriel, telling her she missed everyone, but did not miss the snow and ice. Her room, she said, was small with maple furniture like the room she shared at home with Muriel. She hadn't suffered a cold or an asthma attack since leaving Medford.

For the next two winters Betty headed to Florida, returning to Medford each spring. Eleanor Kurz, a friend of Dottie's, saw Betty often before the war, usually in the restaurant on Salem Street across from the City Hall. Mr. Griffin, the owner, was in his fifties, short and stocky, with thinning grey hair, and he wore gold-rimmed glasses.

The restaurant had only a counter with stools. "I remember I hadn't seen Betty in a while," Eleanor says, "and she was sitting very straight on the stool farthest from the door, dressed to the minute in a leopard fur coat and hat. She made me feel like a country bumpkin. I thought to myself, Dottie's kid sister sure has grown up!"

Eleanor said something about not recognizing Betty and how great she looked. "Some people said that Mr. Griffin was Betty's boyfriend, but I think it was just that he wanted to help her in a fatherly way.

"Betty had her legs crossed, and she wore dark stockings and suede pumps, and a lot of makeup by Medford standards. She was in her teens, but looked older—sophisticated." She had been in Florida, Betty told Eleanor, who replied, "Florida certainly agrees with you."

Betty said, "I'm working as an usherette right now at the Square Theater and it isn't so thrilling. But I love watching the movies." She said she'd done some modeling in Miami. Eleanor told her she could go far with *her* looks. Betty said, "I would like to. Mr. Griffin thinks I can certainly do it."

Eleanor had been one of the first to hear the rumor that

Cleo hadn't killed himself, but was alive and well somewhere out west. Phoebe Short was shocked when she received a letter from Cleo. He said he was in Northern California working in the shipyards, and apologized for leaving the way he did, which, he said, he had not intended. He tried to explain in the letter that he had not been able to face up to the troubles, but knew that in his absence, if it appeared that he deserted or was dead, Phoebe would be eligible for more support than Cleo might have been able to supply by staying in Medford. He asked if she might now allow him to return to the family.

After the surprise and shock of the letter had settled, Phoebe answered her husband with an emphatic *no*. She did not consider him her "husband." He *had* deserted them and she could not forgive him.

Muriel says, "We were older, and making our own way. Dottie and Ginnie were working in Boston. Nonie had a job at the cleaners down the street from the bakery, and I had just turned thirteen and gotten my own work permit. I was working Saturdays doing filing and clerical work for an insurance company in Boston. Mama was proud of our self-reliance and wanted us to be independent, and said there was no longer a reason for our father to return."

The girls were being raised to be modest. "We didn't even walk around in our slips," Muriel says. "We always covered up with robes, even though we were all girls, and we didn't discuss anything about sex with Mama." Muriel remembers being curious about the big Lydia Pinkham bottle and all the pills Betty took for her monthly female complaint. Hardly anything was ever said about it, and Muriel didn't dare ask, but she knew Betty hadn't started her periods. That is what all the secrets were about.

Later, when Betty started buying feminine pads, it seemed to Muriel that the Lydia Pinkham pills had taken care of the problem. Betty would linger over feminine supplies in the drugstore, often buying her packages of sanitary napkins and hygienic items in a gay, flamboyant manner that usually embarrassed the young man working behind the counter.

Now that she had spending money, Betty took Muriel on

shopping sprees or trips to Boston for lunch at Schraft's and to the theater. Betty loved the movie palaces with huge carpeted lobbies and ornate ceilings with crystal and gold chandeliers. She'd often try to impress on her younger sister the "specialness" of the movie palaces, something Muriel didn't understand.

One time while shopping, Betty bought Muriel a pencil box, one of the more expensive ones that she knew Muriel secretly wanted—something that was considered extravagant.

With five girls of dating age, the Shorts' doorbell was always ringing. They still couldn't afford a telephone, so friends would push the downstairs buzzer and yell in the intercom, "Is Shorty there?" One of the girl's would yell back, "Which one?" and the yelling would excite the dog, Penny. The white Pomeranian would start barking and pulling at Muriel's socks as she ran down the hallway trying to get away.

The news about Japan bombing Pearl Harbor broke while Betty was in Florida. The rest of the family were eating Sunday dinner and listening to the radio. When President Roosevelt's voice came on the air, Muriel felt that everything was going to change—probably for the worst.

The draft age dropped to eighteen, and while Phoebe had no sons, she still displayed a flag with one blue star in the window. "When Dottie was told she was too skinny for the service," Muriel says, "she went on a binge of milk shakes and double malts to gain weight." Dottie enlisted in the WAVE's and became a cryptographer stationed in Washington, D.C. Phoebe placed a photograph of Dottie wearing her blue-and-white WAVE's hat proudly on the mantle with other family portraits.

In the spring Betty returned from Florida and worked as an usherette in Boston, replacing a boy who had been drafted. She then took a part-time job at Child's Restaurant, where she met a man who lived in Somerville. Sometimes she'd take the long way home, catching a trolley at Lechmere Square and traveling the entire length of Cambridge and down Highland Avenue in Somerville. She would get off the trolley to meet the man in Donald's Cafeteria. He was an elder in the Seventh Day Adventist Church, and Betty would join him for lunch. The man collected celebrity autographs, mostly sports figures, and

Chinese carvings. Some were very tiny and made of ivory, and fascinated Betty. After several weeks he bought her an expensive coat and matching hat, which she proudly wore walking down the streets like a fashion model.

Remembering how Betty looked, Muriel says, "She'd go to work all dressed up, and sometimes stop by Liggett's Drugstore on Tremont Street. She'd sit at the lunch counter drinking coffee and talking to the waitress or anyone who sat down beside her." The manager didn't like Betty, believed Ruthie, the waitress, because Betty never gave him a tumble. "She didn't try to pick anyone up," Ruthie says. "That I could see. She was just friendly to people, and to me, too. I wore a beige and green uniform with an apron and a little starched doohickey on my head, and I thought it looked ugly, but Betty said it looked cute, that she liked it better than the uniform she'd wear at Child's. That made me feel pretty good. She went shopping with me the day I bought my peacoat. It was like what the sailors wore, except it had plain buttons, not the ones with the navy insignia. If you weren't in the service, you couldn't wear the official uniforms. I decided to wear the peacoat home and had my old coat put in the box, and we were going out when the store detective stopped us. He took us into a room and I was very nervous, but Betty was calm and almost cheerful. Even after I showed the detective the sales slip, he kept asking questions, but seemed to be asking her more questions than he was asking me, and he didn't seem so worried about the peacoat anymore."

Betty said very little to anyone about the man in Donald's Cafeteria because he was worried about his reputation. It would not have been proper for him to be socializing with her because he was rather elderly, and she was still so young at the time.

Betty would often take long walks by herself, or she would walk and talk with Muriel or the neighbor's little girl, Mary. A large brown police dog followed Betty home from Medford Square one afternoon. "They weren't called German Shepherds during the war," Muriel says. "The dog wouldn't go home, just looked at Betty and hung his tail and kept following her. He had no collar or tag, and she said he was as gentle as a baby, so she called him 'Baby.'"

Phoebe told the girls they couldn't have two dogs. One was enough with the rationing. He'd want bones and they couldn't afford all the food he'd need. Betty took Baby outside so the dog would go home, but he sat beneath her window howling. Phoebe worried about the neighbors complaining, and told the girls to bring him back in. She said they'd have to find the owners right away.

The dog stayed that spring and into the summer, usually trailing after Betty. He would wait outside stores and at trolley slops with her, and though sometimes he'd disappear for days, he'd always return, howling beneath her window. Betty and Muriel finally found the owners, who lived in South Medford, two miles away. "You call him *Baby*?" they said. "His name's Tiger! He's one *mean* dog."

Cleo's next letter spoke of an abundance of jobs in California. Betty had written to her father in Vallejo and he had answered, telling her he was working at Mare Island Naval Base, and asked if she wanted to come and stay with him. He suggested Betty keep house for him until she landed work. He would send Betty's train fare in the next letter. Betty wanted to go, but Phoebe had mixed feelings: California was the opposite end of the country. Betty convinced her mother that her father would look out for her—that she would be "safe and sound," as she put it. Muriel says, "Mama never would have let her go, if she hadn't thought she was taken care of." Betty was insistent about wanting to work in the movies and she had to go to California to do that.

Mary, the little girl next door to the Shorts, remembers the week Betty left. "She was all dressed up in something light blue, and she took my hand as we crossed Salem Street and headed toward the gas station. I remember the station manager stopping his work to come over and talk to her. I guess I stood there shifting from one foot to the other as they chit-chatted and he made a date to see her before she left for California. She said something about Hollywood, and as we walked to United Farmers, I asked her if she was going to be a movie star. She laughed and told me that's what she hoped to do and if you wanted to be a movie star, it wasn't going to happen to you in Medford. She'd have to go to Hollywood."

But Vallejo was far from Los Angeles, and Betty's yearned-for reunion with her father turned into a strained situation at best. Cleo would later explain that they did try to adjust to one another. He *did* make an effort to be interested in her modeling ideas and theatrical ambitions, though he knew nothing of these things except what he read in the paper or heard on the radio. He had been working at the shipyard for several years and Phoebe's refusal to take him back into the family had embittered him more than he realized. Maybe he needed a little time off, he felt—time to get to know his beautiful daughter. Although there was a family resemblance, she was not like her sisters, at least in the way she looked. He knew so little about his own family, and it seemed that he never would. A friend and co-worker at Mare Island lent Cleo the key to a Los Angeles apartment that the friend still rented but had not occupied since taking work at the shipyards. The friend said, "Take your daughter to Grauman's Chinese and let her see if her shoes match the movie stars' footprints."

Betty was excited about a trip to Hollywood, and planned to see if she could get work as an extra in the movies. Cleo said he could apply for work at Lockheed Aircraft, which he had been thinking about. But whether or not he traveled with Betty is uncertain, and friction quickly developed over his delaying the "vacation" and his fear of spending money on something he could not use. The more they found themselves in disagreement, the more he criticized her—her interest in going out on dates, her untidiness. He accused her of being lazy, and of having "bad morals" because she was dating sailors from Mare Island. In a very short time Cleo forced her from his own house. He would later say, "I told her to go her way and I'd go mine. We didn't get along and I wanted nothing more to do with her."

A soldier from Vallejo drove Betty to Camp Cook, an armored division training base, where it was possible for her to get a job as a civilian and be eligible for a room on the base. He took her to the post exchange and she told the manager she had come to California for her health, but was fine now. She needed a job so she could stay in the good climate. "At home I'm called

Betty," she told the manager, "but I like to be called 'Beth.'" From then on she wanted to be called "Beth" away from Medford. Her hair was braided and pinned up and her smile was winning. "I've worked as a clerk and a waitress, and I can run a cash register," she said. The manager told her he needed another cashier, and Beth was hired for the job.

The soldier (he was not stationed at Camp Cook) told her if she got down to Santa Barbara to look him up. He'd show her the town—if he was still stateside and not in the Philippines or Guam, "or in the woods in Czechoslovakia somewhere," he said. "And remember, if you want a GI escort, I'm the best in Santa Barbara."

Within two weeks Beth was the talk of the base. Word spread— "look but don't touch." The new gal at the PX was as "cute as all get out, but she wasn't putting out for anyone." Because the housing shortage was bad on the base, Beth hadn't been assigned quarters and was sleeping wherever she could find the space. One sergeant tried to stake a claim on her by appearing generous, sympathetic. He said he felt sorry for her since she couldn't get quarters and offered her the spare cot in his house trailer temporarily, if she wanted it. She eagerly moved in, but she thought he understood the situation: it wasn't romance she was after—just a roof over her head while she tried to save enough money to get to Hollywood.

The manager was disappointed the day Beth notified him that she wasn't well and couldn't show up for her shift. Whether the sergeant thought she'd been overly encouraging or not would never be clear. She rebuffed his advances—he called her a "tease" and struck her, giving her a black eye.

She complained to the commanding officer and quickly was moved into quarters with Mary Stradder, a WAC sergeant. Listening to Beth talk about men, and about her father having kicked her out, the WAC was concerned that the girl seemed to lack the "tougher" veneer she'd need to do the things she claimed she wanted to do.

When Beth won a beauty contest, "The Camp Cutie of Camp Cook," the WAC told her that prettiness alone might "carry her through," but she had to be careful of the men she hooked up with.

The manager would later claim that, because of the shortage of housing, he was faced with the possibility of civilian cutbacks. Beth started looking for a job off the base. She stayed temporarily on a ranch a few miles from Santa Barbara, sleeping in the old bunkhouse with a girl she'd met in Casmalia. From the ranch she looked for work in Santa Barbara and bedded down on the couch of another girl's apartment.

It was toward the end of September that Beth ran into some trouble with the police. She was with a group of soldiers and girls, drinking and "getting a little loud" at a restaurant. The police broke up the party, but since Beth was under legal age and unaccompanied by a parent or legal guardian, she was taken into custody and charged as a minor where liquor was being served.

Policewoman Mary Unkefer realized Beth was no one's version of a typical barfly. The girl was soft-spoken and had the blackest hair the policewoman says she ever saw. Beth was booked and fingerprinted. She was frightened and worried about what her mother would say when she found out.

Policewoman Unkefer arranged to take personal custody of Beth until the charge was ruled on. She could not return to the girlfriend's apartment—a soldier was living there with the other girl. Because they were not married, the conditions legally prohibited Beth from returning, except to gather her belongings. She stayed with the policewoman until arrangements were made at a Santa Barbara neighborhood house where jurisdiction would be taken over Beth and she'd be fed and taken care of.

She was nineteen years old and her father refused to take custody of her. It was decided that Beth would be returned to Massachusetts to remain under her mother's custody. Unkefer drove her to the Greyhound bus depot and saw her safely on board. "I want you to take this," the policewoman said, folding ten dollars in Beth's hand. "Your mother doesn't have to know about the trouble here, unless you want to tell her. There won't be any reports being sent to Massachusetts, so you don't have to worry.

"But it won't be a good idea for you to come back to Santa Barbara and get yourself in any more trouble. What we're giving you is a warning." Recalling that conversation, Unkefer says, "She looked at me with those wonderful eyes and said, 'I'm sorry about the trouble.' She was so pretty and had her heart so set on staying in California—being in the movies. I suggested she wait a couple of years, then give California another try."

3

Glenn Miller's "In The Mood" was blaring from the portable radio as the young bombardier danced dangerously along the edge of the pier.

Beth had written that she'd met the bombardier after a long drive to Tampa Bay. She made the trip with a couple of soldiers and a strawberry blonde named Sharon Givens. The station wagon had no rear window and the exhaust kept blowing into the back, so they'd cranked open all the other windows and laughed like they were flying low over some Philippine jungles.

The guys wanted to fish off the St. Petersburg municipal pier, drink beer and listen to the portable radio while Beth and Sharon fooled around feeding pelicans. When the girls got hot dogs for all of them and headed back to the end of the pier where the guys were fishing, they could hear the music halfway to the beach. The bombardier, whom they'd never seen before, wasn't even dancing with a girl.

He was kicking his legs and jitterbugging on the water side of the guard rail with his toes hopping along the edge of the pier. Shouting above the music, Beth said, "There's sharks down there in the water."

Sharon Givens says, "I'll never forget the way that kid looked—pausing and sort of teetering his balance, and grinning at her. And he said to her, 'Shucks, honey, I got sharks in my hip pockets.'

"I wouldn't have stood a chance with someone who cut a rug like that kid, and then he climbed over the pipe, back onto the pier, and went like this with his hands—coaxing and waving sort of gimme-gimme to her, and even Beth couldn't keep up with him."

A squadron of airplanes flew overhead and everyone stopped and looked up. The bombardier identified them—all single-engine fighters he called "flyswatters," because he rode a B-17 with four radial piston engines called *Sweet Bottom* and had his "own special sharks earmarked for ratso and fatso."

By the end of the afternoon, the bombardier was in the station wagon with the others, talking the whole ride back to Miami Beach. He slouched down in the rear seat alongside Beth who was no longer bothered by the exhaust, while Sharon and the two soldiers rode in the front seat, listening to the radio. But the bombardier kept talking above the music while the soldier Beth had first dated in Tampa kept turning the volume up to drown him out. Sharon later said the ride back practically made her deaf.

The bombardier showed up again the following Saturday in Miami Beach to take Beth to lunch *and* dinner. She told Sharon they were going dancing at the park as soon as the sun went down and invited her to come along. The USO and volunteers had strung up colored lights and laid out a very large platform like a boxing arena. The band for the evening was setting up on the bleachers at one end of the constructed dance floor. That night so many servicemen showed up that the dancers spilled onto the grass. During the dance Beth inserted white flowers into her upswept hair.

Sharon asked Beth if she wanted to model ingenue and misses clothes for luncheons in the cafeteria of the department store where Sharon worked. Beth had worked as extra help at the cosmetic counter during the holiday season and Sharon's manager remembered her as having a "real flair about her." The only problem, he felt, was that people would be more interested in *her* than in what she was modeling.

Since Beth was leaving Florida at the end of the season, Sharon asked Duffy Sawyer to attend one of the luncheon fashion shows to see what she meant about Beth. "Duffy thought she was pretty young for commercial photography," Sharon says, "but he said he could contact clients in Chicago and Indianapolis and maybe set up interviews if Beth could travel and if she'd obtain written consent from her mother." Duffy felt that she was definitely pin-up material.

Several guys fell in love with Beth in Miami Beach before the season ended. "She was a natural vamp," Sharon says, "one who brings out the wolf in all men, no exceptions, and she didn't even have to try."

It was the time, too, the war, Sharon believed. People made promises of love—a guy and a gal swearing devotion and they'd only met that afternoon. He'd be up in one of those flyswatters the bombardier had talked about, or on the gun-turret of a battleship, or flying over Tokyo or Europe or Iwo Jima, looking at *dying*, day and night. How long did it take to fly like a bat out of hell from Florida to Guam? How long did it take to fall in love with a pretty girl in between flights? You're falling in love and not even knowing if you're coming back . . . or if you *are* coming back, whether you'll be in one piece or just a part of the guy you used to be. Everything was blowing up and blowing everyone else up. A pretty girl was a ray of sunshine, and falling in love could be the closest thing to heaven.

The bombardier wrote one letter from New Guinea. He said, "When you hear Dorsey's "Ain't Misbehavin,'" you think of me hedgehopping out of the blue, 'cause I'm thinking of you, honey." Beth answered his letter but never heard from him again.

Phoebe Short loved the late-night talks with Betty sitting at the kitchen table while she heated Campbell's tomato soup. Sometimes Betty would knock softly on her mother's bedroom door, then sit on the bed talking, telling her mother of the dreams she had to travel and to act in the movies.

Ben Schuman, who owned the neighborhood drugstore, was always excited to hear about Betty's latest adventures.

His clerk had been drafted earlier that year and Schuman frequently advised her regarding the different brands of feminine supplies. He always complimented her on her appearance and was especially impressed with a beautiful pink hat she wore with ostrich feathers that seemed to float as she walked.

The neighborhood women would pause to watch Betty and joke about the way the men looked at her. One said, "It's a wonder we don't have more car accidents when Betty walks down the street . . . whistles . . . horns."

Another said, "She pays them no mind and doesn't miss a step. One moment she's like a grand lady in furs and such, and then the next she's running around my back yard, because she's seen my husband's chickens getting loose. She bolts down the three flights of back steps into the yard chasing the chickens back into the coop. There's Betty running with her breasts bouncing, and the chickens are flapping their wings and squawking, and she's bending over trying to cover that hole in the fence with some cardboard while the chickens are poking their heads out trying to make another run for it."

Sharon Givens was working in Houston, Texas, and was surprised when she received a collect call from Betty, now calling herself Beth, in Los Angeles. She told Sharon she'd traced the number from Miami and said she hadn't been able to get any work from Duffy. He had sent her to Indianapolis to model for a hat company, but an assistant for the manufacturer had advanced her money to get to Hollywood. She was short of cash, though, since the train fare had tapped her reserves. Beth asked Sharon for money until hers came through from her last job. Sharon staked her for a week or two, sending a Western Union money order to the Clinton Hotel in L.A.

Beth had met a slim, dark-haired girl named Lucille Varela who invited her to share a room in the Clinton on Broadway. It was not a residential hotel and the seven-day wartime limit applied. But since Lucille's boyfriend at the time was the desk clerk they were able to get around the limit.

The two girls danced and drank in the downtown cocktail lounges and Hollywood cafés. Lucille, who had tried to be a dancer, an extra, and a singer, says, "Beth wore so much makeup it was really hard for anyone to tell how young she was."

Lucille knew a lot of people on the Hollywood sidelines who were underage but hitting all the spots. She knew a few people in the movies, like blonde Barbara Lee, an aspiring young actress at Paramount who complained, using the old cliché, that she mostly wound up on the cutting room floor. The "gang" gathered at the Four Star Grill on Hollywood Boulevard along with Barbara's "booking agent" and other movie and radio people.

Within two weeks after arriving in Hollywood, Beth was accompanying Barbara to the studios trying to meet important people and be seen in the right places.

Lucille moved out of the Clinton and in with her boyfriend at the Sunshine Apartments—a tall wood-frame building on Clay Street west of Hill Street. It was right next to Angels Flight, and when Beth stayed overnight with Lucille, they would sit on the terrace in the mornings drinking coffee and watching the little cable cars going up and down Bunker Hill.

While Beth traveled back and forth from Hollywood, Lucille found a waitress job at a steak house on Broadway near First Street. She was caught sneaking Beth meals and got fired. Beth had been to the Hollywood Canteen with Barbara, and told Lucille she was on the list to become a junior hostess and she'd be able to get meals there.

Beth met a *very* handsome Army Air Corps lieutenant, a pilot who had taken her to dinner twice. They danced at the Canteen, but she was also dating him on the outside because she wasn't an "official" junior hostess. His name was Gordan Fickling and he'd come up from Long Beach. He had the use of a car and he'd take her to the beach and the amusement pier, or to Knott's Berry Farm for fried chicken. But Gordan was soon to be shipped out, and hesitant about an emotional involvement. Beth told Lucille he was mature and intelligent. "Sure, sure," Lucille said, "aren't they all?"

"She mentioned one of the girls she talked to at the

Canteen," Lucille says, "the one who looked like her, according to Dagwood—Arthur Lake—whom Beth also met at the Canteen. The other junior hostess, Georgette Bauerdorf, was a very wealthy girl but a real regular person, according to Beth."

One afternoon in the Formosa Café near Goldwyn Studios, the actor Franchot Tone approached Beth. She was at the bar as the actor stepped from the inside telephone booth. He pretended to know her, dropping a few names, but Beth only smiled and shook her head. "She said she was waiting for someone," Tone says, "and I said, 'Of course you are, you're waiting for me! And I have just arrived."' He says it was "a ridiculous line" he had used before. The actor insisted he remembered her "very well. . . . Most girls were flattered by it, but this one seemed more concerned that I'd had too much to drink." He told her he had finished a film with director Robert Siodmak, *Phantom Lady*, and convinced Beth that an associate interviewing young women with "your kind of looks" would be most interested in meeting her. He could tell she was impressed and that he was making headway toward a late afternoon date.

He took her to the unoccupied office of the "associate" but she was not interested in cozying up on the sofa, which opened into a bed. Tone says, "I thought it was a pickup from the start—she came with me so easily—but to her it wasn't anything of the kind!"

It was an extraordinary experience, Tone later recalled. Beth believed they had "hit it off" as people. She was disappointed that Tone had only "that" in mind. He tried to kiss her a couple of times and told her she had the most gorgeous eyes in the world, which he thought she did—dreamy eyes that he was almost seeing through smoke. He could imagine her as a siren luring sailors to their death. And then she turned ice cold.

Always the gentleman, Tone turned the situation around and made it seem that he had made a mistake thinking that she was after romance. He did find her most refreshing to "talk" to, he said, but secretly the actor was flustered—a pathetic scene, and the girl seemed so sad and disappointed that Tone had to hold back tears. "She told me she'd been ill," he says, "something about an operation to her chest." He had been used to "a whole different breed," he says. He gave her a phone number to reach him about "the part and the associate. I gave her whatever bills were in my pocket and I had the feeling that I wanted to be away from her—that I did not want to be near her. It was a strange and unsettling experience. Even after I called a cab for her and she was gone, the feeling stayed with me. It was almost as though I had experienced being afraid of her."

The Streets of Paris bar became a favorite hangout for Beth and Barbara Lee. One afternoon while Beth was waiting at the piano bar for Barbara, she noticed a plain-faced man staring at her from several stools away. He was drawing a picture on a pad, and said to her, "I'm sketching you." He asked her if she ever posed for an artist. She said no, she was an actress but she did modeling, too. He introduced himself as Arthur James, and said he was an artist and his oil paintings were being sold at a gallery in Crossroads of the World on Sunset.

He asked if she was interested in posing, and said he'd pay a percentage of what he made from the sale of a painting if in fact he developed the sketches of her into oil portraits. Beth was agreeable. She said she'd love to, but she'd need money—in a few days she'd have to find a place to stay.

James said, "Maybe we can work something out." He lived in the Amour Arms on Orchid Avenue, a building once famous for its floating staircase. He offered her a place to stay in lieu of payment. "You'd have your own small room, on the top floor, and it has a very pretty view of the Hollywood Hills." And he promised there'd be no hanky-panky.

James was serious about painting, fancying himself a kind of Toulouse-Lautrec, sketching and drinking in the Hollywood bars and lounges. He had a makeshift easel, sketched canvas, brushes, and paints in the apartment.

When Beth picked up her clothes and makeup at the Sunshine Apartments, she told Lucille about the artist. Within a few days, Arthur had finished several sketches of Beth reclining "like the *Naked Maja*," he called it—draped, with her arms up and her hands clasped behind her head.

"After a little while of seeing him," Lucille says, "and at the same time she was dating the Army Air Corps guy, she said the artist asked if he could touch her breasts because he wanted to feel for the proportions, and she said he was so shy about it that she didn't feel insulted."

James wanted her to lie on his studio couch with another girl, both embracing while he made sketches for what he said would be a large "Sappho" painting. The picture could be sold for a lot of money, he said, and both girls could get a good share from their percentages. Whether Beth ever got around to posing for the Sappho painting is not known, but according to Lucille, Arthur might have used a Kodak and taken photographs of the girls that he would use for future paintings.

Lucille says, "She told me more about this artist, Arthur, and the sketches. He sounded like a very sad character or some sort of sex screwball."

4

While Beth posed for strange paintings and made the rounds, her acquaintance, Georgette, continued as a junior hostess at the Canteen. Beth had never finished high school, but Georgette had been to Westlake and Marlborough schools, enjoying the advantages of wealth and prestige. Like Beth, she kept a diary and lists of servicemen she dated or became friends with at the Canteen—or entertained in her Mediterranean-style apartment off the Sunset Strip. Georgette drove a green Oldsmobile and, according to her close friends, was very generous to servicemen, not only giving them rides, but often money. And if they needed a place to stay, she'd offer her apartment.

An actress who attended several parties "Georgie" threw for servicemen claims the socialite spread herself wide. But Georgette, like Beth, had one special soldier she cared for, and she planned to celebrate his military graduation in Texas. She bought plane tickets the first week in October.

Georgette's neighbor, actress Stella Adler, was puzzled the morning of October 12th when she noticed Georgette's apartment door ajar. She remembers thinking that if she called Georgette or pushed the bell to alert her to the half-opened door, it might prove embarrassing to someone, so Stella walked away from the building.

An hour and a half later, the housemaid entered through the open door and heard water dripping. She went upstairs into the bathroom and saw Georgette floating face down in the bathtub. Warm, bloody water was overflowing onto the bathroom floor. The maid leaned over, turned off the faucet, and ran downstairs to get the janitor and to summon the building manager.

The janitor hurried into the apartment. Thinking that Georgette had fainted, he started to lift her while the water was let out of the tub. Georgette felt warm, but he immediately realized she was dead. The building manager entered, intending to give first aid. When she saw it was too late, she called the sheriff and the Bauerdorfs' family attorney.

Deputy A.L. Hutchinson responded to what was flagged an accidental drowning. "She was in the tub sort of on her side and face down," the deputy says. He notified homicide and made a visual inspection of the scene while waiting for the inspectors and the coroner.

He noticed she was wearing only the top of her pajamas and was nude from the waist down. He found the bottoms of the pajamas in the bedroom, which was across the hall from the bathroom. The bottoms were torn down the side, and other clothes were scattered around the room. There appeared to be a large bloodstain on the floor. It was still damp, as though someone had tried to wash it out. The bed was messed up, like it might have been used. A newspaper was beside the bed. Nearby was a purse, its contents spilled.

The housemaid told the deputy she had been awakened during the night "by the sound of something making a crash in her apartment, something that sounded metallic. It was in the early morning hours."

Another neighbor said he heard a scream. "I heard a female cry, 'Stop, stop, you're killing me!' The screams then were quiet and I thought it was a squabble and went back to sleep. It was about 2:30 in the morning."

Inspector William Penprase arrived and observed the body. "It looks like she fell in," he said to Hutchinson. "She's smashed her nose against something, and has a piece of towel or some cloth in her mouth. She obviously drowned." He decided not to remove the cloth, but to wait for the coroner. He was then summoned to the phone—the girl's father was calling from New York. George Bauerdorf was a Wall Street financier, independent oil man, and gold mine owner. The family was socially prominent and based in New York.

Hutchinson says, "I heard him talking on the phone with her father. He told him it appeared to be an accident; that she'd fallen, injured her nose, and was probably unconscious when she went into the tub and drowned."

George Bauerdorf stated to the press in New York that his daughter suffered severe cramps and heart pains, and that she had fainted and fallen tragically into the bathtub. Penprase reported that Georgette might have had a bloody nose before the fall. "This would account for the stains on the carpet," he said. He had no idea about the piece of cloth protruding from her mouth. "It's a mystery to me."

Georgette Bauerdorf was brought to the morgue at three o'clock by the Sinai Funeral Home. But because the following day was Columbus Day, the autopsy was postponed until after the holiday.

A preliminary examination was undertaken by Dr. Frank R. Webb, an autopsy surgeon, who said the girl had been dead approximately ten hours. He then interrupted the examination and made the statement that, "There is no evidence here that the girl died by drowning. This is not an accidental death. She was dead before she was placed in the bathtub. What we're dealing with is a homicide."

She was strangled, the surgeon said, with the square of toweling that was thrust deep into her throat. And then she was raped as she lay dying or was already dead.

"It didn't take long to figure out that effort had been taken by the killer to make certain that the front of the apartment would be dark either when he entered or when he left the premises," Hutchinson says. "The automatic light over the outside entrance to her apartment had been unscrewed two turns around so the switch wouldn't turn it on. Prints were lifted off the lightbulb . . . and whoever turned the globe must have stood on a chair or used some other physical assistance to reach the electrical outlet which was nearly eight feet from the floor."

"Or someone fairly tall," says Sheriff's Captain Gordan Bowers, who was heading the homicide investigation. He noted that no attempt had been made to burglarize the apartment. The rape and murder had been the sole motive. A large roll of two-dollar bills and thousands of dollars worth of sterling silver were found in an open trunk. Her jewelry had not been taken, and other valuables had apparently been overlooked. It appeared, from the evidence gathered at the apartment, that there was some cash taken from her purse, along with keys, and that her car was missing.

There were traces of lipstick on her mouth, but the numerous cigarette butts in the ashtrays bore no lipstick stains. Her diary, found in the bedroom, was filled with the names of many servicemen. Fingerprints were taken throughout the apartment—many sets of different prints. The sheriff's department asked the army to help trace the individuals as fast as possible before they might be shipped elsewhere.

Georgette's car was located the next day in the southeast part of downtown L.A., abandoned on East 25th Street near San Pedro. The car was out of gas, with the keys still in the ignition.

Fingerprints were found on the driver's window and on the steering wheel, and prints lifted from the car door were the same as some of the prints taken in the apartment. The prints that were found on the unscrewed light bulb were linked to prints in the car. Bowers said whoever took her car was the one who set the stage for this crime, and was lying in wait for her.

"She screamed once," Bowers says, reconstructing the murder, "and to shut her up, a wad of toweling was forced into her mouth and down her throat. She choked to death, probably in seconds, and was raped *following* death, on the bedroom floor—where the bloodstains were found." The killer attempted to remove the towel from her mouth, but her jaws were clenched shut, and he ripped the material, leaving a short piece of it protruding from her mouth. The rest of the cloth was wedged in her throat.

Bowers believes the killer then, for some reason, used the torn end of the cloth to try to mop up the blood on the carpet. Unable to clean it, he apparently pocketed the piece of cloth, since it was not found at the scene or in the car. He lifted her body from the floor, carried it into the bathroom and placed her facedown into the tub. Whether the water was running when her body was put there or had been turned on by the killer could not be determined.

June Zeiger, a friend of Georgette's who had been with her at the Canteen the night before the murder, told the inspectors that less than a month before "Georgie dated a very tall soldier, a buddy of another soldier she talked about and said she wrote about in her diary." June said Georgette saw him several times, but for some reason she was frightened of him and refused to go out with him again.

Georgette's friends and co-hostesses at the Canteen attempted to recall the various soldiers that she had seen *recently*. Bowers says, "Of all the guys we came up with it was the tall, thin one that June Zeiger talked about that we couldn't pin down."

"He didn't dance," June told Bowers. "He seemed to be drinking a lot; more than some of the others. He didn't take part in anything. . . . He just wanted to hold back, you know."

Following the autopsy, Dr. Webb said there were only a few drops of water in the girl's lungs, and these could have come from the cloth in her mouth. She had struggled against the attack—there were numerous bruises and abrasions found on her body. "The knuckles on her right hand were smashed and bruised," he said, "and there was a large contusion on the right side of her head—apparently caused by a fist striking her, and another on her abdomen. On her right thigh there was the bruised imprint of a hand, even to the fingernails piercing the skin. She had eaten string beans approximately an hour before her death." The inspectors had found an empty can that had contained string beans, and some melon rinds, in the kitchen wastebasket.

The Bauerdorfs' attorney in Los Angeles made arrangements

for Georgette's body to be sent to New York. The Long Island cemetery where she would be laid to rest had served seven generations of Bauerdorfs.

Complicating the investigation, a story emerged from Bauerdorf's wealthy business associates and attorneys contradicting certain facts uncovered by the investigation. Despite the wealth and social standing of the family, Georgette was, "a free-wheeling, dusk-to-dawn, good-time gal," according to Bowers. "We had more than a hundred different sets of prints, different soldiers and servicemen, in the girl's swanky apartment.

"Whether she entertained at home as well as at the Canteen is nobody's business but hers. But if one of those guys happens to be the individual we're looking for, then we have to keep on it if we're going to solve the murder."

On the other side of Hollywood, Barbara Lee and her friends were shocked by the murder. "It was like a helluva pall had fallen on us," Barbara says, "and Bob, my producer boyfriend, kept calling Beth at the artist's place because Beth said she was afraid to go back to the Canteen . . . and was really upset because her new boyfriend had been shipped out.

"I saw her on McCadden a week or so later and she said the artist had bought her some brand new luggage and they were going to Tucson to do some modeling work. I said, 'Tucson? You mean the goddamn desert?' She said it wasn't a *desert*, the city itself, and some important people would be taking the photographs. I told her Bob would miss her. I was being cute, you know, sarcastic, and she said very sincerely, 'Oh, I'm sorry. Tell him I'll be back soon, and tell him I'll miss him, and I'll miss you, too.' I thought, boy, it takes all kinds to bake a cake or fill up the world. And when you think you've got it filled up the right way, with someone like Georgie Bauerdorf, you find out the world's got a way of pulling it out from right under you."

Arthur James had a bank account under the name of Charles B. Smith, but he didn't have any money in the account. That didn't stop him from writing checks.

Nineteen-year-old Bobbie Rey Harris, and Beth, now twenty, boarded the *Southern Pacific Daylight* at Union Station with James and headed for Arizona. They arrived in Tucson on the night of November 12, and the three checked into the Hotel Catalina on Broadway.

Bobbie Rey Harris recalls the arrangement at the Catalina as "two corner rooms that were across from one another because we—the girls—were going to sleep in the one room, the one that had a toilet, and it also had a bathtub. The other room, the one Arthur took, didn't have a toilet but it had a basin, and there was a men's room or bathroom downstairs. I don't remember if there was a toilet upstairs for the other people."

But that night Bobbie didn't sleep in the room with Beth. She says, "Arthur wanted to talk, so I wound up sleeping in his room in the small bed. Often he had oral sex upon me, and then we made love. He asked me to come into his room because Beth was sound asleep."

The following morning, while Beth soaked in the bathtub, Arthur and Bobbie "snuck out," as Bobbie recalls it, and went downtown in a taxi, "just to be driving around and going to stores buying stuff." James was writing checks, and he and Bobbie were in the middle of buying new clothes when two policemen and a security guard asked James to step aside. While one officer put handcuffs on Arthur, the other took Bobbie into a small office. "They asked me a lot of questions about my age, and where we came from and if Arthur'd had sexual intercourse with me," Bobbie says. "They said a doctor would examine me and they would know if I was telling the truth. So I told them we'd had intercourse."

James was charged with violation of the Mann Act—white slavery—for having brought Bobbie across the state line for the purpose of having sexual intercourse with her.

Two detectives went to the Hotel Catalina to remove evidence from James's room. They did not extend their search to the room Beth was occupying, and Bobbie later recalled that it was Arthur's hotel key that had sent the Tucson police to his room. Beth was overlooked because she, and not Bobbie, had kept the key to the room they had rented.

Fearing another encounter with police, Beth packed her clothes in her brand new luggage and called a taxi to take her to the train depot. The trip back to Los Angeles took a day and a half. Upon reaching Union Station, she spent a few hours trying to reach Lucille and Barbara before boarding a train bound for Chicago.

Arthur was held on $5,000 bail in Pima County jail. Bobbie Rey was held as a material witness, and required recognizance in the amount of $500. Failing to execute the recognizance, Bobbie was held in Pima County jail. Arthur, refusing a court-appointed attorney, attempted to defend himself through various ploys, including changes of venue and hardship on witnesses whose appearance in Arizona would hamper the war effort, as he claimed they worked in defense plants. On February 13, 1945, Arthur changed his plea to guilty and received a two-year sentence for white slavery. Bobbie was released, and Arthur was transported to the federal prison at Leavenworth, Kansas. Upon his release from Leavenworth on September 21, 1946, he was arrested for forgery and writing bad checks by California (one of the checks was for Beth's luggage), was found guilty, and received another prison sentence.

5

After two days in Chicago, Beth felt cut off from everything. She felt anxious and hounded and didn't know why. She wasn't like Bobbie Rey—a fact that relieved her but at the same time brought a deep, uncomfortable feeling. Things would change, she told herself, writing a letter; there could come a time when everything would change. Maybe soon . . . She didn't mail the letter but folded it into the *Collier's* magazine she'd bought in the train depot. The train to Boston was on time.

A United War Bond rally was in progress at Boston's South Station when Beth got off the train, and an army captain was speaking into a microphone. In charge of the war bond drive was a tall, dark-haired young man wearing a big "Buy Bonds" badge, and when he saw Beth listening to the captain, he approached her, removed his badge, and pinned it to the lapel of her overcoat.

He introduced himself as Phillip Jeffers and told her he recognized her from the movie theater in Medford. He asked her if she knew what a blockbuster was. "Of course I do," she said. "It's a bomb about as tall as you are."

He said, "We're bringing one in later today. It can't detonate and there's no explosives inside but it's to symbolize our efforts with the drive. If you're going to be here tomorrow, I'll appreciate your posing beside it—with me and the committee. It's for our publicity." He told her it was being delivered at noon the next day.

Beth said she'd try to make it, and he gave her his card. She could call the committee headquarters the following morning. She said, "Do you want me to wear a bathing suit or be a sweater girl?" He laughed—blushing, which surprised her. No, he said, what she had on was fine—without the overcoat, but with the badge on.

Beth spent the evening telling her mother about the promising prospects in Hollywood, but while she was making headway, she felt at a disadvantage due to her lack of professional training.

Phoebe said that she would gain the skills through practical experience. The fact that she'd been ill and hadn't finished school would prove no hindrance to her daughter.

The following day Beth took her bathing suit with her to Boston just to be on the safe side. She had hoped to spend the evening having dinner and talking to Phillip following the blockbuster photo session, but the young man and several of his volunteers were bound for New Hampshire and other states on the eastern seaboard. Beth didn't tell her family about Phillip.

She remained in Medford over Thanksgiving with her mother and sisters, but stayed less than a month before traveling to Miami Beach. Again she stayed with friends of the family, and found part-time work in a café operated by a former show girl billed as "Princess Whitewing." Beth was fascinated with the Princess's tales of show business, and listened to the stories long past closing—unless she had a date.

Almost daily Beth met new servicemen and went on dates, but she liked to think she was keeping a special place "in her heart" for Gordan Fickling.

This sentiment changed on New Year's Eve of 1945, when flyer Major Matt Gordan stepped into her life. A few days later the major asked her to be his wife.

"I'm so much in love, I'm sure it shows," she wrote to her mother. "Matt is so wonderful, not like other men . . . and he asked me to marry him."

Phoebe was very surprised with this news, but impressed with the photograph her daughter sent of herself and the handsome pilot. She wanted to *talk* to Beth about her health, and her growth as a young woman, but believed that her daughter was now old enough to take care of her own personal concerns.

Matt gave Beth a gold wristwatch that was set with diamonds as a pre-engagement gift, and wrote to his own sister-in-law that Beth "is an educated and refined girl whom I plan to marry." He asked his sister-in-law to correspond with Beth and get to know her because, he wrote, "when I return I plan to make her my bride." It was clear that Matt respected Beth's wish to consummate their love the night of their wedding, and he told his soon-to-be bride they would plan their honeymoon once he returned from overseas.

Letters went back and forth between Beth and Matt, and in April she returned to Medford to await his return. The letters continued and in one week she wrote seventeen letters to him. She told Muriel that her love for Matt was like the newsreels they'd seen of Old Faithful geyser in Yellowstone Park—where "the flow just keeps bursting forth."

"My Sweetheart," Beth wrote, "I love you, I love you, I love you. Sweetheart of all my dreams. Darling, those are the words of a new song in the States and believe me when I say that it suits me to a T. Oh, Matt, honestly, I suppose when two people are in love as we are, our letters sound out of this world to a censor. I don't care, though, if the whole world knows it."

Beth found a temporary swing-shift job in a Cambridge restaurant, and on the day Germany surrendered she wrote to Matt: "Please take good care of yourself for me, darling, because you are private property. Today is V-E Day. I feel so happy. People are throwing paper from the windows and are ready to run wild. It is going to be wonderful, darling, when this is all over. You want to slip away and be married. We'll do whatever you wish, darling. Whatever you want, I want. I love you and all I want is you."

Her sisters thought she looked so radiant. She seemed to beam whenever she mentioned Matt's name, or when she'd show the linens he'd sent from the Philippines. Beth carefully packed them in her trunk, telling her mother, "This will serve as my hope chest for now." She planned for an October wedding in Medford, a few months away. After the ceremony she would go with Matt to Colorado to meet his mother, on their way to California. Beth was walking on air, almost singing as she went.

But the war was still going on and personal happiness served only as a thin coating to cover the deep fears that mobilized the home front. Phillip Jeffers, the "war bond boy wonder," was back in Boston on a bond drive with several new supporting businesses. Beth had learned from a recruiting sergeant that Jeffers had a special deferment due to his ability to conduct highly successful war bond drives.

Phillip and Beth met again. She seemed so self-assured and charming that he felt as if he wanted to hide. "I've never met anyone quite like you," he told her.

Although they spent time together the next two months, Phillip would never be able to figure her out. "We never met at her house in Medford," he says, "usually somewhere else, on a particular corner or an out-of-the-way café. Not that I was married, but she just seemed to prefer it that way."

He felt that he could talk to her. She seemed to understand things that he couldn't tell other people. They would drive around in his car, maybe stopping in a drive-in for cheeseburgers, or sometimes parking near the reservoir. There were a few kisses, "just necking a little," Phillip says, "but nothing passionate. We laughed and talked, and we went skinny-dipping a couple of times, but there was no sex involved."

He was a *virgin*, and he told her so, red-faced with embarrassment. She laughed playfully and said, "Well, so am I! I'm a virgin just like you." Phillip would sometimes sneak her into the rooming house where he stayed. There were strict rules for the unmarried males—no females allowed in the rooms.

Beth and Phillip would whisper and giggle but with the shortage of rentals, he had to be careful. They would talk or give each other relaxing massages. They would remove their clothing and take turns trying out Swedish massage techniques Phillip had learned from a mail order course. "It was strange to be content just to touch and look at her body," he says, "and her skin almost like a baby's. . . . All of it was rather innocent, like kids. Nothing ever happened between us—we stayed virgins."

There were moments when Phillip would have a *feeling* about her—he wanted to shake her and tell her to wipe all that makeup off her face. He had heard that she dated a lot of guys, and she always had makeup on and that bothered him. She didn't *talk* about other men, and he knew nothing about that part of her life except rumors. He believed she was a person that never lied. She'd said she was a virgin and he believed her. If she didn't want him to know something, she wouldn't talk about it. But she didn't lie. Phillip was convinced of that. "She was *smart*, an intelligent girl," he says, "but she seemed content to just float."

One night they were laughing and joking and Beth became very quiet. A sadness came over her that he did not understand. "What is it that's bothering you?" Phillip asked. "Please tell me what's wrong." She stared for a moment. Her eyes were watery. "Let's enjoy today, right now," she said. "Enjoy what we have in life!"

Sometimes late at night Beth's silhouette would appear against the drawn window shade of the room she shared with Muriel. Several neighborhood men would hide in the dark of the courtyard, watching her shadow move back and forth, undressing and stretching, and getting ready for bed. It was something the men who gathered in the courtyard did not talk about, though at one point they brought along folding chairs to be more comfortable as they watched.

As Beth saw less of Phillip and worked longer hours at the Cambridge restaurant, she became a regular at the Medford Café, a late-night hangout in the Square. "It would usually be after midnight when she'd come in the café," recalls Joe Sabia, at the time attending Leland Powers School of Radio. He had wanted to fight in the war but was 4-F due to a disability. At night he'd go over to the café or sometimes shoot pool with friends in the pool hall downstairs in the same building as the café. When the hall closed for the night, Joe and his friends would go upstairs to get something to eat.

The café was dark, had high ceilings with globes hanging from chains, and booths on both sides of the room. There were tables and chairs in the center and a row of windows across the front wall. "Sugar was rationed, so *they'd* put the sugar and cream in your coffee," Joe remembers.

Beth liked to sit in a booth, and if she joined Joe and his friends, they'd move over to a booth. Sometimes if the talk got rough or crude, she had a way of freezing a guy with a look, or she'd leave and join someone else. He thought she seemed like a private person.

"I have this clear memory of her, in a light blue two-piece dress or suit that brought out the color of her eyes. She usually wore a raincoat—an all-purpose coat.

"She didn't like a couple of my pool buddies," he says. "One was a wolf and he figured every woman put out, just a matter of the time. . . . He'd say Beth was 'built like a brick shithouse, and every brick lays.' Stuff like that. One of the other guys imitated him, but somehow never could score."

Joe looked forward to the times when he'd be sitting alone with Beth. But often she'd join the police lieutenant who came in around the same time for a late night meal. Later he became chief of police and said he missed talking to Beth in the café.

Sometimes, when Beth left the café, Joe would watch her stroll up Salem Street—her hips swaying. He'd watch her until she disappeared from sight and he could no longer hear the clicking of her heels on the pavement.

Joe knew she wanted to be somebody famous but felt she was just hanging out—with stars in her eyes—dreams instead of plans. "She was like a shadow figure," he says. "There was this void—something missing."

The day the war ended, Medford's air raid siren suffered a mechanical mishap. "It got stuck," recalls Muriel. "You had this horrible noise, a steady wail with no break." People were afraid at first, searching the sky for airplanes, some even ducking for cover. Then one of the neighbors began screaming that it was the *signal*! The war was over! "You couldn't really hear the words because everyone was yelling, but you knew that's what they were saying."

Bells were ringing and cars horns were blaring. People poured into the streets, stopping the cars and trolleys. Most of the Medford Square businesses shut down, and those that didn't had people leaning out of the windows, throwing paper and water balloons on the crowd below. The celebrating went on all night and into the next morning.

For Beth it meant that Matt would be coming home and they would be married sooner than planned. She talked excitedly about a small wedding, the trip to California . . . meeting his mother in Colorado.

A few days later a telegram arrived from Matt's mother. Muriel watched as Beth tore it open, saying it was probably about the wedding. Beth read the telegram, then stood there, holding the piece of paper, staring at it. "It's not going to be," she said. "I can't believe it's not going to be. . . ." She handed Muriel the telegram. Her sister read it out loud: "*Received word War Department. Matt killed in plane crash on way home from India. Our deepest sympathy is with you. Pray it isn't true.*" It was signed "Love," by Mrs. Matt Gordan, Sr.

For days Beth read and reread love letters, or studied the newspaper clipping Mrs. Gordan had sent about Matt. Where it mentioned his bride "whom he was going to meet and marry in Medford," Beth crossed out "*and marry*," later claiming that it was a misprint, that she and Matt were married. She would then begin to elaborate on the dream marriage by talking about her and Matt's baby—born to them after the marriage, but dying at birth.

She tied the letters in bundles with red ribbon and stored them in her trunk. Then she began to try on different outfits and ensembles, and spent a great deal of time smoothing a pale, almost white cosmetic powder over her face. With her mass of black hair and the bright red lipstick, she had given herself the look of something like a porcelain China doll.

Using a neighbor's telephone or the pay phone in the Medford Café, she made collect calls in an attempt to pin down some job possibilities—modeling in Miami through Duffy, or perhaps in Chicago—maybe even something in Indianapolis.

She wrote an urgent letter to Matt's mother, asking if she

could possibly send Beth enough money to "start a new life over again." She had waited faithfully for Matt, she said, but their future together had been taken away by the war.

Gordan Fickling returned one of the calls she'd placed to old friends. She told him she hoped that they could meet again, perhaps soon. Her fiancé had been killed in action, she said, and now she had to do *something* with her life.

Gordan said he was bound to be transferred in the next few months, and he'd like very much to see her. They could keep in contact for now, and when he stopped over in Chicago maybe she could meet him there? Beth said it must be fate, because sometime in the coming year she might have a job possibility in Chicago, modeling hats. But she was spending the winter in Florida.

Gordan Fickling wrote to her, "I have been trying to convince myself that you really want to hear from me again, after all this time, in which I have apparently been ignoring you completely. I have always remembered you. I can't deny that.

"Your letter gave me the impression that you didn't want to consider that you had a particular claim on my heart, and I started letting things drift along on their own. You really should have gotten me.

"I get awful lonesome sometimes and wonder if we really haven't been very childish and foolish about the whole affair. Have we?"

Duffy was back in Miami Beach and Beth contacted him when she arrived in Florida. He promised to advance her enough money to live until he could sew up some work for her in "the windy city," most likely in the spring. In the meantime, he could use her as a hostess, he told her, entertaining business associates until the hat-modeling job came through, which would be for newspaper ads.

Duffy had been a tap dancer years before until arthritis had crippled one knee, forcing him into a new line of work. After nine years in advertising and with three department store clients, his small agency had hopscotched from Houston to Miami Beach and to Chicago where he planned to settle in to renovate an old hotel. The war had dampened the advertising business, but he was now looking ahead to prosperity.

Beth left Miami shortly after Duffy went north. She stayed at home in Medford from February until April when Duffy brought her to Chicago and put her up in the hotel, often taking her to dinner with clients and to a couple of clubs featuring Chicago-style jazz. While she could be charming to his business prospects, Duffy sensed she was too despondent at times. He said, "Honey, people can see that you are *not* happy. This is a time for people to be happy—and I *need* you to be happy." She told him it was the dust in the halls from the renovation. It was causing her breathing problems, she said. She didn't like Chicago and she wanted to do something with her life besides smile at older businessmen.

When she saw Gordan during his two-day stopover, she realized that the way their romance had been developing in L.A. was what she wanted out of life. She could be happy with Gordan, and she knew he would love her and marry her. She wrote to him in Long Beach and told him that she knew he loved her, and that she cared very deeply for him. She wanted to join him in Long Beach. She missed him with all of her heart, she told him. "After all," she said, "You are my beau from the year before."

Gordan wanted Beth to make the trip to Long Beach, but wrote, "Are you really sure what you want?" Did she really want to be with him? If her answer was yes, he said, "no one will be happier to see you than a certain lieutenant in Long Beach." He sent her the one-hundred-dollar train fare and arranged a hotel room for her. She quickly shipped her trunk Railway Express, packed her bags, and boarded the *Sunset Limited* for California. What Duffy had said about it being a time for people to be happy, for Beth seemed once again a possibility. It could be like a dream come true.

But she had not counted on living alone in a hotel miles from the base where Gordan was stationed. He met her at the Long Beach depot and took her to the Atwater Hotel. It was as though he had become a different person from the one that asked her to make the trip.

Beth contacted Lucille Varela and told her she had just

arrived in Long Beach. She said she had gotten together with Gordan in Chicago and had fallen head over heels in love with him all over again, though their relationship was almost "platonic." They kissed, she said, did love one another, but only through marriage could she completely give herself to a man.

And now, having brought her to Long Beach, Gordan was avoiding talk of marriage. He wanted her to be some sort of "concubine," to be holed up in a hotel somewhere, but not his wife.

"I think," says Lucille, "she was really hurt by his attitude, and so she tried to make it seem like her coming out there really hadn't been to see Gordan, as the sole purpose, and that he'd only been helping her—once again, as she put it. She said something like, 'Well, two can play the game as well as one,' and she started dating other guys in Long Beach."

Lucille believes that Beth's flirtations, the result of the vivid impressions she could make on men, were only that—flirtations. But Gordan suspected that she was being unfaithful to him, succumbing to the other servicemen that surrounded her. They argued about her friendliness toward other guys, especially one sailor, just a kid. She'd gone to the Long Beach Pike with him and he'd tattooed her name on his arm inside of a red heart. He'd said, kidding, "You know, Elizabeth's also my mother's name, so if you don't love me, my mom will."

A new movie was playing around the corner, *The Blue Dahlia*, with Alan Ladd and Veronica Lake. Two soldiers started kidding around and called Beth "the *Black* Dahlia." Even the drugstore proprietor and his son were amused by the name. A.L. Landers owned the pharmacy, and often winked to his son when Beth showed up. "She'd come into the drugstore frequently," Landers says. "She'd usually be wearing a two-piece beach costume which left her midriff bare. Or she'd wear black lacy things. Her hair was jet black and she liked to wear it high. She was popular with the men who came in the drugstore and they got to calling her the Black Dahlia."

Other servicemen began looking for her. "Has *she* come in today?" they'd ask Landers, "the *Black Dahlia*?" And they'd tell their buddies, "Wait until you get an eyeful of the Black Dahlia."

6

She knew all the songs by heart—the Andrews Sisters—Kate Smith—Bing Crosby—Jo Stafford—and after finding her genuinely friendly, Hal McGuire told her he had connections with *the* Andrew Sisters' radio show, because he was a radio ad salesman. She said, "You are? Can you get me into the radio station?" Before he could answer she surprised him by blurting out a song—something from *Eight to the Bar Ranch,* soft at first.

"Sing it louder—it sounds pretty good," he said, and she did. She had a fair voice, he told her, and he could tell she liked the lyrics. He said she should at least try for an audition for commercials. A lot of money was being made singing soup and soap jingles.

"I think that's a very good idea," she said.

He wondered why she was hanging around the drugstore. A couple of times he'd been in to buy something for his sour stomach and he'd seen her yacking it up with servicemen.

They had coffee, and she talked about her pending-but-not-so-certain marriage. She said, "It would be my second trip to the altar." She mentioned her first husband, a Flying Tigers pilot killed in action, and while trying to put her life back together she'd met another flyer who wanted to marry her. But she confessed she was nervous about marrying so soon after her first husband's death.

Hal remembers her saying something about being "cautious with your emotions." But if marriage wasn't panning out, she still had optimism about her life. She wanted to be an actress, she told Hal. They talked about movies for a while and again he mentioned radio. He was on the salesman side of the mike, he said, but had a connection with the *Great Gildersleeve* show and was working with the *Old Fashioned Revival Hour* out of Long Beach, and that was the reason for his commute from L.A.

He told her whenever she was in Hollywood and wanted to visit the radio station, he'd introduce her to Judy Canova or the Riders of the Purple Sage. She asked Hal for his card. If he wasn't at the station, he said, she could reach him through a friend working at KMPC on Hollywood Boulevard, "The Station of the Stars."

Over the next few days Hal went out of his way to look for her in the drugstore, until some problems arose where she was staying. She was moving to another room on Lime Street. Hal didn't want to get involved in the spats with her boyfriend—whoever he was. She didn't seem to have any regrets or get upset about gathering her things together and leaving the Atwater Hotel. After a few days she told Hal she saw no reason to stay in Long Beach. She couldn't go back home to Massachusetts because of the railway strike, so she supposed the best plan would be to go to Hollywood, since Hal had said he'd help her out as soon as she got there. "It's only an hour away!" she laughed.

He made arrangements for a hotel room at the Dix in Hollywood—she'd be a guest of the radio station, he told her. The morning she left with him she was dressed in black as though going to a funeral. He asked, sort of joking, "Did somebody die?" She was even wearing a veil. He loaded her luggage "and a few dresses still on hangers" into his car.

She didn't have any money, so Hal loaned her some as soon as they reached the hotel and said to her, "I'd like to get to know you better." They made a date for dinner the following evening, but she didn't show up.

Almost from her first day back in L.A., Beth began to tag after Barbara Lee through the lunch stands, soda fountains, and bars. "She was no teetotaller prohibitionist," Barbara says, "but neither was she a lush by far. She liked going to the spots; it wasn't the drinking she was after but the going and gabbing and living it up. . . .

"She liked to sit there looking gorgeous and being looked at, being admired, and I'd see one guy after the other, like they were standing in line, and she was not promiscuous or overly inviting, though that in itself gave her an allurer air, you know, the hard-to-get one.

"She called me the first night she was at the Dix on Cahuenga and when we connected the next night—after maybe a year or a year and a half—she said she was being shown the town by a salesman with a radio station."

Though Beth had stood Hal up on the dinner date, she did see him several times at the Four Star Grill. She did not let him forget he had promised to take her by the radio station. She had called his friend several times at KMPC, and each time, Hal says, "She left some urgent message as though things had to be handled immediately. In the very short time since I knew her, and gotten the room for her, she seemed to be running in ten different directions, and always with several other people. Her manner was that she could be friends with you right from the start—guys as well as girls, only with the guys, I guess, they felt that right away there was interest on her part in them as boyfriends, but in fact, you quickly learned that wasn't what she had in mind. It was more like you'd all been at a church social or a girl-scout meeting. . . . What you had was this beautiful girl that would light up so bright when she saw you, it sort of caught you off guard, and had you thinking she'd taken a turn for you. When you saw that wasn't what the case, it was pretty disappointing."

To Hal she seemed mixed up with a crowd that bar-hopped the nights away and slept till noon. She renewed old friendships, like with Lucille Varela, now living with some guy in a room near

Sunset and Vermont. "Both girls came with me," Hal says, "to lunch and then to the station where I finally introduced Beth to Judy Canova. . . . I left them there because I had some meetings."

Lucille remembers that Beth seemed shy and quiet when she met Judy Canova, but after a moment was chatting away, Lucille says, "without even stopping to take a breath. The two were laughing and it was like they knew each other from someplace, though, no, Beth said she had never met Miss Canova in her life."

Marjorie Graham, from Massachusetts, was sitting at the lunch counter in Woolworth's on Hollywood Boulevard when she saw Beth walking past. Marjorie called to her. "When Beth saw me," Marjorie recalls, "she looked shocked at first, and then she got very excited. I told her I'd come out to join my husband who was stationed in Long Beach and I'd gotten a job in Hollywood."

Beth told Marjorie about her movie plans, and when they left Woolworth's after an hour of talk it was decided that Beth would stay with Marjorie. She was already sharing a hotel room with a girl named Lynn who was trying to be a singer. "Rooms were really hard to find," Marjorie says, "and when you did find one you could only stay a few days."

Lynn Martin was not twenty-two years old, as she looked—she was not even sixteen that September. Blonde and pretty, she said she couldn't walk down the boulevard without being propositioned by at least ten guys old enough to be her father—ready to splurge on a dinner, a date, a night in the clubs. And while waiting for her lucky star to shine, Lynn had no intentions of going hungry or doing without a pair of nylons. "I'm not going to be using any of that tan makeup and drawing lines down the back of my legs so someone's thinking I'm wearing stockings." She'd fluff herself up to look larger than she was, but still she looked like a small canary. "I'm going to be a nightclub singer and I'm going to have lots of clothes and I'm going to spend money on anything I damn well want to!"

Beth later told Marjorie she found herself drawn to Lynn even though there was a lot about the girl she didn't like. Lynn's back and shoulders were badly scarred from attempts to remove tattoos. But there was a sparkle to her; she was far away from where she belonged (Lynn would never say where that was) and both of them had something in common: they kept secrets.

Marjorie would later recall that there were times when Lynn and Beth were like little girls—giggling and doing things they weren't supposed to do.

But there were problems, like Lynn wanting to wear some of Beth's clothes. Lynn was too small, and Beth had developed the habit of traveling fairly light—making the most of what she had and keeping it ready for sudden moves. She gave Lynn a few things she felt she had outgrown, that Beth now felt were too childish for her. Lynn was excited over a choker that had glass reflectors on it, but Beth still wondered whether to keep it or not—it had a sort of flashiness that caught some of the highlights between Beth's face and her hair. Beth told Marjorie that sometimes she felt that her neck just seemed to disappear into her collar because it was so pale, and she felt that it needed some sort of accent.

While Marjorie worked nights, the other two girls seemed to roam. Only a few times did Marjorie accompany Beth on walks along Hollywood Boulevard. One day she walked with Beth to a fortune teller's parlor in a little building off an alley north of the boulevard. "We entered through a door into a dark, odd-smelling foyer no larger than an elevator," Marjorie recalls. "We went up some stairs to the second floor. I remember a window was open and a bird had flown in—it wasn't a big bird, but it was making noise as it flew back and forth between the walls. Beth had been to the fortune teller's before. She pulled a small chain that was hanging down the wall and a bell rang behind the door."

Marjorie says she was bothered by the bird and kept ducking as it flew past. "But Beth wasn't bothered and tried to chase it out the window. She even pushed the window up more so the bird wouldn't hit the glass."

An older dark-haired woman opened the door and when she saw Beth she smiled, then pushed between the two girls and chased the bird down the hallway. She ran after it making sounds like someone chasing away a dog.

Beth had seemed bouncy and in high spirits that day, but after a little while with the gypsy woman she seemed saddened and uneasy. "Whatever the woman told her had disturbed Beth," Marjorie says. "She seemed to have other things on her mind the rest of the day—and was depressed." On the sidewalk, Beth stopped and stared down at her shoes. She said she hated her shoes and was going to give them to Lynn.

Thirty-seven-year-old Martin Lewis co-managed two Hollywood shoe shops, one on Cahuenga south of the boulevard. "We were down from Macy Jewelers," he says. "Every few days or so I'd see this girl coming past the window, looking at the shoes. She'd come in and she liked to try on the most expensive ones. They'd fit her, but she'd make up some reason why they didn't because, I figured, she didn't have the money to buy them." One day she suggested that Martin set aside a particular pair, claiming she'd left her wallet in another purse, along with the keys to her apartment. "She said there was no one at her place, and the manager of the building was out, so she'd not only have to do without lunch, but she'd have to walk more than a mile to borrow streetcar fare for a job interview in downtown L.A. She told me she didn't even have a token for the fare box.

"I said if she had time for lunch, she could join me. She said that was very nice of me, but she wouldn't have time to go for the carfare if she had lunch with me. I said that was not a serious problem and I could loan her carfare." There was a small cafeteria with ogee or Arabian-shaped windows that faced Selma Avenue on the block south of the boulevard. Martin placed the "OUT TO LUNCH" sign on the shop door and walked Beth to the cafeteria.

Beth wanted to sit at the front window table. Martin "didn't feel comfortable sitting there," but he thought "what the heck." She might be a good-looking kid, but she was, after all, potentially a customer that he'd invited to lunch. It was a convenience for her. . . . He usually took lunch when the part-time employee came in and then he'd go to the other store—Leeds Shoes on the boulevard. But, he said, the situation merited his taking an early lunch.

She told Martin she was trying to be an actress and a model, but work had slowed down. She told him about possible leads she had for movies, and dropped a couple of names familiar to Martin. He said he knew a few people working in pictures, character-actor types that were hardly ever out of work. He suggested that at some time he might introduce Beth to a friend who could perhaps give her advice. "I said there were a couple of people." She wrote down their names in a little book, saying she'd look up something about them at the library or at the movie magazine shop by La Brea, so when the time came to meet the people she'd have something to say about the work they'd done. Beth told Martin she thought it was very important for an actor to know that someone had an interest in what they'd done. He said that was a good point, and when they left the cafeteria Beth walked back to the shop where Martin gave her some money for carfare.

"The other salesperson had opened the door while we'd been at lunch, and I slipped the girl a few dollars without anyone else noticing. She took several business cards from the dish at the register and put these in her purse. She asked me to please hold the shoes she'd admired. Even though she'd said they pinched her heels, she believed they'd be all right. Her feet were swollen that day, and she really had to try them on again. If they fit, she promised she'd buy them. I told her I'd set them aside—she could try them on again and if they were okay, she could consider them hers.

"She was back in the shop a day or so later and we had lunch again. It was about the same time she'd come in the last time. The first thing she did was hand me the money I'd loaned her for carfare. I said that wasn't necessary. She insisted, and then wanted to try on the shoes I'd put away for her. I went into the back and brought them out. She sat down and I slipped the shoes on her feet. She stood up and walked around on the carpeting, looking at her legs and the shoes in the mirror. Then she sat back down and had this big smile. She said she had a part in a movie, and I congratulated her. It was just a small part, she said, and she'd have to pay to join the guild, so she wanted to know if she could take the shoes and pay for them later. She was sitting there and the slit in the dress was open above the top of her stocking—these were dark stockings that you fastened up with black garters, but part of her leg was exposed.

"I was thinking about what she'd asked me when she said, 'Do you like what you're seeing?' That was what she said—just like that, with her voice lower like she was whispering it. I hadn't been prepared to get it coming at me like that and I said, 'You're a very attractive young lady, and it would be difficult for someone *not* to enjoy looking at you.'

"Then she said, 'Would you like to look at more of me?' She had on a little jacket, a little bolero kind of jacket like a Spanish dancer wears, and she placed her hand right against her breast. Because of the jacket, you couldn't see that from the side—like from the window or the doorway. She was smiling, and she said she sincerely liked me, and that she wanted me to like her. I asked her what she had in mind about the shoes—how she saw she could work that out. She answered by asking what *I* had in mind.

"I told her I didn't know what I had in mind, but if she came back later to the Leeds store I could give her a ride home and we could talk. I said she could come back about five-thirty."

Martin put the shoes in the box, and told her either way she should come back and he'd drive her home and the shoes would be hers. She said she only lived a few blocks away from Leeds, and he said they could take a drive somewhere. He could show her the lights of the city that were soon to be hers when she became famous.

"She seemed to have a lot going for her. I kept thinking about her: was she hustling me for a pair of shoes or wasn't she? That's what troubled me—I didn't know. They weren't *cheap* shoes, but they weren't the best in town either. The classy way she looked and her personality just didn't figure with hustling for a pair of shoes. But I swear, it was like she'd gotten me shaken up. I couldn't get her out of my mind. . . . Whatever her game, I told myself, she'd sure as hell hit a bull's eye. . . . Later, just a few minutes before I got ready to leave, I told myself to hell with it, I wasn't going through with it. If the girl wanted the shoes that bad, I'd just give her the damn shoes and tell her to get lost. I'd be doing her a favor maybe . . . and maybe I *wouldn't* be doing her a favor.

"But she was right on time—*exactly* on time—and with a smile that would've sent a ship's deck of sailors cheering with joy."

Inside the car Martin handed her the shoebox, already bagged and stapled with a sales slip inside. "She didn't notice the receipt because it was down in the sack," Martin says, "but she opened the box and slipped her feet into the shoes. She turned on the radio and was very happy in her new shoes. I was surprised when she moved over and cuddled against my right side, getting her arm around my arm and putting her head on my shoulder. I drove up through Outpost and parked in a little spot off the road that looked out over Hollywood. We sat for a few minutes and I had my hand on her leg, just feeling her leg, and one thing led to another. I reached over and grabbed her hand, putting it between my legs and moved her hand up and down. She sort of looked down at what we were doing. I got my zipper open and put her hand inside my shorts.

"I guess I just sort of sat back—and she leaned over from her side of the car, and I pushed her head down by the steering wheel, my hands feeling her hair. She didn't resist. Acted like it was what she wanted.

"I gave her my handkerchief and she kept that. I remember saying I didn't mind that she kept it. We drove down to Franklin Avenue. . . . Took her to where she was staying, not directly in front of the place, but a few doors down. When she got out of the car, she leaned in and said she cared for me. . . . Something like that, and in a manner that made me think maybe she did feel that way. It sure wasn't a problem for another person to feel that way about her."

Martin suggested she pass some of his cards out to girls she knew, for Leeds and the Cahuenga stores, but not to advertise to any girls that might possibly have been "working" the boulevard.

"I'd been testing her a little by saying that, and she said she wouldn't have any personal knowledge of girls like that. Her friends were all trying their best to get work in the movies just trying to hold things together until then—the same as she was doing.

"She would come in after that, trying on shoes, and I'd be

helping her if there wasn't anyone else in the store. We'd flirt a little and one thing would lead to another. Maybe three pair of shoes I let her have, and I loaned her money to pay rent—on the second time we drove up Outpost after I'd closed the Leeds store. We got in the back seat that time, but she said it was her time of the month."

Martin claims that he was disappointed, that he'd really wanted to have something more with Beth than what they'd done in the car the last time. She said she couldn't it was impossible because it was her "time."

"I told her to pull her skirt up and I just wanted to admire her legs and the rest of her." He said there were other ways, another way in which he could at least get close to her and that was to do it "the other way—do it by going in the back door," he said.

She said, "Oh, God, I can't do that," and Martin told her she could—there was nothing to it and he had such strong feelings about wanting to experience "*some*thing" with her. And since she was having her period, there wasn't anything to do except to do it that way, or the same thing as before which he didn't "feel comfortable" about.

"I had gotten her skirt above her waistline and she had this belt thing on, that I imagine was used to hold a sanitary napkin in place. It came around the upper part of her hips and fastened in the back, an elastic sort of belt that was gathered in a folded-over part and held with a large safety pin like someone might use on a baby's diaper. As long as I live I will remember that pin.

"Before she'd showed up at Leeds, I'd taken some nips from a bottle and I was very nervous about this girl. When she showed up I did want her, and did not waste a great deal of time about it. She said she was developing strong emotions for me. But in the car I wanted to get my hands around her and get into her underpants, which she was holding up, and she didn't want me to put my hand between her legs.

"She did what happened the time before, and then we drove down the boulevard and she sang a song that was on the radio—Bing Crosby and "I Can't Begin to Tell You." I remember her singing that right along with Bing Crosby. I have never heard the song since that I don't think of her. She asked if I would take her to get barbecued chicken or ribs over on Westlake, but it was too far and I said I couldn't because I had to get over the hill into the valley. I did give her bills for her rent, and I gave her some extra bills so that she might enjoy herself at the barbecue place."

Martin was married at the time and raising three children. He says his in-laws lived near him in the valley. He did not "finagle around," he claims, like some other men he knew. "For a few years there'd been problems in my marriage, but a divorce was out of the question. I had the idea, where was this situation with the girl going to lead in case something should happen—God forbid—like a policeman's flashlight in the car window. I had to be cautious. When I did not see Beth for a week or two, I thought perhaps that it had ended. But then she did show up and I gave her twenty dollars and a new red purse. She came back later that same day wearing a pair of red shoes—which she had wanted the purse to match—which were not the same shade as the purse.

"The shoes to match the handbag, I told her, were still in the stockroom in the larger carton. I said 'When you come back this evening to go for a ride, I'll have the shoes out for you and we can try them on in the car.'"

He took her into the stockroom to show her the shoes, and said he wanted to touch her. "Please pull it up and let me touch it," he said, "and you can have this new pair." But Beth said again she was having her period. Martin said that he didn't mind, he didn't care. "What she did then," he says, "this is *all* that she ever did, was she took my hand and pushed it down the front of her skirt, and under the waistband of her panties, while she held onto my wrist. I remember it felt as though I was touching a child because there was basically very little to feel—it was like the middle part of a child's body. And as quickly she pulled my hand out and she asked if I was satisfied. I thought that was a funny thing to say. I did touch her breasts, she let me do this, and they were very lovely, and very smooth, but the nipples were small and like a girl's, not like a mature woman's at all, and very little contrast to the rest of her breast. . . . I gave her the shoes and another purse that had come in with the shoes from the same manufacturer. It was black, very soft, and the leather was very rich. I said it was a very high-quality piece of merchandise, quite expensive, and she knew that."

She responded with something in French—some phrase he didn't understand. As she went out she was smiling, her body sort of floating, moving back and forth like all the parts of it were somehow very loosely put together and she wasn't really walking on the ground.

7

War surplus and auto parts salesman Ray Kazarian met the Black Dahlia in a Sunset Boulevard bar. He had noticed her days before on Hollywood Boulevard, but their paths didn't cross until he saw her in the Sky Room—next to a drive-in restaurant.

"Kids from Hollywood High School used to sneak in the bar from the drive-in," says Ray. "It was dark and sometimes they'd get booed, depending on which waitress worked the afternoons. The boys would huddle in the back booth—it was the darkest area, lit only by a red glow—and they'd snicker when girls walked by. Usually they'd get kicked out.

"The jukebox was always playing songs like 'Always,' and 'Near You,' and 'The Glory of Love.' This guy, Whitey, kept plugging it with nickels while he made book on a phone in the front booth. He also had a magazine rack up the street. When he saw me that day, he did this Eddie Cantor bit he used to do, wagging his hands and making with the eyes, so I sat down."

Ray recalls that when his eyes got used to the dark, he looked across the table to the girl facing him, the girl he'd seen before. "And Whitey said, 'Some guys call her the Black Dahlia.' She had long black hair and a flower behind one ear. This flower looked pink or like iridescence in there, and the light took the color from her lipstick and she looked all pink. I remember a Spanish kind of blouse, and the choker high up on her neck that was studded around, and flashed when she'd turn her head, the light catching on it. There were two other girls laughing, and the squeaky little blonde asked the black-haired one something, and I saw her give the other two a look and a smile.

"A few minutes later I could see her better, and she had this black mascara and some accents on her eyes. She said her name was Elizabeth—'Beth for short,' and she laughed some more. I asked her what was so funny, I knew a gal I almost married named Beth. And they all laughed at that. But Elizabeth—or Beth—said they were all laughing because Short was her last name. 'You know,' she said to me, 'Beth for *Short*.'

"I got the joke, and laughed. It was all very relaxed, and Whitey was scribbling down phone tips. The third gal was skinny, but had a kind of double chin. They all were sort of horse-looking compared to Beth. I asked if I could treat them to a round and they, Beth and the blonde, said they were waiting for friends.

"The skinny one was Midge, on a lunch break from a building on Yucca that had to do with music." Midge would swing past the hotel where the girls stayed and pick up whoever happened to be there, to join her at the Sky Room.

Ray could see Beth pick up her glass a few times, but mostly she ate a grilled cheese—with a tomato in it. She told him she was from "here and there—awhile back," and everyone laughed.

He noticed her teeth were a little crooked but she had a terrific smile. He figured those could be fixed, and told her what a great smile she had. She acted flattered and he said, "I haven't forgotten seeing you on the boulevard a few times, the last time out in front of the Pig'n Whistle. . . ." Beth said she did remember and her eyes got a little wide and she looked straight past Ray, like she was thinking about it.

He watched her, how she acted, how she talked and laughed. She was nervous, worried about her hair, and bit at her fingernail, anxious about the friends they were waiting for. She kept looking at other people in the lounge.

Whitey ordered more drinks, but Beth didn't have another. He was telling the girls that Ray had been in some westerns, and Ray said, "Don't believe him. I've worked in a movie *theater*, but Whitey's notorious for pulling legs, and that can be a bad flaw for a guy making book." They joked around until a couple of young guys came in, both in uniform. They had a car outside, and Beth and the blonde got up from the booth.

As they were leaving, Ray stopped Beth. He told her he stayed across the street at the hotel, and suggested that whenever she was in the neighborhood she should stop by and they would grab a bite.

She said, "Well, golly, maybe I *can* do that sometime, but I'm pretty busy trying to get into a movie." Ray told her she was standing in a *long* line, especially with the strikes pending. He said, "But you're better looking than half those in line." He asked her why she was called the Black Dahlia, and she said, "I don't know why some people say that. It's just a joke from the Alan Ladd movie called *The Blue Dahlia*. Someone just made up the joke a couple of months ago.

Ray said, "Well, any time you want to grab a bite is okay with me." He told her not to worry, "'cause he didn't bite," and she said, smiling, "Oh, I bet you do—I'll bet you one buffalo you do." She said it was nice to have met him, but she had some place to go with the soldier. She identified him as "the one with the Pepsodent smile" and said something about him being jealous and wanting to marry her. He had proposed marriage the day before. Ray said, "Congratulations! He's a lucky young man." She laughed and squeezed Ray's arm, in a comradely sort of way.

There was no hope for Hal McGuire, who found that following Beth around was as hectic as "jumping like a fast bouncing ball in a pinball game—that's how she was living." She still hadn't managed an income on her own and the small but frequent loans made to her by Hal and others had quickly mounted to a good-sized sum. Nobody for a minute thought they would get their money back.

Despite her optimism and the assurances of booking agent Fred Sherman, whom she'd met through Barbara, Beth was walking a thin line, trying to look the part—measuring up to the flash and verve she generated.

Sherman planned to have Beth meet an associate of actor Bob Steele, who was producing at an independent studio. Sherman, too, advanced Beth some cash for expenses and some additional clothes that were requested for a possible photo session. She was told, "Whatever you do, do *not* get in the sun. And if possible, use something on your hair that will create a shine to the black. It is important that your skin be very white and your hair as *shiny* black as you can get it."

The photographs were to be taken over a weekend near Newport Beach. More money was promised following the job, but Sherman believed the photographs could lead to more work for Beth. The money she got was to be reimbursed to Sherman by Steele, once the photos were taken.

Sherman arranged for her to meet Mark Hellinger at Universal. "He was a real hellion," Sherman says, "crazy as hell. He got stopped in his car speeding in North Hollywood and the girl was in the car with him. There was a record of it at one time, but the girl was here one day and gone the next. She was operating on her own personal wavelength. You couldn't figure out what she was going to do next, and half the time I don't know if *she* knew until she'd gone ahead and done it."

Martin Lewis kept watching out the shoe store window for Beth. In his thoughts, she had become his girlfriend and they were having "this temporary wing-ding—damned if I didn't see it that way . . ." he says. "She didn't present herself as someone that just anyone could get with a pair of shoes. She was not a tramp, but someone that you were having a *personal* relationship with, and the gifts to her, or cash loans, were more of a personal understanding—a friend, something like that. I *felt* friendly toward her, and *caring* toward her, someone *close*, certainly more than getting sexual favors for some merchandise. And the 'loans' were hardly what you'd call bonuses."

Martin reasoned if she could get the shoes or the money

without prostituting herself, that was okay. "So it was not a direct cash and carry situation," he says. She played games. She had an attitude that she didn't do things, but at the same time she was doing them, and taking some pleasure in it. Maybe a base quality—a lowering of herself wasn't possible. He believed that what she was doing was *different* from what she was.

"There was this star-struck or princess notion, and she had what you could call *disdain*, people that she knew or chummed around with were not the same measure as herself. Maybe that's how she saw someone as myself," Martin says. "I don't know what one really calls a girl like that nowadays; nose in the air, like a doe with that white tail straight up—you never catch her."

Martin saw Beth on and off for a few weeks. Once she was with a fellow the police had under surveillance. Martin found out who the man was from a friend who had an insurance agency on Selma. "He was supposed to be a part-time musician and a photographer," Martin says, "but he was a phony. I would've turned him in if I'd had a reason, but I wouldn't have involved her in something unnecessary. Perhaps she didn't know he wasn't any good. When you deal with the public such as I have, you know if something is fishy—you learn to know what a real grifter is, and a bad egg. Hollywood was full of them during and right after the war, or maybe they were just more obvious since the real fellows were overseas."

Martin didn't have to turn the man in—he wound up in prison soon enough. He had sold Martin's insurance friend a stag movie and packages of girlie photographs. "My friend told me the girl I knew was in the stag movie," Martin says. "I didn't believe him. This was a very dangerous time to have anything like that around because the police were being especially hard on pornography. It was a felony. Any kind of pornography was a felony. *Oral sex* was a felony. *Sodomy* was a felony. I was a felon for what I had done to the girl. That's how the police would have seen it.

"My insurance friend took me into the back area of his office where there was a small kitchen, and he projected the part of the film with the dark-haired girl in it. I watched it a couple of times. It showed her head—her body diagonally across the frame to her navel in the left lower corner of the picture. Her chest was not visible because a large dark skinned man, possibly Filipino, was on his knees straddling her body. His bare bottom and her forearm and hand were visible. You could see he had a long wango, and the head on it was inside the girl's mouth, and for a few seconds, he moved his cock in and out of her mouth, going fairly deep into it at one point, and she looked like she was gagging on it."

Martin was sure it wasn't the girl he knew, but his friend said he thought it was. "I argued that it wasn't," Martin says. "The black hair looked like a wig, and she had heavy makeup like a black mask over her eyes. Her hair looked stuck against her forehead, and her eyes were partly open. They looked darker in color, and the black makeup had a shine to it. It didn't look like her hand—the fingernails didn't look bitten down, the way Beth had been biting hers. The nose was similar, but different. For a second you could see her stomach and belly button, and some black lace that looked like the waist of her panties.

"He said he'd have a couple of the frames cut out of the film for me, in case I wanted to have a photograph made from them. The Hollywood Camera Exchange would splice it together. I said I'd take them when he got around to doing that, but I didn't think I wanted to make a photograph. I'd show them to the girl and ask her if this was the sort of movie work she was doing.

"I did not show Beth the frames, but I teased her a little and said that I had heard from someone that they thought she had played in a stag movie, and she said, laughing about it, that did I think *she* would do something like that?

"She was running around in a loose circle, with people that were broken up, or not working. I don't mean employment as we think of it, but getting settled somehow within the law, you know, being *legal*. She did gravitate in that way, and ran around getting rides and being picked up by men to get from one place to another. She had a way of walking—of advertising her ass, certainly drawing attention to it.

"One time, two or three men were across the street fixing a roof when she came into the store, and they were whistling and hooting, and she was getting all flustered—not upset, but enjoying the attention. They came across the street and looked into the store window, and I told them they were bothering the customers. But she liked it, she liked them drooling over her.

"Like a whore, is how *I* wanted to see her. Perfume reeked off of her, and she always had so much makeup on and that very peculiar white powder, and putting that black shine on her hair. And the black dresses.

"And always looking; those eyes going here and there looking around, talking to her and she'd be looking past you or over your shoulder, as if to be giving some guy over there the eye; it was that sort of feeling. Yet she could be as sweet as honey, and kind, I mean truly *kind* and thoughtful, which I have not seen in the Hollywood whores, despite what some people like to say about them.

"I know she wasn't a tramp, and I do not have any way to say that she was—expect that was how I *wanted* to see her, even while another part of me was so drawn to her in a way that had nothing to do with any sort of sex."

One night, a couple of weeks after they'd met in the Sky Room, Ray Kazarian saw Beth in Steve Boardner's bar. "We looked at each other through the back bar mirror and I made eyes at her," Ray says. "She looked right at me, and with that smile that got you right down there in the old apple seed. I was making love to her with my eyes and the way we were looking—she was making them right back. I finally gave her a look saying, 'Hey there, honey lamb, here's your daddy here, and come on over and I'll show you a thing or two.' Something along that silly line, and we fooled around like that for a minute or so. She dished it out in the same manner as I did, so I knew she was no shrinking violet. But not hard by the standards of what I'd known or the kids that were hanging around in the bars after sailors or whatever else was prowling by then. But the Black Dahlia had something that was real exciting in a younger woman like she was."

She was sitting with someone, and Ray wondered what had become of the soldier fiancé. "As soon as the friend moved farther down the bar, I asked where her intended and soon-to-be was. She said, 'My what?' and I said her fiancé, the soldier that came in the Sky Room. She said he'd gone up to Monterey. He'd be back, she said, but he wasn't her fiancé. I said I'd thought he was, and so did he. She said it was just a matter of his having entertained the notion. She went on to explain her ideas about someone else proposing marriage to her, as happened often, she said, but she wouldn't accept someone now who was still in the service because she had come to realize that she was still in love with her husband.

"I said, 'Your what?' and she told me she was widowed, and showed me a clipping and photograph. She had a bunch of photographs in her purse. I said, 'The guy was a major'— her husband. The other kid was a private. She was playing a pretty wide field. She acted like she wasn't interested in talking about it and didn't want another drink when I ordered it. She said she was craving something special, 'like a banana split or something like that, maybe a sundae, a cherry or strawberry one.' She said she shouldn't eat it but she *really* wanted it.

"She didn't want to walk a few blocks, so we hopped on the streetcar and sat at the window. The traffic was bottled up because of a premiere at the Egyptian, and we got off a couple blocks more by Grauman's Chinese and I took her to a little ice cream parlor, very old, with high ceilings and dark wood booths that pretty much shut you off from the others in the place. She told me she'd been there before. I said I wanted to know where she hadn't been and what she hadn't done, and she smiled and cocked her head but didn't say anything."

She asked Ray how old he was, and didn't believe him when he told her. She thought he was older, and to prove he wasn't, he pulled out his driver's license, and she said, "Well, you act so much older than that." It seemed to Ray that she was somehow trying to please him, and he wasn't going to object. He said she was probably used to young soldiers and she said, "Not especially." She didn't go out on dates that much, she said, and she'd had to wait for her husband for a long time while he was overseas. Since his death there had been one other guy that had fallen in love with her.

"She couldn't think of herself as having really ever lived

anywhere," Ray says. She had the feeling that her home, back east, what she'd known as home with her sisters, had never really belonged to her—nor had *she* belonged to it. She said there was nothing very much holding her there. She always felt cut off. . . . Then she laughed and said she's always wanted to be famous and knew it was going to happen. In school she'd decided to hit out on her own. She said it hadn't always been easy, since before she was ten years old she'd had asthma and she'd almost had tuberculosis.

Ray told her he understood health problems because he'd had enough of his own. He told her it was the reason he'd fouled out at getting overseas. "I got a spine that can't take any strain," he says. "I told her I tried like hell. Three times I tried to con my way into the army, and three times they shut the door in my face.

"She told me there was nothing wrong with her now, that she was cured of her illness. I told her I thought she was very beautiful, and that she'd survived very beautifully.

"She had ladyfinger sandwiches, sort of like tea sandwiches. Then after that, she had some ice cream. I watched her lips as she ate, and the way she'd put the spoon in her mouth. She was very careful to wipe at her lips with the napkin. She was very proper.

"I used the word *plebian* about something and she took a pen and a little pad out of her purse. She wrote it down and said, 'I do this if there's something I'm not sure about. I like to look it up when I get a chance.'"

Beth said the girls she knew weren't her friends. She told Ray she wasn't close to any of them. They just happened to share the same room from time to time. She said she wasn't sure where she was going next because of arrangements in the east.

"I didn't know what she meant," Ray says, "and she didn't explain when I asked her, and she kept asking what time it was and checked her lipstick and her makeup several times. I got a feeling at times that she was alone in the booth, and she'd glance off to the sound of voices, as though she'd been sitting over there moments before and knew them—and she'd smile or react to something the people over there were saying or laughing about."

She asked him what connections he had with the movies and he said he'd been in and out of it but mostly was a fan himself, not of the current stuff, but of the older cowboy stars.

Suddenly, with a spurt of energy, Beth said, "You see, you *are* older." She said she didn't know very much about Westerns, but said it in a way that suggested she was interested if he wanted to tell her about it, but she wasn't going to ask on her own.

In the moments that followed, Ray was just making conversation with her. "We were just sitting there," he says, "and there was no cute stuff between us at all. It wasn't that at all."

He felt that he'd wound up with some teenage church matron, and he didn't know how she'd managed to pull it off.

8

Like a lot of cut-loose GIs, Edwin Burns was looking for the girl of his dreams to chase away the blues. He was twenty-four and in Hollywood since his discharge trying to forget the South Pacific. He was learning to dance by hitting all the clubs and small ballrooms that had cropped up during the war.

Before he'd gone overseas, Burns' girlfriend wrote to him that she was being true and would wait for his return, but "she was really out on the town," he says. "Then she'd gotten pregnant by another guy, and actually *married* the guy and had his baby. She said she was sorry and she hadn't wanted to make me feel bad while I was rotting in the jungle dodging snipers. She said, 'I mean, after *all,* it's not like you were going to get involved with someone *else* over there.' I was pretty much down in the dumps and I couldn't shake it off. And while I say I wanted to find another girl, I wasn't really flirting or trying to take anyone serious, at least not for a while.

"I was at the Shanghai Dance Hall on Hollywood Boulevard and there was this black-haired girl, one of the prettiest gals I've seen in my life. The fellows moved around her, and the more they closed in, the more of them there seemed to be and the more she got a kick out of it. But it was fun and kidding around."

Burns didn't chase after her, but stayed back by the counter where refreshments were sold. Maybe he was the only guy standing off to the side and not trying to get around. Then she came over in *his* direction. "I was not very tall and I had buck teeth," he says. "When I was little they said I looked like a rabbit." The girl was smiling with her head down a little, and her eyes were looking directly at him as if she knew him.

"There weren't many girls like her," Burns says. "One of those that when you meet, it's like you have known them somewhere before. And someone you sincerely could have liked. It was a particular look, and the way she was staring at me and smiling; it made me think we *had* met before, but I couldn't remember her name."

It was Beth, she told him, short for Elizabeth. Every guy in the Shanghai wanted to dance with her, but when she chose Burns, it was like he'd been blessed by the gods. It was that kind of feeling, he told himself; she'd make a guy lonely for her company. "And then the funny part was," he says, "that even when you were with her, and even holding her as when you're dancing together, man, oh, man, you were lonely for her even then."

There was a very sharp-looking guy there that night who knew his stuff. And though Beth did dance with him a couple times, she kept going back to Burns. Pretty soon he felt there was no other place for this gal but to be with him, he'd found the pretty girl he was after, and they were going to be flying to the moon. "But," Burns says, "there was tomorrow morning and the next day and like they say, the cold facts of the real world.

"But that night at the Shanghai, she made me feel proud and good, like I was tall and had Charles Atlas muscles and wasn't a rabbit. She had class and she was *smart*, and the other girls she was around just sort of faded away. I think they were jealous of her because it seemed like she could take the guys away from them without ever thinking about it."

Meanwhile, there were problems. Marjorie didn't want Beth using all the nail polish, and began to criticize her, saying the blood red lipstick was too dark for her face, as dark as the paint on her toenails—the same color on her fingernails. She should stop using Marjorie's nail polish, and buy her own. But Beth insisted she had her own, and that in fact, Marjorie and Lynn had used up her polish the week before.

Always ready with an answer—that was Beth. Or with a white lie. It wasn't true that she'd had her own bottle of nail polish. In fact, the other girls had used nothing of hers, except a pair of cream-colored slacks which Marjorie had squeezed into and worn to the movies at Paramount where she got butter spots on the lap from the popcorn.

Beth was bothered about the men Lynn would meet or date out of the hotel. They didn't know that Lynn was only sixteen, and Marjorie didn't seem to care.

There were days when it seemed that Beth hadn't eaten anything. She'd stay at a small table writing letters or scribbling in a small notebook she wouldn't let anyone see. The others would often go together for dinner and invite Beth. "Most of the time, if she didn't go out on dates," Marjorie says, "she wasn't eating."

But, toward the middle of the month, things changed considerably. Beth was dining at La Rue's on the Sunset Skip with nightclub owner Mark Hansen and Mark's girlfriend, Ann Toth, a bit player.

"If you were just a little older," Beth told Lynn, "I'd introduce you to Mark because he has clubs all over town and all he'd have to do would be pick up a phone and you'd be singing in one of the clubs. But unless you have some sort of consent form from a guardian, you're going to get yourself in trouble along with the people that hire you."

"I never pushed anything with the Black Dahlia," Ray says. "She was getting herself in tight spots, and when she called me for advice, I said I'd talk to her. We met at the Ranch restaurant by the post office."

During breakfast she seemed cheerful and bright until he placed two crisp twenty-dollar bills beside her plate of ham and eggs. She drank a large glass of orange juice as he talked to her about her fingernails, bitten down to the quick.

"Her thumb-nail looked like it was bleeding," he says. "And before I handed her the money, I told her she should use false nails and keep them painted. The false nails would keep her from chewing her own nails and give them a chance to grow out." Ray told her she had the kind of looks she could capitalize on. He didn't know what she would look like if her hair was blonde, "but the coloring and her skin, and especially her eyes," he says, "it's as good as a lot of people I'd seen working in pictures. She could've been posing for magazines, I told her. I said I'd steer her to a few people." Then Ray passed the twenty-dollar bills to her.

She stared at the money, then picked at her food "like she was caught in a kick," Ray says. "She looked puzzled. It made me feel good to see that I'd puzzled her. So I said, 'This has got nothing to do with any proposition.' It wasn't why I was giving her the money."

Ray wanted to be certain that she understood what he was saying. "I told her it was a gift to her. There was another holiday coming up—Valentine's Day—Christmas or something. . . ."

That made her laugh. She opened her purse and brought out a small black book that she opened and placed the bills just inside. Ray could see pages of handwriting but he couldn't read it from where he was sitting.

"She told me," Ray says, "that she wanted me to please remember that she was not a prostitute. She didn't go out with men to have them giving her money." Ray told her he already had said that the money had nothing to do with their friendship.

After breakfast that morning, they walked a half block to the boulevard where Ray waited with Beth in the safety zone for the streetcar. He couldn't remember what was said, if anything. He only recalls waiting as the trolley came down Hollywood Boulevard; it stopped and she climbed on board. She'd put on a pair of gloves, Ray says, and he can still remember her opening and closing her hand with the token against the palm of the glove. She dropped the token into the fare box and turned sort of looking back over her shoulder, and down at Ray, just as the doors were closing.

"She said she would call me," he says. "She promised to call.

But of course, she never did. . . ."

Marjorie was in Lee's Drugstore on Highland when Beth told her she didn't have any money. But a day later when she paid the gypsy fortune teller, she brought out a couple of twenty-dollar bills folded neatly in half, and peeled one off and gave it to the woman who then gave her ten dollars back—a five, a two-dollar bill, and three singles.

After the old woman had closed the door, Marjorie said to Beth, "I thought you said you didn't have any money?" Beth said she didn't, not the night before, but she had managed to find the money that morning. "You must have forty or more dollars there," Marjorie said, and reminded Beth that she owed her five.

Beth unfolded the bills and gave Marjorie some singles, a two and a five, saying, "Here's ten. The five is for you, and the rest is for when I'll need it again. . . ."

Marjorie said something about Beth's purse having a hidden talent to manufacture money while she slept, and she'd have to let her in on the secret. She hoped Beth might confide where she got the money, but she only smiled, and said, "Everything's all right now. At least for today."

The last time Martin saw Beth, he says, "She brought a guy into the store with her—greasy-looking with wavy hair. He looked like he had a lot of Vaseline on his hair, or pomade—he was small and he dressed flashy. She had this brand-new dress on that was chartreuse, and it had some sort of camisole top with something like laces across the bust. Some laces at the side by the hips, if I remember exactly.

"He was older than I was, and a lot older than Beth, and short, with funny shoes, black and white wing-tips, but quite old shoes. She came in this day and there was no familiarity between us, other than she had been in the store before. She was just a customer this time, which by her attitude I guessed is what she was up to. I had the feeling that he might've been carrying a gun.

"So I was this salesman and we chatted for a moment and she bought a pair of shoes. The guy was all concerned, saying, 'You sure, honey?' Something like that. 'You sure this is what you want?'

"I'll never forget her eyes. She looked at me, smiling and mysterious as this little guy pulls out a wad and starts peeling off bills. She is looking up at me, secret-like, and her eyes are smiling at me. That's as clear in my mind now as it was back then.

"She had some skill—some way of getting someone to feel something for her, and to worry about her. Maybe it was an angle, but what made it so special is that it wasn't something that is just passed off—because of who she was, whatever she was, and what the world she walked in was like."

Edwin Burns claims that he "probably" knew Beth less than a month: "maybe just a little more than three weeks." He'd picked up an older truck since his discharge and on a couple of occasions had driven Beth from a hotel in Hollywood, "just down that street east of Grauman's," to an apartment flat near Ocean Park, "by the amusement pier." On another occasion Burns drove Beth from another hotel to a house on Carlos Avenue that was situated behind the Florentine Gardens nightclub.

"She had a lot of luggage this one time, and some clothes stacked up which I put on top of one of her suitcases, and then the other luggage on top of her clothes to keep them held down and from blowing out. She seemed very nervous about what she was doing, and talked about the famous names of people she'd met—and the man that owned the house where she was going. It sounded like a touchy situation having to do with this guy, like hanky-panky she didn't want to get caught up in. She said that he was very fond of her and she was going to be working for him in the nightclubs. But she said that she was having trouble—she was in some kind of trouble, but she didn't tell me what it was. You just sense those things. I only said something like if there was anything I could do I'd try to help her. . . . They were all chasing rainbows. . . ."

One of the times Burns drove Beth from Hollywood to Ocean Park it was late, he recalls, dark, "because I had to use my headlights and one was cockeyed. I couldn't gel it in low beam. When I parked on this little street at the beach, you could see the amusement pier to the right and all the lights were shining, and the rides were going on. You could hear people yelling all the way from where we were, and the sound of the roller coaster.

"The two-story building she was going into was one of those bungalow buildings, with probably four flats in it. She was going up to the one on the water side. The windows looked out over some of the roofs to the ocean and the pier. There was a porch, or a verandah, and I remember a glass wind chime hanging there and making these tinkling noises.

"She looked so pretty from her profile, her nose was cute and she had such a beautiful mouth. I wanted to kiss her and I put my arm up around her and she looked at me and said I was very sweet and she really appreciated my helping her. There was a light on upstairs and it was showing through the window shade.

"But I can remember shadows up there like they were figures, but they weren't moving, and I got the idea that they were statues. But I remember the wind chime and the roller coaster in the background, and people yelling. She said that she didn't want to hurt me. She liked that we were friendly, but if she kissed me, she said, I'd start thinking about her more and it would lead to my getting hurt, and the last thing in the world she wanted to do was hurt me like I'd been hurt before . . . like I'd told her about the other gal. So I never even got a kiss . . . and I had it in my mind that she was this new girl of my dreams ."

Barbara Lee thought it was a bad idea for Beth to move into Mark Hansen's place, although a number of young actresses were staying there. "It was like someone's selling the idea of the old Hollywood Studio Club that had been right across from Hansen's for years," Barbara says. Beth wanted to get into the movies and it was important to be seen in the right places with the right people, and Mark Hansen had all the contacts. He owned nightclubs—including the Florentine Gardens—and movie theaters, and some dance halls. Beth could make herself appear to be the most charming person in any group of people, and she'd charmed her way into Mark Hansen's. She had her mind set on things and the way she wanted to lead her life, and Barbara felt that Beth's way did not always jive with how other people wanted things done.

Ray Kazarian was still seeing Beth in some of the boulevard bars. He didn't think the Mark Hansen situation was such a hot idea. "I told her one time when I took her for a bite at the Spanish Kitchen. She was nuts over the albondigas soup. She just kept eating it and didn't answer back to my gripes about her staying at Hansen's."

It was just a few days later when he ran into her in Cardo's bar on Spring Street. "She was with a soldier, and an ex-Seabee who lived in a little trailer with a kid that sold papers on Seventh. I drove her from Spring over to Beverly because she was going into Hollywood, but she wanted more of that meatball soup. So we went back to the Spanish Kitchen and cozied up a little in a booth just under that stairway that went up to a second floor of the building."

Ray had begun to feel old, in his thirties and still hitting the spots. "Most of her friends were just kids in their twenties," he says, "Ann Toth and Lucille, and the other gals, and the young fellows, some still in the service." Ray could see that Beth enjoyed these people, a kind of closeness, the way they'd all bunch up at the bar. There seemed to be no other place in the world for these unanchored drifters, except floating, moving from group to group—laughing, talking, buying each other rounds of drinks. So many people and places were compressed into such a short period of time, the two or three months that Ray actually knew Beth.

He gave her some more money and she rented a place on Cherokee Street. It was $1 a day, a week in advance, and she would share the room with three other girls.

The cage elevator was too slow and the room was on the fifth floor. There were two sets of bunk beds forming an L shape in the rear corner of the room. Windows on the opposite wall faced the alley. One girl living there worked for the Max Factor makeup company, and was soon intrigued by how Beth applied her makeup.

She'd later admit the effect was startling, "like a geisha," the girl said. The other roommates couldn't help noticing that Beth worried about making a good impression. "The way she fusses over little details," one said, "and spends three times as long as anyone I know with her makeup. I can come and go and she's still in the bathroom putting on her face."

It was the candles another complained about. "Everyone waxes their teeth to make them shine but I saw her filling in the cavities with the wax," the girl said. "Sometimes she uses the pink stuff like the dentists have, or she'll light a candle, let it burn for a minute and then pinch off the wax and carefully push it in the cavities. Then she'll smile into the mirror, and examine her teeth."

Beth told one girl she had gone to college. But later someone else said that Beth hadn't finished high school.

"If I try to talk to her about it or be friendly about what she's doing or where she's going," the girl would say, "she'll just laugh or smile."

They were getting fed up with Beth's coughing keeping them awake some nights. And then, too, there were her late hours. Where Beth went, and who she was with she'd never tell her roommates. She never had her dates come by, but always met them somewhere else. "Probably told them she lived someplace fancy," one girl says. "That's how she thought of herself."

They were tired of Beth's "important contacts" and the small loans, not only the few dollars, but the soap or toothpaste or the sanitary pads that Beth would somehow forget to repay. They didn't think that she was *completely* stuck on herself. She had a helpful, concerned way about her, but things didn't seem to get through to her.

Gladys, a neighbor on the fifth floor, remembers a "terrible row" in the hallway one night. "Beth came to my door earlier, a little while before the commotion, and she had been crying. She told me the manager wasn't in her apartment downstairs and she wanted to leave a small suitcase with me. She said she'd accidentally locked herself out. She left and then came back, very excited and scared. She said her boyfriend was jealous and he was chasing her. She wanted to know if she could hide in my apartment until he left. I said it was all right."

The two women sat in the kitchen drinking coffee, trying to ignore the pounding and yelling down the hall. After it was quiet, Beth left. "She didn't take her suitcase with her," Gladys says. "I saw her a day or so later when I was leaving the building and asked her if she wanted the valise. But she said she would pick it up later, and hoped that it wasn't in the way. I asked her if everything was settled between her and her boyfriend and she said that it had been a difficult night, but that things were resolved. She said, 'I have broken off the engagement.'

"I didn't know she'd been engaged. I'd sometimes see her with men—model and actor types, or older guys. There was the tall lean guy with the accent, who'd give the girls tickets to radio shows. He said he was German—an *American* German. He seemed very refined." Gladys saw him once, later, after Beth moved out. He was asking about Beth. "He had tears in his eyes—must've been fifty years old," she said.

Days later Beth showed up at Alex Constance's rooming house on McCadden Place. It was near Don the Beachcomber's restaurant and Al Green's Night Spot. She told Alex she was working in a small restaurant in North Hollywood, "but that she was getting tired," Alex says. He was older than the "crowd," a dress extra with plenty of costumes who wanted to be a studio hairdresser. "I'd practice hairstyles on the girls," he says. "Wouldn't charge them, you know."

He'd noticed Beth was coughing more than usual. "Beth talked about her boyfriends, and I warned her that she should be careful. You might get some guy mad, I said, playing them off each other. And if they think you're a tease, some guys can get awfully ugly." Alex says he liked Beth a lot. "But somehow or other she'd get problems." He'd tried more than once to get her to tell him what was bothering her, but she wouldn't say. He'd make fresh coffee and sit there quietly while she let herself go, "tears running down her cheeks," he says, "and she'd keep saying, 'I know things will work out.' But it all seemed so hopeless to her sometimes."

Alex arranged for her to stay at the rooming house for a few days. "Cheer up," he told her. "So you might have to move again. Remember Paul Burke, that nice-looking young guy I pointed out to you in the hall a few days ago. He's trying to break into the business, too, and he's had to move *seventeen* times this year." The next coffee klatch Beth had with Alex, she told him things were looking up, that she'd found a drama coach through Ann.

Lauretta Ruiz was a retired actress, getting into coaching and producing plays. Lauretta thought Beth had a pleasant voice, though on the slightly higher, thin side. "There was an aristocratic air about her, in the tenor, but she needed to concentrate on something to modulate her voice."

But there always seemed to be something that held Beth in check. "I briefly tried to help her out of it—and introduce her to people. I was planning on doing a Leo Gordon play at a Hollywood theater, and we wanted Richard Carlson in the cast along with Hedy Lamarr. I was trying to convince Richard to do the play—he was very attractive, and an excellent young actor. We met in a restaurant once, and Elizabeth and another young actor were with me. Richard showed up and said he had met Beth before. He was standing politely as we slipped into the booth, and he had recognized Beth immediately. But he seemed unsettled. Beth asked him if he remembered the bracelet, and she said she still had it. I had no way of knowing that they'd met before, but I sensed something out of the ordinary had gone on between them. To this day I can't imagine what it might've been.

"Richard later told me he didn't know Beth 'at all.' He said he had only given her a ride once, 'just a few blocks from somewhere on Vine Street up to somewhere on the boulevard,' and she spotted a red box on the seat and asked if it was a fountain pen set. Richard said no, it's just some gimmick from the radio station, a charm bracelet, and he told her she could have it.

"A theatrical agent friend of mine met Beth and wanted to arrange for her to have professional photographs taken. She had several unprofessional shots, and he didn't think they were suitable. He said she had an interesting presence, and that he was intrigued by a femme fatale quality she possessed, but I thought that part of her might have been a cover-up for what I sensed as a real conflict inside of her—or contradictions. . . ."

Lauretta recalls how Beth was drawn to the unusual—such as the broach she wore in the shape of a large black flower with a sterling silver Egyptian face in the center. When asked where it came from, Beth just smiled and wouldn't say. Once she showed Lauretta an ivory-colored cigarette case in the shape of two clasped hands, which she used to keep business cards in.

"She was unusual wherever she went," Lauretta says, "and for Hollywood, especially at that time, that's a bold statement." The drama coach saw Beth as exotic—"some people would say eccentric. But definitely a show person. She simply *had* to be in show business. She should have been on stage! There was no other salvation for her, and it is a crime and a waste that she wasn't brought forth.

"Beth seemed attracted to odd types, as well as odd objects," Lauretta says. She was told that Beth dated men other girls would have nothing to do with because they served no purpose. They would hinder one from reaching goals, the other girls would say.

Lauretta recalls giving a fine piece of lingerie to Beth. "She adored black lace. Elizabeth was of the night. She was the dark. . . ."

It gave Barbara a terrible feeling to think Beth had been suckered in by Mark Hansen, becoming one of his "cutie pies," as Barbara put it. And that, in no time at all, Beth would have to be "singing for her supper." But Beth shook her head and told Barbara, "I'm not going to have any part of *that* stuff. I just have to move around and be seen. That's all there is to it. It's a nice place to stay, and there's some nice girls there and I'm sharing a room with Ann, and *she's* Mark's girl, not me."

Barbara's friend Bob tried to get Beth on as a Paramount contract player through an associate, hoping it would give her the money to be independent and get her foot in the door. "But it didn't pan out," Barbara says. "A couple of times we'd get together at the Vagabond Isle—a bar east of Vine, and she'd be talking about the big shots *she* was hobnobbing with—Mark Hansen, of course—and living over there at his house. I didn't like Beth's set-up with Mark Hansen at all. It gave me just plain bad feelings. Maybe she was bringing out the mother in me—I was never much of a mother."

Actor Kevin Wilkerson remembers when Beth moved into Mark Hansen's and started showing up at the Florentine Gardens. "She was being called the Black Dahlia, but my girlfriend said that Mark was calling her the *black-haired eight ball*."

Most of the girls staying at Mark's were pretty young, and as far as Kevin knew, they were working the bar, sometimes just decorating the place, encouraging drinkers—not exactly B-girls, more like "*fancy* B-girls." They were lured there with the promise of making it into the chorus at the Florentine Gardens. Any girl who was lucky enough to get into Mark's *house* believed she was in line to be "discovered"—usually by the Garden's impresario, Nils T. Granlund, "master of ceremonies *deluxe*." He gave a lot of big show business names their "break" and he was quick to publicize the beauties he'd made—Yvonne deCarlo and Betty Hutton, Jean Wallace, Gwen Verdon, Marie 'the body' McDonald, and Lili St. Cyr. He was like another Earl Caroll or Flo Ziegfeld. He was "N.T.G., Cabaret King."

He also lived in a small apartment over Mark's garage, and off and on he'd have the latest 'discovery' visiting him privately. One ex-showgirl-turned-prostitute who had, as 'Granny' Granlund would say, sought greener pastures, says she "was supposed to have been another Betty Hutton." He promised her spots in the chorus at the Gardens but instead she wound up "wet-nursing servicemen as a taxi-dancer in one of Mark's downtown dime-a-dance joints."

Wilkerson went to the Florentine Gardens for drinks and dinner and the floor shows—beautiful girls dancing around almost naked and the crowd going wild. "N.T.G. ran the place like a camp of good will," he says. The master of ceremonies would point out celebrities in the crowd (and the people on the rise), inviting them up on the stage to join in the singing and dancing. "There'd be people jumping up on stage—which was shaped like a top hat—and they'd be trying to climb over the brim part. But I was gun-shy of all that," Wilkerson says. "I didn't like to get up there, so I'd just watch the acts and watch the celebrities making fools of themselves.

"Mark was planning the *Beautiful Girl Revue for 1947*," Wilkerson says, "and Ann said he'd promised Beth a part in it, featured in a gardenia or a big flower opening and she'd be in the heart of it, wearing a thin G-string, and a flesh colored flower in her crotch. She should be a stripper, Mark was telling her. He talked about the *Flesh and Fantasy* revue, where she'd wear high heels and ankle straps like Ann Jeffreys in the *Dillinger* movie."

In early November of 1946 Barbara wrecked Bob's car, following a long alcoholic "blackout" in the desert. The car was towed to a Mojave garage, and after a few more drinks at the local tavern, Barbara wandered off into the desert. She left behind the car, her agent, Bob, her ambitions, and her career.

Around Thanksgiving Wilkerson ran into Beth in a bar near Sunset and Gower, a hangout for radio people from KMPC. "She was sitting in a booth with this guy Ray, and a man who was a singer, John Frizell. He was working pretty steady as an extra," Wilkerson says. "A few nights later, I saw Frizell at a party in the Linola Apartments on Carlton. Beth was there with Ann, and there was a man with them. He wasn't much taller than Ann, and seemed more friendly with her than he did with Beth, who sat on the rug. She had her legs bent to the side, and was leaning on one arm and seemed very gay, smiling when you talked to her. She cocked her head to the side and back and forth, funny-like, as if she was trying to please the guy who kept talking to her, like it was an effort she was making to make him feel she was paying attention to him—or to you in particular. I wanted to know more about her. I disliked the man she came to the party with—he chased a cat off the arm of the sofa by blowing cigar smoke in its face.

"But Beth had dark circles under her eyes. Not baggy, but more like she wasn't well, or else she hadn't gotten much sleep for a few nights. She looked like a lot was bothering her under the smiles and all that." The party was at a musician's apartment. He had a wire recorder in a large wooden cabinet. During the party he had the recorder on and he thrust the microphone in Beth's face asking her to say something into it. She didn't know what to say and started laughing. He said, "That's a beautiful laugh!" She laughed again. He asked her what her name was.

"Beth," she said.

"What's that?" he asked.

"Elizabeth—or Beth," she said.

"Beth?"

"Yes, that's who I am."

"Beth what? What's your full name? We need full names here," he said, acting like he was interviewing everyone for a program.

She leaned forward to the microphone and said her name was Elizabeth Short. "Elizabeth Short?" he said. "But you're not very short, are you?" They both started laughing over his joke.

He was fiddling with the recording, rewinding the wire and playing the sound of her laughter. Then the wire started coming off the spool.

Wilkerson saw Ann Toth a week later and asked her about Beth. "She told me that someone had said she was going back east, but someone else had said she'd gone to San Diego."

"San Diego?" he asked Ann. "What the heck's in San Diego?" Ann said something like, 'Who knows what there is *any*where for that girl.'"

9

She left Hollywood so abruptly it was as though she was being chased. Before leaving she called Ann and they met in the Brown Derby coffee shop. Beth told her about a "new romance." He was Lester Warren—a Navy officer. Beth said he had suggested that if she made it to San Diego he might be able to get her a job at the naval hospital. But, more importantly, Mark Hellinger had been constantly after Lester to act in a movie. Beth said Les had invited her to San Diego to discuss their relationship because, he admitted, he was getting serious about her. She smiled and said it was very possible he'd announce an engagement, and she held up her ring finger.

"I said it sounded swell," Ann says. "With the strikes there wasn't any work, and I said the news was worth coming to brunch for. I didn't know what else to say." First, Beth said, she had to get to San Diego. Ann said, "That's fine," and asked if she was planning on landing on his doorstep.

"No, no," Beth said, "our meeting has been taken care of." But she was a little short on cash and needed a few extra dollars for a hotel—just a simple room, she said, something like she'd had in Long Beach. Ann didn't know anything about Long Beach, but gave her twenty dollars, which Beth promised to return when she got work in San Diego.

Two days later, on the afternoon of December 8, 1946, Beth walked into a café in San Diego with her suitcases. She sat at the counter for almost an hour. Then, according to the waitress, she made an unusual request. "She asked if she could leave her tab on the counter with the exact change, but that she did not want to be excused as a customer. She said she might return and have something else added to her check as soon as she'd checked her luggage. I had never seen the girl before.

"After apparently checking her bags in the bus depot, except what looked like a makeup case, she came back to the café and asked for more coffee. I asked her if she wanted anything else. She said she didn't know where he was and whether she should wait or not. I didn't have any idea what she was talking about, but I figured she was meeting someone. I said, 'Well, that's a guy for you,' or something like that."

After leaving the café, Beth walked up Fifth Street to the Aztec Theater where a double feature was playing. The sign outside said "OPEN ALL NIGHT." She bought a ticket, and soon after settling into one of the plush seats, fell asleep while the movie was playing.

Twenty-one-year-old Dorothy French worked as cashier and usher at the Aztec. When the houselights came on she saw the girl sleeping near the front row, the only person left in the theater except for Dorothy and the janitor.

Dorothy woke the girl and told her the theater was closed. Beth seemed confused and mentioned the sign that said the movie house was open all night. "I have to apologize for that," Dorothy said. "The sign is not supposed to be out there. The policy has been changed because we're under new management." The girl began to cough and asked if there was any water. Dorothy walked back out to the lobby and got a paper cup, which she filled from the drinking fountain. She returned to Beth who swallowed some water and said she was sorry she'd fallen asleep. She told Dorothy she had traveled from Hollywood—she hadn't made her connections and didn't have any money left. She said she'd been an usherette and cashier in a theater back east and asked if any temporary help was needed.

"When she said 'temporary,'" Dorothy says, "I thought it meant she wasn't looking for a permanent job. I suggested she talk to the manager the next day. There was something so sorrowful about her—she seemed lost and a stranger to the area and I felt I wanted to help her. I wasn't sure how. She apparently had no place to stay. I suggested she come home with me and get a night's sleep on our couch, if that would help. She said she was thankful for my generosity. She used the word 'generosity,' and said things were difficult in Hollywood because of the strikes."

Dorothy had read about the strikes and listened to news on the radio, but personally she knew little about a struggling actress's life in Hollywood. It seemed far away to Dorothy—far from the small, cardboard-like house she shared with her mother, Elvera, and her younger brother, Cory, in a tract area outside of San Diego called Pacific Beach—erected during the war for shipyard workers.

The bus Dorothy had to catch for the half-hour ride left in less than twelve minutes and she quickly closed the lobby, leaving the theater with her new companion, Beth. On the bus, Dorothy pointed out the harbor and the lights of ships as they went along the coast.

"Beth didn't say much," Dorothy recalls. "She seemed sad, like someone with no one to turn to. I was taking her to my house for a place to sleep, but I felt like she was all by herself on the bus."

They got off at Balboa and Pacific Coast, a dimly lit intersection with a gas station on one corner and Sheldon's Sandwich Shop on the other. They walked the short hill, and Dorothy said her mother was still up because the kitchen light was on.

Elvera French was sitting in the kitchen with a cup of coffee and the newspaper. She apologized for the mess in the house—she had not expected company. Dorothy quickly told her that Beth was going to "camp out" on the couch for the night since she'd missed a ride and was a little stranded.

It seemed as soon as Dorothy brought her a blanket and

pillow, and Beth lay down, she was already fast asleep. In the kitchen, Elvera told her daughter that the girl looked "pale." Dorothy said Beth had been coughing, and it sounded like some sort of congestion. Her mother suggested the girl should see a doctor.

When Elvera left for work the next morning, Beth was asleep. Later in the day Beth was surprised to learn that the woman was a civilian employee at the naval hospital. She told Dorothy, "Your mother will be able to get me in to see the navy lieutenant I've been looking for." She told Dorothy what Lester Warren had suggested about civilian work. "It's the reason I came down here."

By the next afternoon Dorothy's younger brother, Cory, took a bus to the Greyhound station for Beth's suitcases. They were so heavy with clothing, the boy said it felt as though the bags were filled with rocks.

Beth called from a neighbor's telephone about getting a money order sent Western Union, or to General Delivery at the post office. Elvera suggested that Beth could have the money or letter sent to the house. She was making herself at home, but assured Elvera that her stay wouldn't be more than a day or so, until the money arrived. She offered to pay the Frenches for any inconvenience she was causing.

"I told her that was not necessary," Dorothy says. "A lot of people were having a hard time—the housing and apartment shortage was bad, and my mother also told her not to worry about putting us out, and whatever she needed we'd be able to take care of it."

But then a few days later things seemed a little different than Dorothy had anticipated. Beth slept till half-past eleven almost every morning. The evening before she'd told Elvera that she was probably starting a new job the next day with Western Airlines, and though she wasn't sure of the duties, she would begin training soon. Elvera came home for lunch and she found Beth sound asleep on the couch, her clothing spread about the living room—hanging over chairs, on top of the radio, and laid out as though on display. "There was a strong, sweet-smelling scent in the house from her perfume," Elvera says. "It was as though she had sprinkled perfume everywhere. She hadn't, of course, it was just her way of using it. Her clothes looked quite expensive, especially the lingerie. There were brand-new black *silk* stockings. I could tell they weren't nylon, but silk."

Beth had been out until two in the morning. She said the date was with a prospective employer. Then she told Dorothy she would meet her at the Aztec, but instead she ran into the theater manager and left with him. She stayed up most of the night on the date with the manager, and slept most of the following day. Still, Elvera felt bad for the girl. She'd look at her sleeping—often on her stomach with one arm cradled up, the forearm sort of supporting her chin. Even while the girl slept, Elvera noticed that her lustrous black hair seemed to remain perfectly in place. When she'd brush or comb it, it was more of a primping or patting, and never did she see the girl take long strokes of the brush as Elvera did and had taught her daughter to do.

The manager had invited Beth to his house for shish kabob, Beth told Dorothy. She said he gave her "too much to drink," and that he scratched her arms as he was grabbing her.

"I was puzzled about that," Dorothy says. "Beth had long, red scratches on her upper arms, and she said the manager told her he was in love with her, and that was what he would do to her if she stepped out on him." Elvera urged Beth to use peroxide on the scratches to keep from getting an infection.

Later, in an "innocent" way, Dorothy asked the manager about Beth, but the man seemed quite unconcerned. He said she had just kept him company for dinner. He also said he wasn't hiring anyone else to work at the movie house. "When I mentioned this conversation to Beth," Dorothy says, "she said he told her he was not going to hire her because other guys would be bothering her if she worked there, and he'd not be able to control his jealousy."

Despite the questionable behavior of the manager, Beth dated him again, and other men almost every night. "Even if we were riding the bus," Dorothy says, "guys would stare at her and it was like she was putting on an act, and they'd try to get a date with her."

Sometimes Beth would be lounging in her pajamas until past two in the afternoon, writing letters and sipping coffee. She wrote home to her mother, mentioning she'd be working at the hospital. "I am going to make every effort to save every penny," she wrote, "so when the strikes are over and I go back to Hollywood, things will be easier for me." She said she would be punching a regular clock at the hospital. But to Dorothy it appeared that Beth did not punch a time clock or work at any other job while she was in San Diego. And as Christmas approached, she seemed no nearer to making a change—lounging in a black Chinese robe with flowers and dragons on it that she seemed to acquire while staying with the Frenches. Dorothy remembers her mother asking Beth to dress a little less casually when Cory was in the house. "She'd noticed my brother going out of his way to look at Beth," Dorothy says. "It wasn't that my mother was a prude, but Beth was *very* eye-catching, and when only partly dressed, it was difficult *not* to pay attention.

"She'd talk about her Hollywood connections while painting her toenails or putting on makeup. Often she'd use cold cream to take it off and then start all over again. She used a jar of cold cream I had, and then asked if she could use my mother's Noxzema."

Beth carefully matched articles of her clothing into different outfits for her nights on the town. Dorothy thought the embroidery work and the fine pearls on one of Beth's sweaters were beautiful. There were tiny embroidered loops and circles around the sequined and beaded parts. Beth would dress up for dates and stand before Dorothy, turning one way or the other like she was modeling, and say, "Well, what do you think?"

Dorothy told her she'd feel out of place in some of Beth's outfits, but that Beth could bring it off. She felt that Beth asked those questions to be admired and to involve Dorothy in her decisions of what to wear. Except for the Aztec manager, Dorothy didn't know any of the other men. Elvera said that, for someone who was a "lost soul" when she showed up, she'd gathered quite a circle of admirers.

Dorothy's brother, Cory, was thirteen at the time. He told his sister that Beth and he had talked about her staying in his room, instead of always sleeping on the couch. Cory said, "It's okay if I sleep on the couch, isn't it?"

"Why do you want to do that?" Dorothy asked him. He replied that he thought she was funnier than the "guys on the radio," and she did imitations and made him laugh. He said, too, because she was such a nice person and he felt like he could really talk to her—"not like she's a grown-up," Cory told his sister, "but more like she's someone that *I* know, too." Cory felt it was fair if he shared his room with his new friend.

"She is a friend to all of us," Dorothy said to Cory.

When Dorothy told her mother what Cory had suggested, Elvera said, "That's *his* room, and for the love of God, we'll *never* get things back to normal around here if she moves in there."

Elvera found herself tiptoeing through the living room while getting ready for work. She'd ask herself why she was tiptoeing through her own house—the girl should have been up, dressed, and looking for work instead of sleeping or fancying herself up for dates.

"She should return to Hollywood," Elvera said. "She talks so much about working in the movies, she should go back there and get a job in one of the studios!" Dorothy found herself defending Beth when she really didn't intend to. Her mother said all the talk about Hollywood was "next door to bragging," but Dorothy thought it was more likely Beth was trying to believe it herself, as if she said it enough, and believed it enough, it would come true—the same as with the couple of men she claimed to have been in love with.

If only she could meet some handsome army officer or sailor or airman who'd love her like she knew she could love him, and marry her—then maybe tomorrow her life could be different.

She'd told Dorothy that Gordan Fickling was still in love with her. He was out of the Army Air Corps, and now was a commercial pilot flying between North Carolina and Chicago. Dorothy says, "She would sit at the kitchen table with my mother and me and talk about her husband who died, and how much she still loved him and how this kept her from falling in love with someone else. And she'd unfold that newspaper clipping and read it to us, always saying the same thing about the crossed-out place—the paper had made a mistake. She'd talk about the baby dying, and that was why she couldn't find the *right* situation for herself."

At other times the Frenches wondered if Beth had been in some kind of trouble in L.A.—and was hiding out in some way. She wrote Gordan for money. "If something could be possible for you to send me, please, please wire something to me," she asked. She wrote to Ann, telling her she would repay her as soon as she got back to Hollywood, but she needed anything Ann could manage to send.

Gordan replied that her request was impossible "at this time." He could not send her the money. "Darling," he wrote, which made Beth feel good, but the rest of the letter disappointed her. "Other obligations have me against a wall. Please try to make other arrangements. I'm concerned," he wrote, "and I am sorry, believe me."

Shortly before receiving this letter she'd written to him and spoken of her love. "Have we been foolish?" she asked. "Is there something we could share, is there something, some way for us to be happy?"

He'd wondered the same thing. Gordan wrote, "My feelings for you are such that I'm afraid that if we spend any more time together, I am going to be falling in love with you all over again, and it will be the same problem we have faced before. I know you care deeply for me, and you know that I care for you. I do not know if there can be any future in it at all. You want us to be good friends. I want nothing more than that.

"Are you sure what you really want? You've got to be just a little more practical these days. I am glad you have ambition to be a cover girl. You deserve to be a success. After all, you have a lot to work with.

"You know how I feel about you, but I don't think I can simply be good friends with you since I care so much about you. I don't know what we can do about it. I am worried about you. I am concerned about you. I will try to help you in all ways and any way that I can, but Beth—Beth—please understand that no matter how much my caring for you is, I cannot be optimistic about a future together. . . ."

Why? Why? Dorothy wanted to know. Why didn't he think there could be a future with someone like Beth? But Dorothy had no way of knowing what it was that so troubled Gordan, that kept him torn about the girl he claimed he had loved, and still cared for—but could never be close to again.

Whatever was wrong just kept getting more wrong, Dorothy felt. "My mother and I had a couple of arguments. You just couldn't tell someone to go away once you'd asked them to stay." The Frenches hadn't intended on Beth staying long. They kept hoping one of her contacts would come through. But instead of going out and "making things happen," as Dorothy put it, Beth occupied her time writing love letters which she'd hide away, saying she was going to "post" them later. "She said to me in the kitchen that she'd send Gordan the letters, and that with him she could have been living in a little house somewhere . . . that it could've been a little house like ours."

Elvera mentioned the temporary employment agency and Beth said she'd go next door to use the phone, but Elvera suggested it would be best if she applied in person. Beth said, "Oh, of course, what could I have been thinking?" Then after an hour or more doing her makeup, she finally left, wearing gloves and a hat with a veil. The truth, Dorothy felt, was that neither she nor her mother knew where Beth was going. They weren't sure if Beth herself knew where she was going.

10

Red-haired Robert Manley was soon to find himself in the worst predicament of his life. It began casually enough; he hadn't been *intending* to pick up a girl. But there she was—and there was no avoiding it.

He was driving on San Diego's Broadway in his old Studebaker coupe on a business trip from L.A. Stopping at a signal, he glanced to his right as a car turned the corner. When it passed, he was looking at a very pretty black-haired young woman standing on the corner near the Western Airlines window. At twenty-six, Red didn't whistle at girls, but if he did, *she* was someone he'd certainly have whistled at.

The car behind him honked its horn and Red drove ahead, looking more closely at the girl. He turned the first corner past the intersection, then made another quick turn and drove two blocks further to go around once again and see if she was still there.

It was as though she hadn't moved a muscle. What was she doing there? he wondered. She wasn't waiting to cross with the signal. The street he'd just turned onto was one-way, so if the girl crossed the street when the light changed, he might not be able to get around the next block to catch her before she disappeared into one of the office buildings.

He pulled over to the curb at the corner, leaned to the passenger window, and said hello to her. "Can I give you a lift?" he asked. She turned her head and wouldn't look at him.

Edging a little more toward the window, Red told her he was serious, that he didn't know the town. "I'm here on business," he said, and if he gave her a lift somewhere, maybe she could help him find his way around.

Without looking at him she said, "I'm on my way home."

"Well, then, let me give you a ride *there*," he said. "I really just want to find out the directions around here." She looked at him for a moment, then stepped down from the curb and got into the car. Once in, she pulled the door shut and adjusted her skirt, looking at Red with a slight tip of her head. He told her a ride in the car was better than waiting on a street corner.

"What makes you think I was *waiting* on the street corner?" she asked. Her manner embarrassed him. He said he didn't mean it *that* way and introduced himself. She said her name was Beth Short, and reached out her hand. Red shook it briefly, almost awkwardly turning his hand away.

"I don't live in San Diego," he said. "I'm a hardware salesman." He asked if she knew where Huntington Park was—east of the downtown Los Angeles area. "Further south than downtown," he said, "but in the eastern side of the city."

She said, "I don't know if I do or not."

"There's no reason you should," he said, "unless you happen to live there and work for a hardware company. My firm deals in pipe clamps." He said it wasn't something he intended to *do* the rest of his life. "It's just a job," he said. Then he told her again he didn't know the city.

"I don't know the city either," she said. "I'm visiting with some friends in Pacific Beach."

"That's right off the coast highway," he said. "I saw the sign coming down here." She said she had been seeing about a clerical job at Western Airlines. "You married?" he asked, glancing at her hand. She said, no, and then said yes, she was, but her husband had been killed in the war—an officer in the Army Air Corps. It wasn't that she *wasn't* married, but that they were no longer together, she said, "at least, in this life." Before she got around to asking if he was married, Red changed the subject. He was thinking that he just wanted to forget about that part of his life for the moment—his wife and baby. There had been problems between them since the baby had been born. Red had been telling himself it was only a "readjustment" period.

He told Beth he'd been a musician in the Army Air Corps band. "I'm discharged now," he said. "I try to keep up with the music, but it's pretty hard to do it as a profession—unless you've got something special." She asked if he'd been an officer, and he said no, just a corporal. She asked if he knew about the Flying Tigers. Red knew something about them, mostly what he'd seen in the movies. She said her husband, a major, had been with them. She asked how old he was, and when he told her she said he was very young. How old did he think *she* was, she asked? He couldn't tell. He thought she was young—younger than he was, but not too young. He said she had a very glamorous air about her, and that sometimes made it difficult to tell the age of a very attractive young woman.

She laughed a little. "You think I'm very attractive?" she asked. He said sure, and that she knew it herself without having to ask. Then he laughed a little, too, as though they'd shared a joke. She directed him to the Frenches' house where he parked and shut off the motor. He then asked if she wanted to have dinner with him. "I don't have anything else to do until I make some calls in the morning," he said. "We can have a few drinks and maybe dance."

She said she was concerned about what to tell the people she was staying with. He suggested she could introduce him as a business associate. That didn't sound right to her, she said. She'd tell them he was someone she was working with at Western Airlines. "It'll seem like we're associates that way," she said, "and we have things to talk about, and you've asked me to dinner."

There was nothing wrong with that, he said, and suggested picking her up at seven o'clock. She said, "Fine," and got out of the car. "Don't walk me up there now. You come to the door at seven."

Red felt good. He drove to a motel and rented a room for two, writing his address, car model, and license number on the registration card. He then walked back to where he'd spotted a café called Harry's, ordered a beer, and asked about a "nice place to eat—for dining and dancing." The Hacienda Club was one of the best, he was told. It was out near the Mission Hills area.

After listening to a couple of songs on the jukebox and thinking about the date, he finished his beer and walked back to the motel. He took a shower and was in the midst of shaving when he began to think about his wife, and it was hard to think about her without thinking about the baby. He had a pretty wife, though she wasn't as pretty as the girl he was seeing at seven.

He had been married just shortly over a year. He had never stepped out on his wife, but he had lost interest in her. He didn't want to have sex with her anymore and he tried to avoid her as much as he could. He would find himself wondering why he was doing this. He believed that part of it was the pregnancy—things had changed, and he'd been nervous a lot. The baby made him nervous, and he felt guilty about that. He thought of himself as a rat. He had been over to the veterans hospital a couple of times, and each time the doctors told him that he seemed to he having "the same old problems." He hadn't been able to take the army, even though he'd felt *good* at times as part of the band. But he hated the restrictions—the discipline.

He had received a "Section Eight"—a psychiatric discharge. It was his nerves. Once or twice during the past year he'd said to himself, "Look out, Red, you're going off the deep end!" But he hadn't gone off the deep end yet. It was just nerves. He had a bad case of nerves.

The air in San Diego was terrific. He sat on the motel bed breathing deep before the opened window. There were a lot of things that had to be ironed out in his marriage. Maybe many were just small things, but they seemed to get all tangled up. They became a big ball of tangled loose ends that seemed to get away from him when he knew it was important that he keep them all straightened out.

Stepping out on his wife troubled him, but he felt he was facing a kind of test, to see if he still loved her. He changed his shirt, slapped some Aqua Velva lotion onto his cheeks, and made the decision that he wasn't going to give any more thought to his wife or to the job or to the condition of his nerves. He was just going out to have a little relaxation and a couple of laughs.

He showed up at the Frenches' a few minutes before seven, and introduced himself as someone from Western Airlines. He did say that he had worked for a hardware manufacturer previous to the airlines, but to the Frenches he didn't seem to know much more about San Diego than Beth. Both of them were like strangers from some other place, and meeting in the Frenches' living room as though it were some kind of play they were performing. "Beth was almost brusque," Dorothy would later recall, "and she walked out before Red could give any details to Elvera. 'I'll try to stop by the movies and say hello,' Beth said."

"I feel bad about fibbing to them," Beth said in the car. "They have been very helpful to me. But I think I've outworn my welcome."

"Well," Red said, "maybe you'll feel better after a bite." He wasn't sure of the directions to the restaurant and by the time they arrived at the Hacienda Club it was almost nine. Jerry Leonard's Band was playing, and after a couple of drinks Red and Beth danced. He had the feeling that she was watching him, sort of measuring him as though looking for mistakes he'd make. She asked if he was married and he said yes, but they were at a halfway point—and maybe it wasn't going to work out.

Beth opened her purse and brought out a clipping, handing it to him. He read about Matt Gordan and asked about the scratched out part. She said the paper had made a mistake. He mentioned in the car she'd told him her name was Short. She said she returned to using her maiden name. Red said it was too bad about him getting killed, just as the war ended. He ordered more drinks, and she put the folded clipping away and said she was hungry.

"This place is dead," he said, and asked what she wanted. But she said she didn't want anything on their menu. "I want a sandwich or something," she said. "Something that's simple. I'm not hungry for a fancy dinner. . . . Why spend money on a fancy dinner anyway? I've been having it pretty hard, and staying where I am isn't easy. I'm out of work. And it isn't a good idea to spend a lot of money on something that's probably not any good."

"How do you know it won't be any good?" he asked.

"Well, look around," she said. "What do you see?"

"I don't see anything," he said.

"That's what I mean," she said. They found out the kitchen was closed for the night, so they finished their drinks and left. Beth said she was a little tipsy and he said they'd find a restaurant on the way back to town.

He pulled into the first drive-in, leaving the radio on because she liked the music. She ordered a sandwich and Red had a hamburger.

"Halfway through the meal," Red says, "she heard the guy on the radio say the time—which was almost one o'clock, and she said she had to get back. I told her I had to get up pretty early, so maybe it was a good idea to call it a night. I didn't ask her to stop back by the motel for a nightcap—though that had been in the back of my thoughts since I'd taken the room that afternoon."

At Pacific Beach, Red parked the car and took her hand. He told her he would like to kiss her. She turned, facing him, and he bent forward a little and put his lips on hers. After a moment she drew her head back and said she had to go into the house.

"What about one more kiss?" he asked. She leaned over and kissed him on the lips, but hers were cool and hardly moved. Then she opened the car door. "I'll walk you to the house," he said.

She smiled and took his hand after he came around the car. He said, "After I finish some business in the morning, I'm heading back up to L.A. You haven't got a phone here, so how can I call and leave a message for you?"

The Frenches didn't have a phone, she said, and she'd been using the neighbor's, but that was becoming difficult. Red said he'd send a telegram to the house, letting her know when he'd be down. "We can have dinner," he said. "I'd really like to see you again."

It was okay with her. She wasn't sure how long she'd be staying where she was, but she'd expect his telegram.

Red drove back to the motel and sat in the chair feeling awful. He'd only kissed the girl. Feeling awful was stupid, he told himself.

The following morning, after grabbing breakfast at Sheldon's Sandwich Shop on the highway, he drove to the Pacific Beach area and stopped at the house. When he knocked on the door, it was opened by the young woman he'd met the night before. Dorothy told him that Beth wasn't there. She said she thought Beth was at work, but wasn't sure. Red asked Dorothy to tell her he had stopped by and would see her later.

The first telegram that came for Beth was not from Red. It was an apology from Gordan, and contained the one-hundred-dollar money order. She told Dorothy, "I'm shocked. I didn't expect Gordan to wire the money."

She walked to Sheldon's, where she made a number of collect calls and told the waitress that she was expecting a long-distance person-to-person call. The waitress said, "Don't worry, honey, if your call comes when you're gone I'll put the message on the spindle at the register. It'll be here late tonight or tomorrow for you."

Back at the Frenches' she wrote again to Gordan. "I think I'm going to be coming back to Chicago to do some work. . . . I am sorry that you feel as you do, and I hope that you can find a nice young lady to kiss every New Year's Eve. I believe it would have been wonderful if we belonged to each other now. I do want you to know that I'll never forget coming west to see you. Even though it has not worked out that you did take me in your arms and keep me there. Honey, it was nice as long as it lasted. . . ."

She folded the letter into her handbag, along with the other unmailed letters. It was Christmas Eve, and Beth waited at the movie theater for Dorothy to get off work to return to the house with her. But a young man stood talking to her for a little while, and then Beth told Dorothy that the young man had asked her to have dinner at his house. Beth did not return to the Frenches' until late Christmas day, with small presents for everyone.

The following week was difficult for everyone. Dorothy saw

that something had happened with Beth and she had no way of knowing what it was. It was as though Beth had suddenly pulled down a window shade on anything to do with her life or what she was planning to do. She lounged around the house most of the time and fiddled with her clothes, laying them out again and looking at them, or ironing. She wrote letters and read magazines, and sent Cory on errands. The boy didn't mind, but Elvera felt it was wrong for him to be used as a *coolie*, which is what she told Dorothy. Beth had asked him to buy sanitary napkins and scented stationery. Dorothy suggested that she could buy those things for Beth, since Cory wouldn't understand what he was buying. Beth took Dorothy's hint as an offer to do something for her and was glad, she said, "because you could pick out better things."

Beth wrote a letter to her mother, and another one to Gordan, then another one to Duffy in Chicago. Dorothy mailed the letters on her way to work at the movie theater.

"On New Year's Eve she was at the El Cajon Club with a date, and she became drunk and passed out," Dorothy says. "Her date brought her back early in the morning, and Beth slept until almost noon," and then spent the rest of the day in her Chinese robe chatting with Dorothy or Elvera—flighty or nervous, Elvera observed. Later in the day she wrote to Ann Toth again, asking her to send some money that she would repay when she was back in L.A. Beth didn't have any of the hundred dollars left and she had not given any money to Elvera or Dorothy.

Dorothy recalls, "A couple of days later some people came to our door and knocked. There was a man and a woman, and another man was waiting in a car parked on the street in front of the house. Beth became very frightened—she seemed to get panicky, and didn't want to see the people or answer the door. They finally went back to the car and drove away. Even our neighbors thought all of this was very suspicious."

Western Union delivered a telegram on January 7th. It was from Red. He hadn't been able to forget the girl he'd met in San Diego. A few days before he sent the telegram he complained to the veterans hospital that he thought he was having "a nervous breakdown." The doctor told him he seemed in control. Perhaps it was the job—or the stress of his marriage problems. He certainly loved his infant son, but there seemed to be a lot to think about. He needed time. He needed a break. He wanted to see that other girl again.

On January 8th Red covered the territory he'd been assigned in San Diego and arrived at the Western Airlines office about four in the afternoon. He waited for about thirty minutes, but Beth didn't show up. He then drove back to Pacific Beach, to the house where she was staying.

As soon as he climbed out of the car he saw her at the front door. She looked upset as she came to the car and said, "I have to make a call. Will you take me down to the highway so I can make it?" Red wanted to say he'd do anything she asked. She climbed in and he drove down the hill. When they reached the highway she seemed to have relaxed a little. She asked what time it was and he told her. "It's too late now to make the call," she said. She seemed worried and he wanted to know what was wrong. "Well," she said, "I'm leaving here. I'm really glad you sent me the cable. Maybe you can take me someplace to get a room for the night and I can take a bus in the morning." She said she had to get back to L.A.

When they returned to the house for her luggage, Red walked her to the door. Beth's suitcases were just inside and he said he'd put them in the car.

He put the suitcases in the car and glanced back to see her talking in the doorway to the woman. Beth was giving Elvera a hat—saying something about it wasn't much except she knew she liked it. Beth seemed happy, almost laughing when she got in the car. Red started it up and drove down the hill toward the highway. "When I didn't find you downtown, I thought it was best that I went out to the house," he said. "I guess that shows how much I wanted to see you."

"I appreciate that," she said. "You're being very sweet. I'm sorry if things are a little mixed up."

"I'm concerned about what you're going to do," he said to her. "I'll get you a room for the night and maybe you'll want to go out to dinner."

Once Beth got her room, she brought in her makeup kit, sat

on the edge of the bed, and began to comb her hair. He asked if she was getting hungry and she nodded, smiling, applying lipstick, and using a small dauber to touch up the corners of her lips.

"Do you feel like something fancy or just grabbing a bite?" Red asked. But before she replied, recalling how she got tipsy the last time, he said, "We can go over to the Hacienda Club again. You feel like doing that?"

She said all right, "I'd like to stop at Sheldon's on the way." Red said that was fine with him, and when they got to Sheldon's Beth wanted to sit in a booth and order a sandwich. Red got a couple of beers and played the jukebox with Beth picking out the songs. Red kept checking his hair in the mirror behind the counter, and she was laughing. She told him he seemed to comb his hair a lot. "It's lying wrong," he said, and he needed a haircut.

He told her he was glad that she was feeling better and maybe they could make a grand night of it. But he didn't let her know that he was thinking about the motel room. Then she said there was another place she'd like to go, since she wouldn't be coming back to San Diego for a while—the U.S. Grant, a big hotel that had a band. Red said it sounded like a good idea, and asked the waitress for directions.

It didn't take them long to find the hotel, but while the band was there the dance floor was almost deserted. Red ordered drinks and soon noticed that Beth's mood had changed. She became quiet and kept glancing to the door or to the back of the room as though looking for someone. It gave him the feeling that she'd wanted to stop there to see somebody else before leaving town.

Next they drove to the Hacienda Club, where people were dancing and the music was playing. Beth's mood again changed, and to Red she seemed to be having a swell time. They danced and had more drinks; it was getting late. Beth told him she wanted to leave. Back in the car, she said, "Maybe I should take a bus."

"You mean *tonight?*" Red asked. She didn't know. He said, "We've got the room—maybe a good night's sleep. . . . I'll take you to the depot, if that's what you want, but I'll drive you to L.A. in the morning. You'll probably get there sooner than the bus."

They didn't say anything for a while, and then he asked if

she was hungry. She said she was. "Let's grab something to eat," he said. "Maybe taking a bus isn't such a good idea."

"Maybe not," she said. "My stomach is bothering me." Red suggested getting something to go and taking it back to the motel where she could relax. "Maybe that's what's wrong with me—I need something to eat," she said.

They drove to the highway café where Red asked them to bag a couple of hamburgers and sodas. When they returned to the motel, Beth changed into a sweater and pushed the sleeves up when she tried to eat. Noticing the red scratch marks on her arms, he said that one of them seemed to be bleeding. She looked at her arms and, smiling a little, said, "I have a jealous boyfriend." "You mean to say someone *did* that to you?" he asked.

"He's Italian," she said. "He's not a very nice guy at all." She said it had happened quite a while ago, but she'd been picking at it, and it started bleeding. Then she started to shiver and said she was cold.

She picked up Red's topcoat and put it around her shoulders to keep warm, saying she wished they had some heat in the room. He said, "You want me to light the fire?" She said please, in a soft voice as though suddenly tired, and sat in the chair with her legs curled up under her. He lighted the fire but she didn't seem to get any warmer. She nibbled on the hamburger as Red moved the chair right in front of the fire. He sat on the edge of the bed and tried to make conversation with her, but she was shivering.

"I'm very cold," she said, and he took two blankets off the bed to wrap around her.

"Is that better?" he asked. She nodded. She wanted her suitcase out of the car—the smaller one—and asked if he could get in. Red wanted to know if she wanted something from the drugstore—was there anything he could get that would make her feel better?

"No," she said, huddling in the blankets. She just stared at the fire. Red got her suitcase and the other things from the car, and then drank the rest of the soda. He was thinking about how gay and lively she'd seemed at the Hacienda Club. She hadn't been cold or sick then.

He sat down on the bed and said, "I'm going to try to get some sleep. Do you want to lay down and try to get some sleep? I can sleep in the chair—it's okay with me."

"No, I'm too cold to sleep right now," she said. "You go ahead and sleep on the bed."

While her back was turned, Red removed his shirt and trousers and climbed quickly into the bed. He felt peculiar. He thought about his wife and the little baby and he felt sad. It wasn't his nerves—just kind of sad, like he had burdened himself in some way with this girl. In the back of his mind he'd pictured romance, and he kept thinking of how they'd danced, how he'd felt her breasts against him and the aroma of her hair and whatever that unusual perfume was.

Shutting his eyes, he felt as though he was still back at the Hacienda Club dancing with her. How well she danced and how easy it had been—and her laughter, her head going back slightly and all that black hair fanning out about her head. He had an image of a bottle of thick ink turned upside down and the way it would spill and spread out.

Now he didn't feel romantic at all. He just felt tired. He couldn't even remember falling asleep.

When he opened his eyes again it was daylight but he didn't know how early it was. His muscles jumped slightly like he was suddenly falling and had to catch himself. He raised his head. Beth was propped up with a pillow on the other side of the bed, wide awake. "How do you feel?" he asked. She had chills all night, she said. "You haven't slept?" he asked. She shook her head and he looked at his watch. "I'm late!" he said. "I've got an appointment!"

He was going downtown and they decided she'd wait in the motel room until he returned. She asked if he would take her shoes to a shoe repair and have new taps put on the heels. "When you come back," she said, "we can leave and go up to Los Angeles."

"That's the plan," he said, taking her shoes. "Noon is checkout time, and I'll be back by then."

But it was almost twelve-twenty when Red returned to the motel. His business appointment had run longer than expected.

There were new taps on the shoes and she was ready to go. She looked lovely, he thought; a black tailored cardigan jacket and skirt, a white blouse with a very fine sort of lace at the collar. She slipped her feet into the black suede pumps and offered a beautiful smile, thanking him for the taps.

Within minutes they were heading north on the coast highway, and Red said, "I've got a call to make on the way. It's business and I'll try to make it fast." She didn't say anything, just kept staring straight ahead.

The stop at a plumbing supply company took a little while, and when he got back into the car she said she was hungry. "We'll get something first place we come to," he said.

It was twenty minutes farther, and before they got out of the car at the restaurant she reached down and straightened the seams of her stockings. She looked at Red sadly and said, "It's the last pair of stockings I have."

They got a quick sandwich, then drove as far as Laguna Beach where he had to stop for gas. While the attendant was filling the tank, Beth told him she wanted to write to him, if that were possible—with the situation with his wife. "I don't know," he said. "Maybe it would be better if I wrote to you."

"You can give me your business card and I'll send a note there," she said, "telling you where I'll be." She smiled and added, "You don't have to worry—I'll make it sound like it is business." Red said all right, but then he couldn't find a card. He tore off the company name from a slip in his salesbook, and she folded it into her handbag. "You're very sweet," she said.

Still on Highway 101, they stopped for some more coffee and something else to eat. When they came out Beth said she had to make a phone call, and Red waited by the car while she gave a number to the long-distance operator. He got into the car and waited for her. When she got back in, she had a small address book open and said her sister lived in Berkeley and was married to a professor from the college there. She told Red his name was West and that her sister was going to meet her in L.A.

"I feel better about that," he said. "Are you going to Berkeley with her?"

"We have to talk about that," she said. "I'm sure I'll probably be up there with her for a couple of days, and then I'll be going to Boston." "*Boston*?" he said. "You really move around." "That's where my home is. I'm from the Boston area."

Red said he didn't know that—she didn't talk like someone from Boston. "Well," he said, "it's on to L.A, for now. Where are you meeting your sister—" and without waiting for her to answer, he added, "—at the Biltmore?" He didn't know why he asked that. He was being a little sarcastic.

She said, "Yes, that's where I'm meeting her." That sounded funny, but Red said that's where he'd take her. She said she'd appreciate that very much.

They continued to drive north, but before arriving in downtown L.A. Beth opened her suitcase and took out a beige topcoat, then drew on a pair of white dress cotton gloves. She said, "I want to check my bags first. Can we do that?"

It was between four-thirty and five. The traffic was bad. Red parked in front of the Greyhound Bus depot on 6th Street. He got out and carried her suitcases into the depot so she could check them. She checked the hatbox with the suitcases and said he had better move the car while she was checking her bags. He said he would go around the block and pick her up in front. It was a kind of bad area, he said. She was smiling as she checked the luggage, he noticed, and then he went out and drove the car around the block. He stopped again in front and waited several minutes until she came out. "Biltmore Hotel, right?" he said, still feeling funny about that. She nodded and sighed like she was suddenly tired again. It had been a long drive. "Okay," he said.

The Biltmore was only a few blocks west. Red found a place to park and they walked around the corner of 5th and Olive, going into the Biltmore Hotel lobby. "I have to go to the little girls' room," she said. "Would you mind checking at the desk to see if my sister has arrived?"

The desk clerk told Red that no Mrs. West was registered, nor was there a message for anyone from a Mrs. West. While waiting for Beth to return from the ladies' room, Red wondered if perhaps her sister had not registered but was somewhere in the lobby—waiting for her.

He noticed two blonde women who looked like they might

be waiting for someone. He asked each one if they were waiting for their sister. One woman seemed to get annoyed, and Red sat down in the lobby.

When Beth returned, he told her what the desk clerk had said. "I'm probably too early," she said. She would wait there, she told him, but it wasn't necessary for him to stay. Red had already done enough for her, she said. He looked at his watch. It was six-thirty. It was getting late, he said, and he had to drive to Huntington Park.

She was just looking at him—smiling at him. Her eyes looked very clear and blue and they seemed to be shining. He said, "Well . . . all right," and told her she could send him a letter at the business address, and let him know where she was going to be. She said she would do that and he turned around and headed for the Olive Street door. He glanced back to wave to her, but she was talking to the cashier at the cigar stand. She handed him a dollar and he returned some change. She was still standing there when Red left the hotel.

Several of the Biltmore Hotel employees noticed her waiting in the lobby. A number of times she walked across the marble floor to the telephone booths, and seemed to be making calls. The desk clerk would remember her sitting opposite the bell station for some time, then getting up and walking to the Olive Street door.

Outside, the doorman greeted her and watched as she walked toward Sixth Street. He would become the last known person to see her alive. Elizabeth Short would seem to vanish—to disappear. Her mutilated body would be found six days later in a vacant lot.

11

The Los Angeles County morgue, where the questionable deaths and murder victims were delivered pending identification or burial, was cramped, dingy, and had leaking water pipes. Glass panels in many of the doors were fogged over with a sticky moisture. The foul air reeked of decomposition and the constant electric fans only blew the odors from one hallway or room to another. The fumes of formaldehyde partly masking the smells "was like a gas that stuck to your clothes," says Detective Herman Willis, who had been transferred from the metro division to assist in the investigation.

Willis had been summoned to Central during the night to assist in the search of missing persons files in an effort to identify the victim, and to join in picking up and questioning more than a hundred "sex degenerates and suspected sadists." Other divisions had been pooled for the task, but Captain Jack Donahoe had requested that Willis, the "bright kid" of metro, who was to work with detectives Finis Brown and Harry Hansen, was to report directly to Donahoe.

"I didn't like going to the morgue," Willis says. "It was an awful place." For ages there had been threats to shut the morgue down—plans for condemning or moving the facilities. Time and again they got out of it with improvement schemes, but nothing was done. "There were other changes going on in the city, but a lot of things were staying the way they'd been—pockets were being filled and the dead weren't going to kick."

Rooms opened off halls that were filled with deputy coroners drinking coffee, joking, and talking, while in some rooms the bodies were stacked two and three deep— "stacked up like cord wood," Willis says. "I once had a judge order a check on a particular decedent in a case, and a deputy took me into one room and dumped one body off the other like you'd roll logs to get to the one on the bottom. I never found the right corpse. When we left the place he didn't bother to stack them back up again, but left them where he'd turned them over looking for the one I needed."

Often it would seem almost hot and humid in the halls. At one point the incoming cases became so "bottled up" that, with the severe shortage of equipment, the autopsies were performed on the gurneys. The rims around the table edges were too shallow to contain the fluids spilling over. "The examiners didn't seem to bother with their own regulations," Willis says.

Civilian mortuaries had grown to hate the county morgue—hated the surgeons *and* the deputies. "Guys at funeral parlors griped that bodies were sent over half the time without being sewn up or put back in shape." Willis says. "Sometimes body parts were put in wax paper—especially with traffic fatalities—or put into boxes for the independent undertakers. I remember one incident where the face was still folded back over the top of the head, which they'd sawed through, and the body was sent out like that, with the wife and relatives waiting for it at the other end."

Sometimes the morgue would release the wrong body. "If it was not detected, they'd cremate the one remaining behind," Willis says, "using the ash to fertilize the county rose bushes down by Exposition Park."

On the morning of January 16th, Willis joined Brown in the examination room where the autopsy on "Jane Doe Number 1" would be handled. She was on the table with her head to one side slightly, the cut through the mouth now gaping open, exposing the teeth. The lower section of the body angled up at the hips—somehow locked in that position so that the severed portion appeared at about a 45-degree angle to the opened area of the upper torso. This angle would puzzle investigators and lead them to the belief that the body had been in a semirecumbent position at the time of death.

Deputy Coroner Victor CeFalu was leaning slightly over one leg, holding a metal instrument between the thighs. "The other guy with CeFalu was Louis Delgado," Willis recalls, "and he wore an apron like CeFalu's. They were passing instruments back and forth because they hadn't been able to get a body temperature from the rectum the day before. The problem that morning had to do with some sort of blockage, CeFalu told us, even though the opening to the rectum appeared unusually dilated. CeFalu was attempting to clear this before the chief surgeon, Frederick Newbarr, began the postmortem. We were told that there appeared to be a blockage of both the rectum and the vagina and the chief surgeon was consulted earlier than scheduled."

According to Delgado the rectal obstruction was attended to by inserting a circular clamp in order to enter the area with forceps. "With several jerking motions," Willis says, "like pulling hard on something, what was brought out looked like pieces of skin. These were put into a white pan along with the forceps, and Delgado said it was epidermal tissue, with muscle fiber, or that part of the flesh that seemed attached and intact with the surface of the skin. These pieces that had been inserted into the dead girl's rectum—like setting pieces of a puzzle together—when they were rearranged in the pan, it looked like these were parts of the flesh that had been gouged out of her left thigh."

The next concern of CeFalu was what the surgeon had described during the cursory examination as an "apparent blockage" of the vaginal area. Brown wanted to know what it was, but CeFalu said Newbarr would have to make a determination on the condition of the body, or the possibility of sexual assault.

As a homicide investigator, Brown had spent a long season in the shadow of Harry Hansen. Brown gambled often, sometimes to his own serious disadvantage. He owed people to whom it wasn't smart to be indebted. He'd eventually have to pay what he owed, and he wouldn't be able to hide behind his older brother, Thad Brown, deputy chief of police and one of the most highly respected California lawmen. There was never a day that Finis didn't watch what he was doing so nothing would cast a bad light on his brother's unblemished reputation.

On the phone with Donahoe, Brown said it wasn't possible to know for the moment whether she'd been sexually assaulted. Donahoe said, "It's either a sex crime or it isn't. Half the department's interviewing perverts and the chief is pushing the net state-wide. She's mutilated and cut in half and if we're not dealing with a *sex* crime, Brownie, you tell me what we *are* dealing with so I can tell the commander."

"Of course it's a *sex* crime, sir," Brown said, "and we're looking for a pervert. We're not on a limb with that." Brown told the captain that the killer had pushed up into the girl's hind end the flesh he cut from her leg. "It's like they could belong in that wound to the leg. Some part of it's still missing. But no one can know this except the killer—and us. Hansen isn't even aware of it yet. Willis was with me when they found it." Donahoe told Brown to have Willis call in as soon as the autopsy was done. He wanted Willis to have full disclosure to the information shared between Hansen and Brown.

"Do you think that's the best policy?" Brown asked. "We don't know the guy that well."

"He's to be involved in all phases of the case," Donahoe said, and added that if either Hansen or Brown didn't like that, they could bring their grievances directly to the commander, who was in full support of Donahoe's decisions.

Brown felt that the captain had developed, like an overnight fever, some sort of mistrust for Hansen and Brown and had assigned a third leg to walk them through the case, as though they were all in some potato race.

Surgeon Newbarr, a short, balding man wearing gold-rimmed glasses, began the autopsy and the recording of his findings at 10:40 that morning, describing the body as being "that of a female about 15 to 20 years of age, measuring 5'5" in height, and weighing 115 pounds. There are multiple lacerations in the mid-forehead, in the right forehead, and at the top of the head in the midline. There are multiple tiny abrasions, linear in shape, on the right face and forehead.

"There are two small lacerations, one-fourth inch each in length, on each side of the nose near the bridge There is a deep laceration in the face three inches long which extends laterally from the right corner of the mouth. The surrounding tissues are ecchymotic and bluish purple in color.

"There is a deep laceration two-and-one-half inches long extending laterally from the left corner of the mouth The surrounding tissues are bluish purple in color. There are five linear lacerations in the right upper lip which extend into the soft tissue for a distance of one-eighth inch."

Examining the interior of her mouth, Newbarr noted that the teeth were in an advanced state of decay. "The two upper central incisors are loose and one lower incisor is loose." The rest of the teeth showed signs of decay, with "areas of subarachmoid hemorrhage on the right side and small hemorrhagic areas in the corpus callosum. . . .

"No fracture of the skull is visible. There is a depressed ridge on both sides and in the anterior portion of the neck. It is light brown in color. There is an abrasion irregular in outline in the skin of the neck in an anterior midline. There are two linear abrasions in the left anterior neck. There are two depressed ridges in the posterior neck, pale brown in color. The lower ridge has an abrasion in the skin at each extremity. The pharynx and larynx are intact. There is no evidence of trauma to the hyoid bone, thyroid or cricoid cartilages, or tracheal rings. There is a small area of ecchymosis in the soft tissues of the right neck at the level of the upper tracheal rings. There is no obstruction in the larynogotracheal passage."

CeFalu had stated the previous afternoon that the victim might have suffocated or strangled on her own blood as a result of the extensive lacerations to the mouth area. But with her throat opened, Newbarr could find no obstruction nor the residue of any coagulation.

Examining her upper chest, he reported "an irregular laceration with superficial loss in the skin of the right breast. The tissue loss is more or less square in outline and measures three and one-fourth inches transversely; and two and one-half inches longitudinally. Extending toward the midline from this irregular laceration are several superficial lacerations in the skin. There is an elliptical opening in the skin located three-fourths of an inch to the left of the left nipple. The opening measures two-and-three-fourths inches in a transverse direction and one-and-one-fourth inches in a longitudinal direction in its midportion. The margins of these wounds show no appreciable discoloration . . ."

With her chest opened, Newbarr examined the heart and lungs. "The left lung is pink in color and well aerated. The right lung is somewhat adherent due to fairly firm pleural adhesions. The lung is pink in color and well aerated. There is calcified thickening of the ninth rib on the right side in this scapular line. The heart shows no gross pathology."

As to the severing of the body, Newbarr recorded that "the trunk is completely severed by an incision which is almost straight through the abdomen, severing the intestine at the duodenum and through the soft tissues of the abdomen passing through the intervertebral disk between the second and third lumbar vertebrae. There is very little ecchymosis along the tract of the incision. There is a gaping laceration of four-and-one-half inches which extends longitudinally from the umbilicus to the suprapubic area. On both sides of this laceration there are multiple superficial lacerations. There are multiple criss-cross lacerations in the suprapubic area which extend through the skin and soft tissues. No ecchymosis is seen."

Examining the vagina, Newbarr said, "the labia majora are intact. There is an abrasion which extends through the lower half of the labia minora and the margin shows some bluish discoloration. Within the vagina and higher up there is lying loose a piece of skin with fat and subcutaneous tissue attached. . . .

"The anal opening is dilated and the opening measures one-and-one-quarter inches in diameter. The mucous membrane is brown throughout the circumference of the opening. There are multiple abrasions and a small amount of ecchymosis is seen at the margin."

Her hair was parted across the top of her head, and Newbarr quickly cut the scalp from one ear to the other. One piece of the scalp was pulled to the front, the other to the back, exposing the skull. With a small electric saw, the surgeon circled the scalp bone in a disk, which, about four inches across, was chiseled out and her brain lifted from the cavity of her skull.

The clock in the morgue indicated 11:45, and the time was recorded by CeFalu as the brain was labeled "specimen number 7569," to be submitted to the toxicologist for determining the presence of alcohol or any other compositions.

Opening the stomach, Newbarr noted that it "was filled with greenish brown granular material, mostly fecal matter and other particles" which the postmortem would not be able to identify.

Following the autopsy, Newbarr met with Hansen, Brown, and Willis. Hansen resented being overridden by his superior officer and forced to accept the presence of a subordinate policeman. According to Brown, he kept himself ramrod straight and condescending, while Willis seemed indifferent to Hansen's attitude.

The immediate cause of death was hemorrhage and shock due to concussion of the brain from blows on the head, and lacerations of the face, Newbarr told the detectives.

"It is impossible to tell you if she was *raped* because traces of spermatozoa are negative, and she did not *have* fully developed genitals. . . .

"There is no tumor or growth or even an accumulation of tissue from lesions, with the exception of the piece of skin inserted into the vagina. The area is shallow indicating that she did not have a completed vaginal canal.

"There might have been the possibility of spermatozoa traces from the laceration of the area below the navel down to the pubic area, if the attacker had some sexual usage of that area of the body. It would have been impossible for him to have inserted his penis into her vagina. "But, he said, "the body was then completely washed—removing all traces of semen or blood."

"Are you saying," Hansen asked, "that she could not have

normal sex?"

"There would be the possibility that there might have been problems in that area," the surgeon said. "The rest of it is a field I'm not well versed in and I will need to consult another—"

"—no!" Harry said so sharply it startled the man. "If all of this is on the level we're one up on the killer. The sonofabitch is out there and *he* knows as much as we do—I don't mean medically, but if you say she's missing organs, and some of the others he's taken out, and cutting her open in the stomach and possibly using that area and using her rectum—anal sex—because he couldn't get it into her vagina—and inserting pieces of her skin into her—*he* knows stuff *we* do, and we're the only ones that *know* it—insofar as any damage that was done to the girl."

Hansen said the feces in her stomach was troubling. "There's nothing to suggest what she might've taken into her stomach, as a meal, or a time she might've eaten something?" he asked.

"No," Newbarr said. "The fecal matter had been introduced into her mouth. She had ingested it and taken it down into her stomach previous to death." There would be no way to determine what she might have eaten last in the way of food, he said, as there was very little in the stomach except the greenish undetermined matter and the feces.

"Would it be her own excrement—or someone else's?" Brown asked. Newbarr said he had no way of making that comparison, though the specimens would be examined along with any possible smears for spermatozoa from other areas of the body. He suggested that these results would probably be negative and the possibility that some other particles of a meal might've been in the small intestines was impossible to determine since those organs had been removed.

"The conversation was confidential," according to Willis, and the indication of an abnormality to do with the vagina was not the only unusual thing discussed. "That would've been playing with firecrackers for a lot of people," Willis says, "including the fact that human shit had been *forced* into her mouth so that it was ingested down into her stomach before she was killed. I say forced into her mouth because I personally couldn't imagine her taking it in and swallowing it on her own."

There were missing organs, the detectives learned. "The killer had cut out parts of some basic female organs," Willis says. What seemed to emerge from the discussion was the possibility that the organs were missing because they had not *been* there to begin with. "This was the speculation as if for argument's sake," Willis says. "Harry looked blank—stone-faced about what was being said. But he was all itchy and clicking away."

Brown asked if they were talking about a surgically altered body "before the condition she's in now?"

"No," he was told. "Organs that had been present were removed for some other alternate reason."

"Whatever it is," Hansen said abruptly, "I don't want *anyone* to have details or information on the condition of the body. This is dynamite and it's got to be kept quiet. The point of the situation is she might not have been able to have satisfactory intercourse. Whatever it is, I think it's best that not a word of this gets out—not right now. I'm asking you to keep this sealed up," he said. "I'll talk to Donahoe and see what he can get—if an order might be needed here tomorrow—tonight, maybe. Not a word of this."

"There's already a thousand photographs," Brown said. "You can see most of what's been done, but there can't be anyone that knows what's inside of her, or what's not developed, that hasn't tried to get intimate with her—in some sort of intercourse manner."

Outside the morgue Hansen watched Willis get into his own unmarked car and pull out of the parking lot onto Spring Street. Hansen slid into his car alongside Brown. "These developments are things that nobody else should know about," Hansen said. "Nobody knows about the skin pushed up into her, except us and the nut who put it there. Now these physical complications—"

"—which I don't understand," Brown said. "But whatever you want to hold back, you realize, we're not going to be able to give it to the captain."

"What we have is what we'll go with. We've got this goddamn killer running around out there right this minute and we have to tag him, number one."

"Whoever he is, " Brown said, "she must've made him mad as hell. She must've given him a bad time, Harry."

"Which is exactly what we're talking about," Hansen said. "And this thing about the sex with her is the key to the door."

A gorgeous female that might have been some kind of question mark, Brown was thinking as they drove out of the morgue parking lot and south on Temple. He'd heard of some anomaly or condition—someone looking like a gal in every physical way except without the equipment to *be* a gal. It came down to saying, oh, my God, what've we got here and what're we going to do with it?

For Hansen, on the other hand, it was as though he'd been gifted with some special challenge. It was unusual for Brown to witness his partner's elation. Hansen said he wouldn't want anyone else to get their hands on what the postmortem revealed. He said it would be a good idea maybe if the chief surgeon wasn't *putting* the facts into a transcript. As he drove Hansen said, "There has to be a way to keep a lid on this."

Brown said, "For God's *sake*, Harry, we've got no jurisdiction to tell the coroner what not to do. If I tried to tell them that, they'd throw me out on my ear."

"They won't throw *me* out," Harry said, "and they certainly couldn't throw out a court order. There's only one person that knows what you and I and the coroner and *junior* Willis knows, and that's the one that killed her—the one that stuck shit in her mouth and skin up her ass and vagina, and cut her in two goddamn pieces! And that's our link, that's the ticket between us, that brings us *together*. As long as we keep together in this, and it goes no further, we're going to get him, Brownie, and *fast*."

Harry was dreaming, Brown thought.

12

Something was going on, Sid Hughes told a photographer, something sneaky that was being kept from the reporters. The chore was to side-step everyone else and find out what the hell it was—what the hell they were hiding. Hughes had doggedly tracked Hansen to Central and then to the morgue. "Stay at the morgue," Editor Jimmy Richardson told him. "Use every means you can to find out what is going on. You're good at that, Sid. I'm depending on you."

Hughes had been crowding the sheriff's press liaison with reporters from other papers. "We haven't started fighting over the details yet," he told Richardson. "But the *Daily News* and a couple of guys from the Hollywood *Citizen-News* are starting to foam at the mouth a little. There's nothing coming out of the morgue, and what someone's doing is shutting off the information."

The editor then got through to Captain Donahoe at Central. "I hear Aggie Underwood's on her way in to see you, Jack. But let me tell you, this one's got *Examiner* written all over it!" He told the captain, "We're going for broke. Whatever *we* come up with is going straight on your desk, Jack, and I'm going to play ball—I mean *ball* on this one as far as you're concerned. You'll see I'm laying it straight with you. A couple of my boys are on their way over now, and I hope to hell they get through to you before she does."

At the *Examiner* it became quickly known that Elizabeth Short was a glamour gal with a shape that would put bathing beauties to shame. She'd done just that on the army base by winning the Camp Cutie contest. She'd been 18—a 110-pound knockout with a face like a movie star. Wain Sutton had rolled out some background about the mother and some sisters in Medford, Massachusetts, and Richardson told him to get the mother on the telephone. Keep her line tied up so no one else could get through.

"But there was no telephone listed for the Shorts in that town," Sutton says. "We tracked down the nearest neighbor with a phone, and it turned out to be a flat in the Shorts' apartment house."

Then the worst thing that Sutton believes he ever had to do was set in his lap by Richardson. "He had me call the neighbor and ask them to go upstairs and get Elizabeth Short's mother to the phone. He told me to tell the neighbor it was urgent. Richardson said, 'Don't tell her the girl's dead.' I said, 'So what the hell am I supposed to say to this woman if I'm not talking about her daughter's death?' He said, 'Keep her on the line, Wain. Your job depends on how long you keep her on the line and get every bit of information you can about the girl—' Just then the mother said hello on the phone. I said hello, and asked if she was the mother of Elizabeth Short, and was her daughter in California?"

Yes, she answered. "She said her daughter was trying to break into the movies," Sutton says. "*Bingo*!' I said to Richardson, my hand over the phone. 'The girl's in pictures—in the movies!' Richardson's eyes got as bugged out as a couple of jawbreakers. I said what was I supposed to tell her mother? She didn't know anything about what had happened. He said to tell her the girl had won a beauty contest and we were calling for background to run a story.

"Damn liars that we were—it worked like a charm. The

mother's voice was all excited and enthusiastic. She was telling the neighbor about it. Richardson said 'keep her on the goddamn line,' and I said 'she's telling the neighbor about it—about the contest and the story the *Examiner*'s running about her daughter.'

"Richardson said, 'Fine, keep her talking and write down every word. Wain, I told you your neck's on the line.' What an asshole he was. I scribbled and talked and she said her daughter had been in San Diego over Christmas because of the movie strikes, and she gave me the name of a girlfriend her daughter was staying with, just outside of San Diego.

"It was another *bingo* and I was repeating what she was telling me so the others could hear it. Richardson was punching me in the back to get the names of the people she knew in Hollywood—movies—the director—the studio—anything! But the woman didn't have any of that information—just something about a screen test. . . ."

Richardson yelled into the city room for Tommy Devlin. It was rumored that if anybody wanted to be a hotshot newspaper reporter, they'd wind up wanting to be like Tommy Devlin. He was the best—but he was considered distant— "far away," Sutton says. Devlin was hard and tough and no other reporter equaled Devlin's sharpness.

"Elizabeth's mother was reading from a letter her daughter had written from Pacific Beach," Sutton says, "giving me the address. Richardson was grabbing the paper as I was writing the address and already had Devlin briefed for a run to San Diego. For me it was time to bring the charade to a close and to tell the woman the truth. I did it smooth. I told her I'd had to make sure I was talking to the right person, and now that she had a letter her daughter had written, I knew for sure she was Elizabeth's mother, and I did, in fact, have some news—but it wasn't good news. It was the worst kind of news a mother could hear."

Sutton said that her daughter had been killed, and that the *Examiner* was going to do everything in its power to see that justice was done. He didn't give her any of the details, and she sounded as though she wasn't going to believe what he was telling her.

He put his hand over the mouthpiece and told Richardson he didn't think he could *keep* her on the line. But the editor said to keep her on the line—to *cry* with her, commiserate with her, talk about money and transportation for her and the other daughters. The *Examiner* would put them up and pay expenses for her to come to L.A., to identify her daughter.

But Sutton didn't know if she heard any of it. She asked him why he was doing this—why this cruel joke? She said she wouldn't believe it until the police came to her door and told her, and then she hung up. When he put down the phone he felt wrung out, dirty and empty. His hands were sweating and he wanted to get drunk.

The previous afternoon's extra edition of the *Examiner* had gone out two hours ahead of the other papers, and became the second biggest run in the paper's history, right behind the 1945 end-of-the-war extra on V-J Day.

Before half of the other papers published the dead girl's identity, the *Examiner* was digging into her life for clues or leads to her death.

The *Examiner*'s phone did not stop ringing. Something big had hit town. That meant big story. It was the sort of story an editor prays for. Richardson would later say, "They don't come that big, maybe once or twice a generation. It was *the* case—the goddamned crime of the century, and it was right on the *Examiner*'s front door." Richardson had hotshot reporters, the hottest in the city—Tommy Devlin, Sid Hughes, Jimmy Shambra—a whole staff of guys that made the front line of the *Examiner*. "Sure it was William Randolph Hearst, sure it was his paper and I worked for the *boss*, but *that* was the real guts of any big story, because the *boss* got personally involved. He'd get all hot around the neck and start shooting out memos every 10 or 20 minutes to all his newspapers—so it was up to us to make the story fit the city and the city fit the story. The game was selling newspapers and who sold the most newspapers got the gold ring on the merry-go-round."

Homicide's Donahoe had recently climbed, transferred from robbery. "Before that he'd been buried in administration where," according to Richardson, "the man's real capabilities rested in pushing pencils instead of people." The editor knew he could *work* the captain—a lot of favors and swapping had gone on, and he knew he could get a hold and play him for what he was worth. "You got people in a line and you push them when you want a pound cake to come down the tube," Richardson says. "Usually with someone like Donahoe, you keep it calm and servile, in a sense of saying, you don't jerk the strings too hard because the guy has a fragile sort of character. He's hungry for press and to see his name and picture in the daily papers. An editor's got to weigh advantages. We got the dead girl's identity for Donahoe, and with a case as big as this one, you lay the trump card straight out—but in a servile way—you call the bluff and figure if you lose the guy you at least got the goods and you can easily, especially in police situations, get another guy to fill the bill.

"The power of a newspaper is to mold—you mold people and you mold minds and you mold wars and battleships and you take the glory and you run. Like they say about the guy laughing on the way to the bank . . . You can call it cynical, but then you got to say the whole ship is cynical. It's a tub we're floating in with a rotten bottom and you've got no room for sentiment or weak-kneed sisters. What we had in Jack Donahoe was a true-blue, weak-kneed sister—like a prizefighter with a glass jaw or a guy who can't take a punch in the stomach."

What worried Richardson during those early hours of the second day was that Harry Hansen had taken charge. Donahoe had *given* it to Hansen because Central took most major homicides out of the local divisions. "There weren't any cops that weren't press-hungry except one—Harry Hansen. Oh, he was *press*-hungry, but you had to play the game the way Harry saw it, or you didn't play it with Harry. What's worse is he didn't give a damn how *you* played it. Harry was a *prima donna*. Once the case got out of University and into Harry's hands, you knew it would be hard-going to get on the inside, so the next best thing was to climb over Harry's head and get it from Harry's *boss*. And if you couldn't get it from Harry's boss, then you went to the damn *chief*, Clarence Horrall—and as long as you got

Horrall looking good, you'd get some cooperation. Harry had the case and you'd look for anybody that's got one up on Harry—step forward for a bonus, even if you haven't got one coming, and boost up a rung or two on the boss's newspaper."

Over at the *Herald-Express*, Hearst's sister paper to the *Examiner*, Aggie Underwood was chasing tips as eagerly as "Richardson's boys." She says, "It was going to become one of those slug-it-out-to-scoop battles between every paper in town. Because of the chief we had expense accounts to run a lot of the other papers ragged, so we had an edge. But something was happening that would bother me the rest of my life. . . .

"All of us—the *Herald*, but especially the *Examiner*, because they set the pace for it—broke off from the cops. Sure, we always worked a little in each other's way, but there wasn't the deliberate *bypassing* that got a quick momentum right out of the gate on the Elizabeth Short case.

"You work with the law—you can't assume the responsibility for being the law or for setting your own code when it's got to do with matters affecting society at large. And when you broke off from the law and went your own way with the attitude of *we*—the power of the press—we'll solve the damned case and then let the law nail the culprit, they began to break the rules that keep us all a little civilized. That's how it took off. Where it was going to land was anyone's guess."

Because Sid Hughes was especially good at police impersonations and eager now to outfox the cops, Richardson called him in from the morgue and gave him the responsibility of a "raid" on the Camp Cook personnel files before the detectives could padlock the information.

Wain Sutton was back on the rewrite desk and recalls Sid "taking off like a horse foaming at the mouth. He was known to create the shortest distance between two points, and he was ordered to call in every 20 minutes once he'd hit Santa Barbara. Sid took a younger reporter with him—Fisher, who looked like a cop because he didn't have any color to his lips. And the guy never said anything either. He just stood there looking at you. You thought he was smart and appraising, but he was really just drunk. He could type better than any of the reporters, and we needed him in the city room right *then* but it was Sid's idea to pick up another car in Santa Barbara and cover two bases with Fisher. The most important thing going on was to get *anything* fast and be *first*."

"Everyone was getting into the act," says Gerry Ramlow, a short, wiry reporter for the *Daily News*. There were lines at the pay phones in city hall and Ramlow couldn't find a phone in Central's squad room that was not being used. He complained to Detective Al Shambra, whose brother, Jimmy, was a reporter for the *Examiner*. But the detective only shrugged and said, " Tough, pal." He was too busy to listen to Ramlow. "When, as if by some miracle," Ramlow says, "a phone on a desk appeared with the receiver in the cradle and I made a grab at it just as someone's hand was pulling away from hanging it up. There were a dozen or so genuine sex flakes being shuffled from room to room, real saps or some of them downright maniacs. I remember they had a drunk in there for taking a leak in the alley. He got out of hand and they shoved him around until he broke the water cooler. We were walking around sloshing in a few gallons of water and kicking broken glass between the detectives' desks."

What it was about the case, Ramlow felt, that had everybody jumping from the word go, and that kicked in the machinery, was "you had this gorgeous dish—at least gorgeous from the airbrushed shot they were handing out—naked and stacked and cut in half like you'd bisect a sausage, and not a single damn clue—not a *single* shred of *any*thing to go on—and divisions wrangling for jurisdiction though it was certainly Central's case because of the enormity of the situation. I'd a lot of time logged in on Central's crime beat but with this one—it had people saying screw you to the law and racing for some scoop on their own. Madhouse wasn't the word. You could see it was going to be a real hard problem to get some control over the investigation."

There were too many detectives from too many divisions, too many policemen canvassing neighborhoods and too much speculation being broadcast by Chief Horrall and Donahoe during the hunt for some basement or hole in the wall where she'd been held prisoner and tortured for hours before the coup de grace of slashing her mouth. Off the record, the chief said, it seemed at least a direction to search in view of nothing else to go on. "And search they did," says Ramlow, "showing pictures, asking if anyone was burning clothes—digging a hole in some yard—burying something suspicious. But the answers were all 'no.' Nobody'd seen the gal or heard any screaming in the night."

After a couple of hours dodging traffic in Central where they were packing up the flood lights and hauling away their lab paraphernalia—it was like going to a sideshow.

Central division detectives did not actually work out of the Central Station building at First and Hill streets. Like the morgue, the facilities had become outmoded and too cramped for the number of personnel needed to handle L.A.'s skyrocketing crime rate. Central homicide had set up on the northwest floor of city hall. The detectives found using the front entrance of city hall too inconvenient and would enter or exit through a side window. That first floor hall was being occupied by the homicide, robbery, and burglary units—all one department at the time.

A row of holding cells in the basement was used to detain suspects, and the deputy police chief's offices were on the same floor as homicide. One police officer recalls that sometimes you never knew where you were going and they kept changing names on all the doors. There would be a lot of ordering of rubber stamps with the new names, but by the time the stamps got there, they'd changed the names again.

The crime lab headed by Ray Pinker continued to occupy the top floor of Central Station on First Street, up three flights of rickety wooden stairs to the lab and the photo department, the scientific investigative department (SID), small-scale ballistics, and latent prints. The three consecutive flights of stairs were exposed in part to the rain and covered with pigeon droppings due to holes in the roof and the city's delays in appropriating funds for repairs.

Finis Brown had worked around the clock while rotating teams of policemen from different divisions worked in shifts, 12 hours on and 12 hours off. The flood of leads from those that had known Elizabeth Short at some time, calling into Central to volunteer information, complicated the investigation almost hopelessly.

"No matter how unimportant each lead appeared on the surface," Brown says, "we had to track it down, and in this case each lead seemed to open into something else, and it went on and on, and none of them were giving a clue to the missing week or to the murder itself.

"What would become embarrassingly apparent as the days wore on was that, in the confusion at the vacant lot, University's police photographers and lab had neglected to take pictures or make casts of the tire track, the heel print, or the blood drops on the sidewalk."

Despite the unusual aspects discussed at the morgue, which for the detectives became the basis of the *undercover* side of the investigation, the case started out pretty much according to standard procedure for sex crimes: they thought the killer would strike again, and there was a rush for clues and leads, first at the scene or where the corpse was found, and then with the coroner. The second phase was again to produce leads that might focus on the perpetrator.

"You had the importance of immediate action," Willis says. "All off-duty officers were called in, and known sex offenders were being picked up, interviewed—alibis established, checked, and rechecked."

More than 150 sex offenders were screened during that first night. "Not one single individual questioned was able to provide the least lead to the murder," Willis says. "And except for those persons with outstanding warrants, the rest pulled in under what we were calling 'Donahoe's dragnet' were released.

"Confessions always surface with sensational murders. Cranks have to be examined by using a series of control questions—how was she mutilated? Questions to do with the crime—usually something only the killer would know, and these facts are not released to the news so only the cops and the killer know about it. Once or twice I've seen it where guys have forgotten what they did—certain things that you know is a fact, and then the guy remembers things you *don't* know, but you verify it and build the case. . . .

"In the Elizabeth Short case," Willis says, "and at the first bull sessions we'd have in conferences, Hansen didn't talk about the case and he was very unavailable about details and speculations; and anything you'd venture he'd tend to dismiss as scuttlebutt-bullshit, or that you didn't know what you were talking about. Harry particularly disliked me because I'd been privileged to some of the confidential information he wanted to monopolize. I was working with Brown, had a couple of meetings with his brother, Thad—assistant chief—about the case. And Donahoe also assigned me to work with Baughm and Wain and Estrada on a county case with a possible link.

"A lot of times a suspect forgets details or just hasn't *absorbed* them. But he'll tell you about the murder and get into some things that only the police know. . . . Harry had an ace up his sleeve, he believed, but I wasn't sure what he was doing as I didn't have the full picture. I don't think anyone did except Harry because he'd put it together himself from the different agencies, and none of these agencies knew what the *other* one had. So he had a lot of those control questions to be used on the crackpots who came in to confess, and they were beginning to stand in line."

The newspapers played up the confessors big: front page photographs and stories pieced together as fast as the facts surfaced, "true or false." Tommy Devlin was in San Diego cornering Elvera and Dorothy French, while Sid Hughes, posing as an LAPD detective, wangled a mug-shot of Elizabeth Short from the Santa Barbara police. He popped into the local newspaper and wired to the *Examiner*. Sid said he'd been taken with the girl's picture, from her brush with the law as a juvenile. "I'd seen her in death and even helped at the paper with that rendering of her likeness before death, the airbrushed morgue shot we used on page one. But we didn't come close to what she really looked like. *Nobody* loves a mug-shot, but that gal's picture could've been used on a magazine cover. She had a haunting kind of beauty—those eyes staring far off, it's the truth—those lips talked sex and mystery without even moving."

Dorothy French told the *Examiner* that Beth's trunk had been shipped from Chicago and held by Railway Express for nonpayment of storage charges. The *Examiner* tracked it to the warehouse in L.A., but called Donahoe at the same time to alert the police that they were not interfering or tampering with evidence.

The Frenches talked to the police about Red and Beth's other dates, and the telegrams from Red and Gordan Fickling. When the detectives contacted Fickling in North Carolina, he at first denied knowing anyone named Beth—or Elizabeth—Short. Then, confronted with the letters he had written to her, and the letters addressed to him that she had never mailed, Fickling changed his story. In confidence, to avoid publicity, he told the detectives about his relationship with Beth. He had never had sexual intercourse with her, he claimed, and could offer no information about her murder.

Red, or "Bob," as Dorothy called him, became the number one suspect. Dorothy said she believed he was an airlines employee in San Diego. Beth had left with him about 6:00 on the evening of January 8. His car, she recalled, was a tan Studebaker coupe with a Huntington Beach or Park sticker in the rear window. An all points bulletin went out over the state teletype system throughout California and Nevada for Red to be held for fingerprinting.

Within hours San Diego detectives had discovered a mid-December registration at a Pacific Beach motel. Red had signed as Robert Manley, with a Southgate address, make of car, and license number. Police wired Sacramento for confirmation on the vehicle. Red had been found.

Beth's trunk was opened officially, revealing clothes, photo albums, and dozens of letters going back over the past few years. "Most of her letters spoke of her disappointments in love," Brown says, "many from servicemen who'd backed out of the relationship before the love was consummated. Every one of the servicemen had to be checked out. Some were difficult to find and you had detectives on phones 24 hours." Brown, Hansen, and the detectives spearheading the case logged in excesses of overtime the first few days of the investigation. The crime lab was going non-stop. More than 15 times Ray Pinker's men combed the lot and the surrounding neighborhood of 39th and Norton.

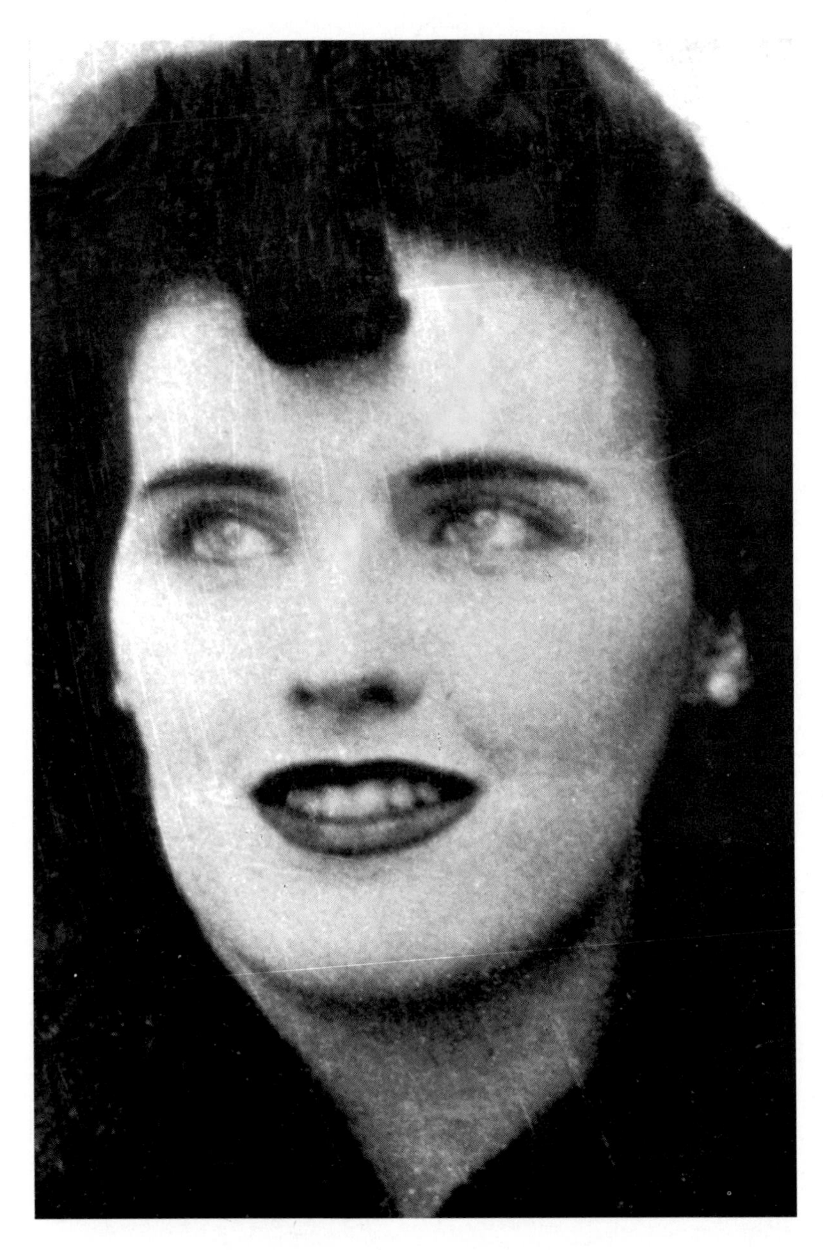

Elizabeth Short, the "Black Dahlia"

The Short Sisters: Dorothea, Elizabeth, Eleanora, Muriel

Virginia, Dorothea, Eleanora, Elizabeth, and neighborhood friend

The Shorts' third floor flat in Medford, MA;
in foreground is neighbor Ron Hernon.

Muriel Short with "Baby" at Medford High School

JUNIOR HIGH SCHOOL RECORD

MEDFORD, MASSACHUSETTS

Name *Short, Elizabeth* Entered from *Swan* Date *1936-9-9 Roberts* JUNIOR HIGH SCHO[OL]

Date of Birth *1924-7-29* Place of Birth *Hyde Park* Address *~~99 Magoun Ave.~~ 115 Salem St.*

Father's Name *Cleo A.* Place of Birth *Virginia* Mother's Name *Phoebe Mae* Place of Birth *Maine*

	Year	Obedience	Co-operation	Courtesy	Respect for Property	Effort	Days Present	Days Absent	Times Tardy	Times Dismissed	English	Latin I	Latin II	French I	French II	General Mathematics	Algebra	Business Arithmetic	Commerce, Jr. II	Business Training	Geography	History	Ancient History	Civics	General Science	Woodwork	Printing	Mechanical Drawing	Practical Arts	Clothing	Foods	Household Management	Art	Arts and Crafts	Music	Library	Physical Education	*Conduct*	Remarks
Gr. I	1/4	S	S	S	S	B	45	0	0	0	C					C					B	B			C					C			C		S	a	a		
1936	1/2	S	S	S	S	B	88	2	0	0	C					C					C	C			C					B			C		S	a	a		*Left May 19, 19[..]*
	3/4	S	S	S	S	B	119	15	0	0	B					C					C	C			C					C			C		S	a	a		*Transferred*
1937	1	S	S	S	S	B	118	36	0	0	D					D					D	D			D					C			E		S	a	C		*Edna Pickard*
	S*																																						
Gr. II	1/4	S	S	S	S	A	45	0	0	0	B					C						C			B						B	C	B		S		A	S	
1937	1/2	S	S	S	S	A	88	2	0	0	B					C						B			B						B	C	B		S		B	S	
	3/4	S	S	S	S	A	133	2	0	0	B					C			B			B			B						C		C		S		B	S	*Promoted*
1938	1	S	S	S	S	A	178	2	0	0	B					C			B			B			B						C		C		S		A	S	*Elsie C. Hiat[..]*
	S*																																						
Gr. III	1/4	S	S	S	S	A	41	0	0	0	C							B		B				C	C										S		A		
1938	1/2	S	S	S	S	A	86	2	0	0	C							D		B				C	C										S		A		
	3/4				S	B	127	3	0	0	C							C		C				C	B										S		A		
1939	1					C	173	4	0	0	C							C		C				C	B										S		A		*Promoted*
	S*																																						*E. Hart[..]*
	1/4																																						
193	1/2																																						
	3/4																																						
193	1																																						
	S*																																						

*Summer School Record

Elizabeth Short's junior high school record from Medford, MA

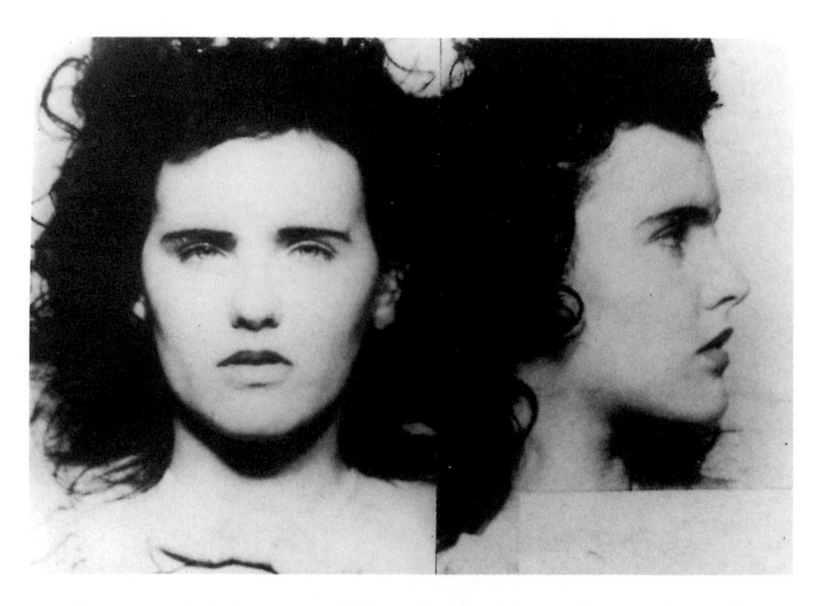

Government photograph of Elizabeth Short for civilian employee ID

Elizabeth in Florida with Airman

Elizabeth Short, Hollywood, 1946

On back of this photo, Beth wrote:
"Hubba, Hubba! Love Beth"

Hollywood, 1946

Elizabeth Short and soldier, Florida, 1945

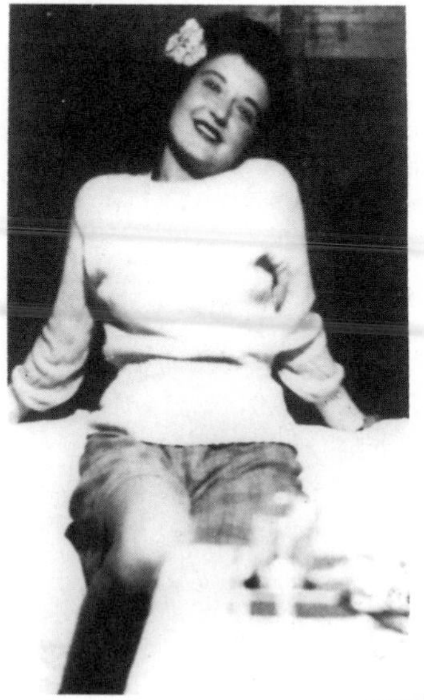

Lucille "Lula" Varela at Sunset Apts.
near Angel's Flight

Pup Café on Beverly/Temple near Vermont;
Elizabeth Short met Lucille "Lula" Varela
several times en route downtown

"On the Town," Tim Mehringer and Beth Short

Elizabeth Short's friends in Hollywood

Photograph courtesy of the Museum of Death

Elizabeth Short and unidentified boyfriend, circa 1946

At Water Hotel, Long Beach, California;
another of Elizabeth Short's temporary haunts

Hot dog stand on Main St. in downtown
L.A., frequented by both Elizabeth
Short and Jack Anderson Wilson

Pig'n Whistle Café

The love she never had:
Army Air Corps Captain Matt Gordan and his fiancée, Elizabeth Short

Photograph courtesy of Tony Mostrom

December 1946
Night on Hollywood Boulevard

Elizabeth Short's body, January 15, 1947

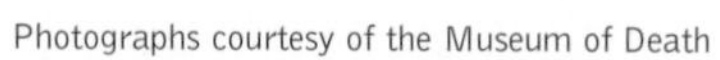

Photographs courtesy of the Museum of Death

Policemen with Elizabeth Short's body

LAPD Detectives Harry Hansen and Finis Brown
with Elizabeth Short's body

Photograph courtesy of the Museum of Death

Café on Crenshaw Boulevard, blocks from where the Black Dahlia's body was found; her shoes and empty purse were found in a café garbage can

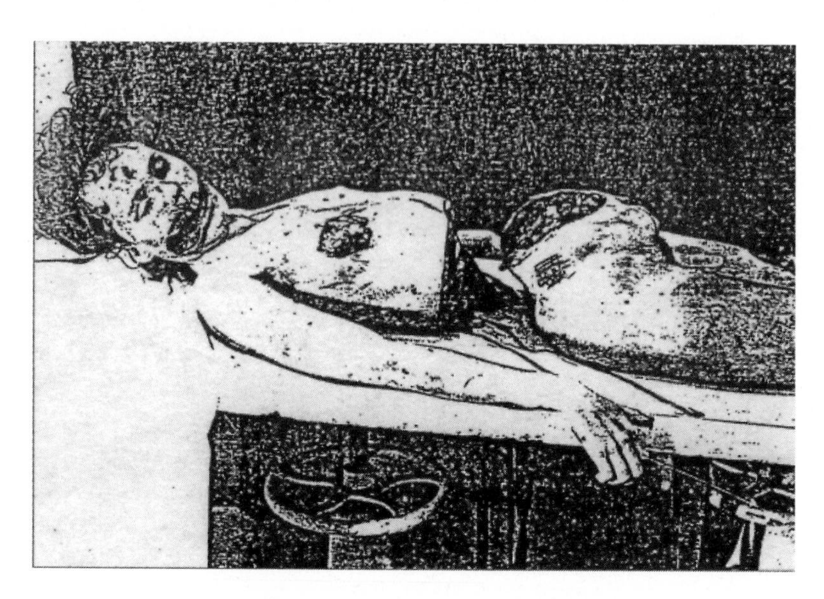

Elizabeth Short's body at L.A. County Morgue; note recumbent position of lower body

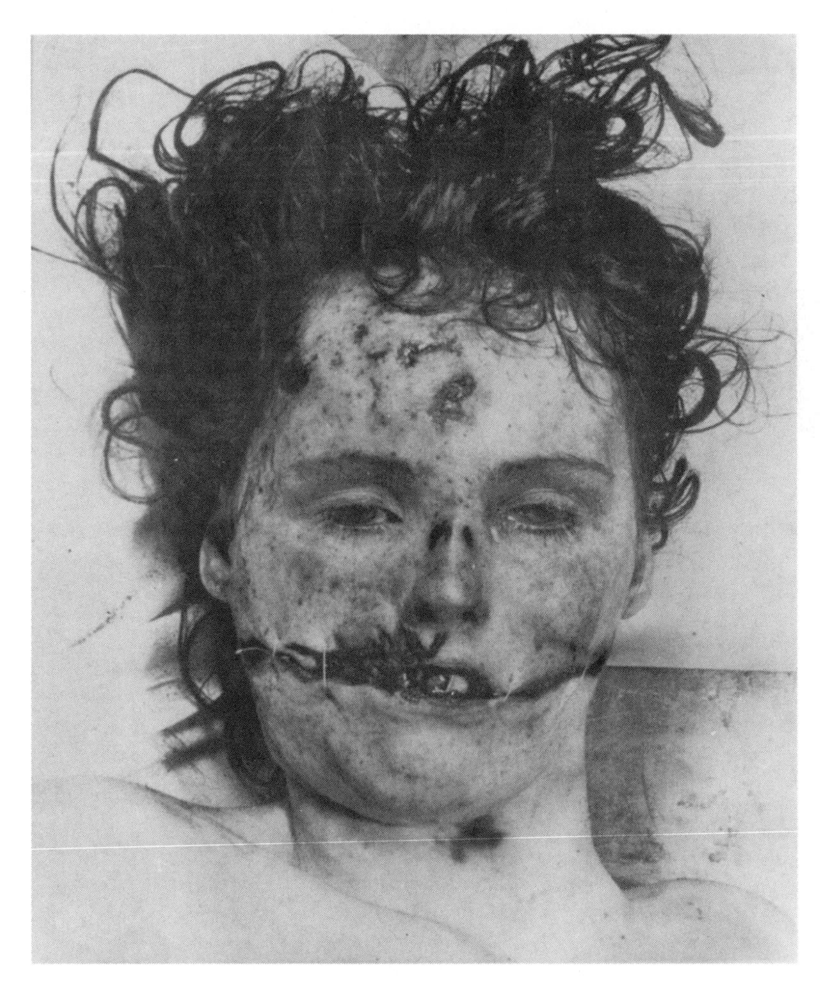

Elizabeth Short in death, at L.A. County Morgue

Photograph courtesy of the Delmar Watson Los Angeles Historical Archives

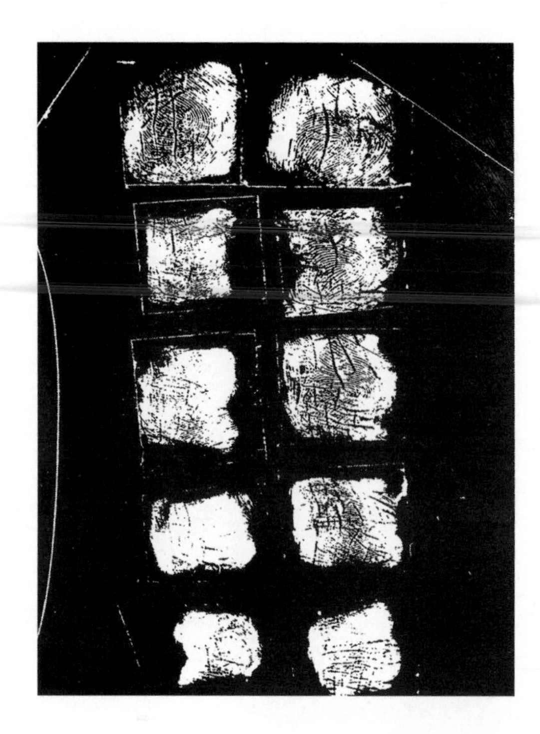

Elizabeth Short's fingerprints, taken in death

Police rendering, superimposed on morgue photograph that appeared in the Los Angeles Examiner

Press hoopla during Black Dahlia inquest

Proprietor in Majestic Malt Shop remembering Beth Short

Sgt. Sam Flowers, LAPD, with Elizabeth Short's scrapbook

Elizabeth Short's funeral in Oakland;
Virginia Short and her husband Adrian at the coffin

Photograph courtesy of the Museum of Death

Police psychologist
Paul de River,
interviewed the dozens
of "Confessing Sam"
suspects

Cleo Alvin Short,
Elizabeth's father at the LAPD;
he did not attend her funeral

Robert "Red" Manley, suspect, undergoing lie detector test, supervised by
Finis Brown, with Ray Pinker of the L.A. crime lab

Questionable packet sent to the Los Angeles Examiner

William Randolph Hearst's Examiner building

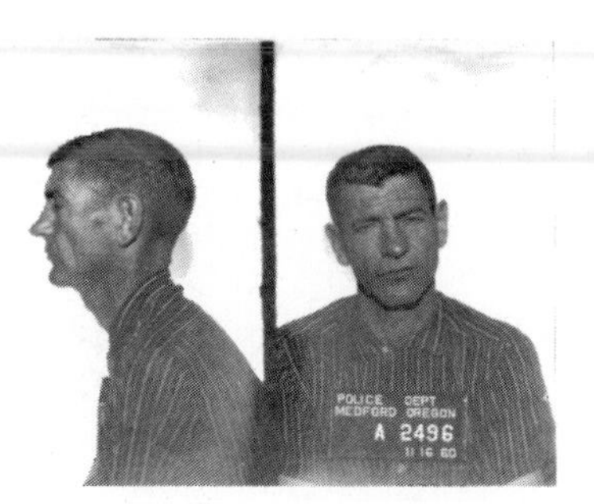

STATE OF CALIFORNIA
DEPARTMENT OF JUSTICE
BUREAU OF CRIMINAL IDENTIFICATION AND INVESTIGATION
P. O. BOX 1859, SACRAMENTO

FBI# 5 119 180
NC SS# 242 22 924
VA SS# 223 22 964
MD SS# 219 38 501

~~The following CII record, NUMBER~~ 524 567 IS FOR OFFICIAL USE ON

20 L 25 - 110 - FINGERPRINT
M 13 U 000 10 CLASSIFICATION

BRN BRN 6-4 170 CALIF 8-5-1924

PEN JACK A. WILSON

ARRESTED OR RECEIVED	DEPARTMENT AND NUMBER	NAME	CHARGE	DISPOSITION
ALIAS: JACK ANDERSON WILSON; JACK OLSEN; HANNS ANDERSON VON CANNON; JACK A.TAYLC JOHN D. RYAN; EUGENE DEAVILEN; JACK MC CURRY; JACK H. WILSON; GROVER LOVING; GROV LOVING WILSON; JACK ANDERSON MC GRAY;				
3-22-43	PD LOS ANGELES 2019-W-31	JACK A. WILSON	SUSP.VIOL. SEL.SERV.	
5-9-48	PD LOS ANGELES 118941	JACK A. WILSON	VAG.,LEWD – [illegible]	
7-26-48	PD LOS ANGELES 118941	JACK A. WILSON	BATT.	
[illegible]	PD LOS ANGELES 118941	JACK ANDERSON WILSON	DRK.	
6-3-50	PD LOS ANGELES 118941	JACK A. WILSON	DRK.	
6-12-50	PD LOS ANGELES 118941	JACK ANDERSON WILSON	BURG.	
6-12-50	SO LOS ANGELES B-148961	JACK ANDERSON WILSON	SUSP.BURG.	
6-21-50	PD LOS ANGELES 118941/R-90151	JACK ANDERSON WILSON	SUSP.211 PC – ARMED ROBBERY	
2-21-51	PD LOS ANGELES 118941	JACK ANDERSON WILSON	WARR.G.T. GRAND THEFT	REL.TO L.A.SO
[illegible]	SO LOS ANGELES B-148961/B-176307	JACK ANDERSON WILSON	G.T.	
[illegible]	SO LOS ANGELES B-148961/B-184157	JACK ANDERSON WILSON	THEFT	
5-31-54	PD LOS ANGELES 118941/R-90151	HANNS ANDERSON VON CANNON	SUSP.487.3 PC GRAND THEFT OR ATT.	
1-4-57	SO LOS ANGELES B-148961/B-461023	JACK ANDERSON WILSON	INTOX.	
		CONTINUED PAGE 2		

ENTRIES INDICATED BY ASTERISK (*) ARE NOT VERIFIED BY FINGERPRINTS IN CII FILES.

First page of Jack Anderson Wilson's five-page rap sheet

Photograph courtesy of the Museum of Death

Suspect in Black Dahlia, and Georgette Bauerdorf bathtub murders, Jack Anderson Wilson, aka Grover Loving, Jr., aka Arnold Smith

Georgette Eilise Bauerdorf, Sunset Strip socialite, oil heiress;
father associated with William Randolph Hearst

Police Hunt Jitterbug Slayer of Oil Heiress

Army Officers Aid in Search; Diary Scrutinized for Clews

[illegible]

SOLDIER QUESTIONED

[illegible]

SAILOR'S STORY

[illegible]

FINGERPRINT CLEWS

[illegible]

Plane Crash Kills Torpedo Expert

[illegible]

Mickey Rooney Going Overseas

[illegible]

Peru Rations Horses

[illegible]

BATHTUB VICTIM — [illegible]

Errol Flynn's Pal in Cafe Brawl

[illegible]

Georgette's car was found abandoned not far from where Beth Short would be murdered

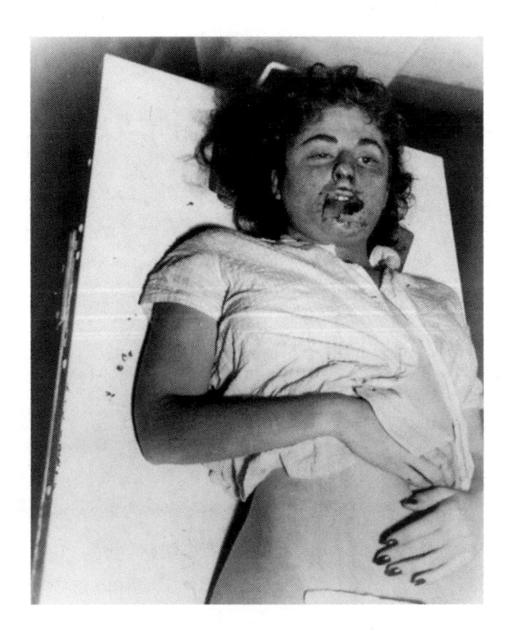

Georgette Bauerdorf at L.A. County Morgue; note cloth wedged in mouth, cause of strangulation

Georgette Bauerdorf in death

North Carolina OHIO DEPARTMENT OF HEALTH
COLUMBUS
STATE OF ~~Avery~~
COUNTY OF Avery ss.
AFFIDAVIT
COPY

I, Mrs. Minnie Buchanan, Wilson being first duly sworn, say that I am the Mother of Jack Anderson Wilson and that (h is) original birth certificate on file with the Ohio Department of Health is incorrect.

The following is a true and correct statement:

NAME Jack Anderson Wilson FILE NO. 80166

DATE OF BIRTH August 5, 1920 PLACE OF BIRTH Cantoh, Ohio.

NAME OF FATHER Alex F. Wilson

MAIDEN NAME OF MOTHER Minnie Buchanan.

REMARKS

(SIGNATURE OF FATHER OR MOTHER) Minnie Buchanan Wilson

Sworn to before me and subscribed in my presence, this 10th day of November nineteen hundred and 42.

My Commission Expires June 24, 1942.

(SEAL)

Green Hampton Lowe
Notary Public
OFFICIAL TITLE

V.S.20 (This affidavit must be typewritten)

Jack Anderson Wilson's strange birth certificate

STATE OF OHIO
BUREAU OF VITAL STATISTICS
CERTIFICATE OF BIRTH

PLACE OF BIRTH
County of Stark
City of Canton
No. Francis Ave S.W.
Registration District No. 1206
Primary Registration District No. 8482
Registered No. 1260

FULL NAME OF CHILD Grover Loving, Jr.

Sex of Child Male | Number in order of birth 1 | Date of birth Aug 5 1920

FATHER
Full Name ~~Alex F. Wilson~~ Grover Loving
Residence Francis Ave S.W. Canton
Color or Race White | Age at last birthday 26
Birthplace North Carolina
Occupation and Industry Machinist

MOTHER
Full Maiden Name Minnie Buchanan (Wilson)
Residence Francis Ave S.W.
Color or Race White | Age at last birthday 23
Birthplace North Carolina
Occupation House Wife

Number of children born and living 1 | 1

CERTIFICATE OF ATTENDING PHYSICIAN OR MIDWIFE
I hereby certify that I attended the birth of this child born to Mrs Alex F. Wilson and that the Born alive at 8 A. M., on the date above stated.
(Signature) A.K. Olmsted
Address 1717 Navarre Rd
Canton Ohio
Filed Aug 12 1920 Margaretta McAbee

Affidavit used in attempt to establish identity as Jack Anderson Wilson

Photograph courtesy of Russell Miller

The Holland Hotel, downtown L.A., where key suspect Jack Anderson Wilson burned to death

"The truth sneaks out:" the author's interviews with Jack Anderson Wilson shortly before his death. (Property of LAPD)

LAPD's Sgt. John St. John, Detective Badge Number One, in charge of Black Dahlia investigation and inquiries into suspect Jack Anderson Wilson

Sheriff's Detective
Sgt. Joel Lesnick

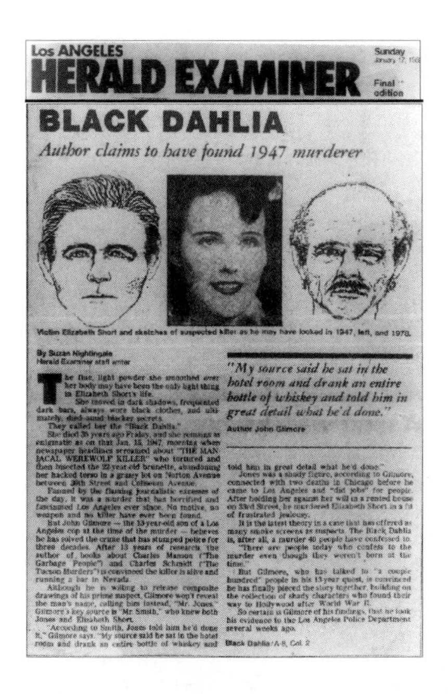

Los ANGELES
HERALD EXAMINER
Sunday
Final edition

BLACK DAHLIA

Author claims to have found 1947 murderer

Victim Elizabeth Short and sketches of suspected killer as he may have looked in 1947, left, and 1978.

By Suzan Nightingale
Herald Examiner staff writer

The fine, light powder she smoothed over her body may have been the only light thing in Elizabeth Short's life.

She moved in dark shadows, frequented dark bars, always wore black clothes, and ultimately, died amid blacker secrets.

They called her the "Black Dahlia."

She died 35 years ago Friday, and she remains as enigmatic as on that Jan. 15, 1947, morning when newspaper headlines screamed about "THE MANIACAL WEREWOLF KILLER" who tortured and then bisected the 22-year-old brunette, abandoning her hacked torso in a grassy lot on Norton Avenue between 39th Street and Coliseum Avenue.

Fanned by the flaming journalistic excesses of the day, it was a murder that has horrified and fascinated Los Angeles ever since. No motive, no weapon and no killer have ever been found.

But John Gilmore — the 13-year-old son of a Los Angeles cop at the time of the murder — believes he has solved the crime that has stumped police for three decades. After 13 years of research, the author of books about Charles Manson ("The Garbage People") and Charles Schmidt ("The Tucson Murders") is convinced the killer is alive and running a bar in Nevada.

Although he is willing to release composite drawings of his prime suspect, Gilmore won't reveal the man's name, calling him instead, "Mr. Jones." Gilmore's key source is "Mr. Smith," who knew both Jones and Elizabeth Short.

"According to Smith, Jones told him he'd done it," Gilmore says. "My source said he sat in the hotel room and drank an entire bottle of whiskey and told him in great detail what he'd done."

"My source said he sat in the hotel room and drank an entire bottle of whiskey and told him in great detail what he'd done."

Author John Gilmore

Jones was a shady figure, according to Gilmore, connected with two deaths in Chicago before he came to Los Angeles and "did jobs" for people. After holding her against her will in a rented house on 33rd Street, he murdered Elizabeth Short in a fit of frustrated jealousy.

It is the latest theory in a case that has offered as many smoke screens as suspects. The Black Dahlia is, after all, a murder 40 people have confessed to.

"There are people today who confess to the murder even though they weren't born at the time."

But Gilmore, who has talked to "a couple hundred" people in his 13-year quest, is convinced he has finally pieced the story together, building on the collection of shady characters who found their way to Hollywood after World War II.

So certain is Gilmore of his findings, that he took his evidence to the Los Angeles Police Department several weeks ago.

Black Dahlia/A-8, Col. 2

A break in the solution of the Black Dahlia murder;
the facts "behind the facts" were laid bare for the first time

John Gilmore on the lot where the house in which
the Black Dahlia was murdered stood until 1960

John Gilmore in Los Angeles Bradbury Building office

All of the leads were cleared or discarded. A Long Beach police inspector named Boynton traced Elizabeth Short's activities to a drugstore on Linden where some soldiers and other soda fountain customers had been calling the girl the Black Dahlia because of her jet-black hair and the black clothing she seemed to favor.

The Hollywood *Citizen-News* and the *Herald-Express* reported the name BLACK DAHLIA, in bold headlines. As one newsman says, "Every other paper jumped on the bandwagon and pushed it to the hilt—STRANGE LIFE OF GIRL VICTIM OF WEREWOLF MURDER." Dozens and dozens of new calls were prompted, delivering more tips leading to more dead ends. The entire homicide detail joined in widening the search for the killer without a single clue to his identity.

More than 750 investigators were on the case including 400 deputies with the sheriff's department, and 250 California state highway patrol officers—hoping to turn up any information about where she was from the evening of January 8 to the morning of January 15. Teams from each division searched storm drains beneath the bridges of the L.A. River, through cellars and attics for the "torture chamber" where the newspapers reported the Black Dahlia had been murdered.

Sixty detectives from vice were hitting Hollywood and downtown bars. There were 30 or so officers searching for the victim's clothing or personal effects, and another 40 patrolmen still going door to door in the Norton area, moving to the Highland Park and Eagle Rock areas.

Willis says, "I went back to vice in metro to go through the downtown bars. Along Main Street there seemed an endless supply of these dinky joints with girls working them. Captain Donahoe assumed the Dahlia had been working as a B-girl in one of the places. She was *known* in a few of them, like the Rhapsody, the Dugout, and the Loyal Cafe. The girls were drawing something like 40 bucks a week working whatever George she could—a split of champagne was 15 bucks and she'd knock it over whenever she had enough to drink. These girls never worked a George out of the joint, just bilked them in the booths or at the bar and got the wallet whenever they could.

"This one kid I got to know, she told me that before the licenses were lost on these dumps, she'd gotten to know Beth Short—called her Beth or 'Miss Upper Lip,' as some called her, because she thought she was better than the rest—and she was favored by the barkeeps, but she wasn't hustling drinks for anyone, and she wouldn't give a George the time of day unless he thought she was really something special.

"One girl, a stripper in between working these joints, said Miss Upper Lip liked to get guys worked up over her, but she'd leave them hanging dry. She said she didn't know her well, but knew Miss Upper Lip hadn't been working for any of the bars. The girl told me Beth was a loner—she was out for a good time, but she was a loner."

The few sketchy *sightings* of the Dahlia during the "missing week" failed to produce any evidence pointing to her murder. "These were uncorroborated maybes that didn't go anywhere," Willis says. "Not a single lead cleared up one minute of the Dahlia's missing week. And the pressure for a good showing—to bring in some hard facts—was unbelievable. And it just got worse. But nothing was turning up."

Councilman Lloyd G. Davis resolved to appropriate a $10,000 reward for the detection of the Black Dahlia killer. A week later the city attorney ruled they could not legally pay rewards for the solution of crimes.

Willis says, "Had they kept the reward, it might've brought someone forward with a real tip; instead, we got nothing. It was the confessors that came forward, not interested in a reward, but desperate to be linked to the Black Dahlia murder." The confessors poured in, sweating, from the dapper to the deranged, spilling their guts without any realistic offering of evidence.

Dr. Joseph Paul de River would join the interrogations and tape record the interviews. Police Chief Horrall approved de River's hiring as "Criminal Psychiatrist and Sexologist, and Consultant Alienist to the Superior Courts." De River originated the Sex Offense Bureau for the city of Los Angeles.

While the city council was critical of his lack of psychiatric experience, de River, an eye, ear, and nose specialist with the Veterans' Administration, applied for and was granted the position of Police Psychiatrist in 1938.

"None of the confessors," says Brown, "came close to answering the key questions that Harry had put together from the confidential files. Asking for details about how she was raped, and what had been put in her rectum, ruled out most anyone who would make a wild guess."

According to Hansen, the odds of an accurate guess would be one in a million. If anyone outside the department discovered and revealed any of the confidential information, the policy was to deny the validity of such information.

De River would recommend committing some of those confessing to the murder. "We started arresting these characters for obstructing justice," Brown says, "and they got a little fewer for a while, like the word must've gotten around to the other crackpots. . . . It almost made you get a little nuts after awhile. It had all the earmarks, at least to me, of seeing us dead before we ever got the real guy in for questioning, let alone getting him behind bars."

The police blamed the press for complicating the investigation. Bevo Means, a reporter for the *Herald-Express*, got it from a deputy coroner that the Black Dahlia wasn't having sex with guys. "It was a leak," Brown says. "And Bevo jumped on it figuring if she couldn't have sex with guys, she was having sex with women. He pegged her a dyke. He told people, 'something in the autopsy indicated lesbian pathology.' You'd have to work overtime to come up with such a stupid statement.

"Then you had Sid Hughes, who grabbed onto Bevo's bullshit, running around to lesbian bars, trying to find someone who'd had a fling with the Dahlia. Places like the IF Club on Vermont. Sid went around impersonating Harry—saying he *was* homicide's Harry Hansen—anything for a lead to beat the other papers. They didn't care what they did. Then they came up with that story about the ovaries being crossed; the killer had crossed her sex organs. The *fact* that these organs might've been missing to start with is where their confusion began."

Brown began thinking that Harry was shifting the files around. He passed the information to his brother, Thad, that

Harry kept saying he's going to lock up the files from the other detectives.

Brown says, "I was personally concerned that Harry kept saying he was going to yank the papers from the morgue. I asked Harry what he had in mind. He said to me, 'A few changes. There's too many people with noses into the case; it's being jeopardized. We're never going to get this bastard if he knows every move we're making.' I asked him what he meant. He was trying to get Donahoe to back off from Richardson at the paper. Then he says to me, 'Now you see it, now you don't.'

"I said you've got to have legal backup to deal with the county. He said, 'We *will*, but I'll have control of the case. I'll know which way is up until we get the sonofabitch and nail his ass. In the meantime maybe nobody is going to know anything, and when they pull these records they won't be getting what they think they're getting.'

"I said, 'Harry, you can't monkey with the county. The coroner runs this whole thing.' He looked at me as if to tell me to keep my mouth shut or I'd be off the case, and that would make Harry and me enemies because I knew almost as much as he and Willis did. He said I was a fine one to talk about ethics, and I was lucky I wasn't in jail or off the force. I said, 'Up you, Harry.' Then he laughed, but he was serious."

Two days later a policewoman from the academy coded the records so only Harry and Donahoe had access to the confidential information. No one could get a straight answer unless Harry wanted to give him one. And Donahoe let him go ahead, placing his trust in Harry's judgment.

"We got down on 6th Street," Brown says, "on a tip and we were interviewing this woman named Hackett, and Harry laid into her. I thought she was going to have a stroke. She wasn't that old, and she was a nice person; she was from back East and her parents—at least her father—was still back there. She had these letters of Short's and some other stuff, and Harry told her he'd run her through a federal wringer for mail tampering and mail fraud."

But first, Brown says, "He'd have to show intent and he'd have to prove the stuff wasn't left with Miss Hackett just like the woman said. Harry snatched—he actually *grabbed*—the mail. That part of it that was open, and he said to her, 'You read this? Have you opened these and read this and broken the law?'

"In other words, he gave her the option to lie and say she hadn't read what was in the stuff, and she'd never know what was in it because if she did she'd broken the law and he'd have her up for mail theft or tampering, and he'd actually have done it just to keep her quiet and sequestered from the goddamn newspaper people.

"I think Harry thought he'd have a fast make on the guy that killed Short, and given all the manpower and control he had, he felt he'd bring it in fast and there wasn't anything going to stand in his way. So while he might've actually had the woman rattled enough to keep her mouth shut, he might well have had her held long enough to convince her to forget whatever she knew was in those papers.

"He didn't want her to remember any of it, or if she did she'd face a federal mail theft rap. He held it like you'd keep it for latents, and put it carefully in a brown bag, saying he sure hoped her prints weren't on the contents of those envelopes.

"She was just all white and shook up and I felt sorry for her. I said it was okay and we'd be checking back with her."

In his gut, Brown knew there would be nothing but trouble ahead.

13

Blanks. They were drawing nothing but blanks. Who killed the Black Dahlia? Who *was* the Black Dahlia? It seemed impossible for detectives and newsmen to get a clear picture of the girl, who she was or where she'd been, or why she'd been heading wherever it was. "She was on the move almost every day," Herman Willis says, "and even the people who *supposedly* knew her didn't know her because she wouldn't level with them or confide in them."

The police files were filling with hundreds of documents—information and possibilities without one conclusive lead to pinpoint even one minute of the "lost week." Not one shred of evidence pointed to a who, or a where, or a why of the murder. "The picture of the victim that formed," says Willis, "was someone living day to day, from hand to mouth, and with a different guy almost every night, as she'd done with Red Manley, the one who'd brought her back from San Diego to L.A."

Sergeant Sam Flowers, who closed in on Manley, says Red insisted on his innocence from the time he was picked up at his employer's house in Eagle Rock and then booked downtown on an open murder charge. Questioned for hours that same night by Hansen, Brown, and Donahoe, Manley underwent two lie detector tests. During the second test he collapsed from exhaustion.

While Red repeated his story, detectives went to the Greyhound depot to retrieve the suitcases checked by Elizabeth Short. Police fingerprint expert George Wheeler, accompanied by Detective L.C. Hull, sorted through suitcases and hatbox—through the articles of clothing, letters, photographs, the candles she carried, and her personal papers. Each item was examined and booked into evidence. Detective Lieutenant William Cummings, Al Shambra, and Hull concentrated on this phase of the investigation.

Aggie Underwood interviewed Manley at Hollenbeck jail with Detective Harry Fremont. Red retold his story painfully, and it remained as unshakable as his alibi. Aggie said she believed Red was innocent, describing him as a "hapless victim of circumstances." After two days he was released.

Les Warren was questioned by San Diego and L.A. detectives, and later by the Hollywood division chief. He said he'd met Elizabeth Short in Hollywood one evening at Earl Carroll's where he was a victory dinner guest of producer Mark Hellinger. The girl was present at the table, and she was attentive and friendly, he said. He danced with her and told her he was with the naval hospital in San Diego. She asked if they accepted civilian applications, and told him she'd been a junior hostess at the Hollywood Canteen during the war.

Warren said that his meeting with Elizabeth Short had been "above board," and that he'd understood she was out of work because of the strikes.

A number of calls from Beth had been made to the naval hospital during early December, but Warren said he was not in San Diego at that time, not even stateside. He'd been transferred to Hawaii. She had not made contact with him in San Diego, and he did not know if she had tried to reach him on the islands.

Cleo Short said he did not want to identify the body. Hansen and Brown found him in L.A., living alone in an apartment on South Kingsley Drive. He said he knew nothing about his daughter's activities in Hollywood, and he had not been in contact with her since 1943, "when I told her to go her way, and I'd go mine. . . . I want nothing to do with any of this."

Phoebe Short arrived in L.A. on American Airlines, where she met with reporters and a deputy of the coroner's office. She signed a release form for the coroner, allowing Pierce Brothers, agents for Grant Miller, an Oakland Funeral Parlor, to take charge of the body when the coroner's investigation was completed. After a few hours wait at Metropolitan Airport, Phoebe then flew north to stay with her daughter Ginnie until the inquest.

On the morning of January 22nd, she returned to L.A. with Ginnie and her son-in-law. They were met at the airport and brought downtown to the Hall of Justice entrance to the morgue. Harry Hansen and Brown were waiting.

"Harry wanted to talk to Mrs. Short personally," Brown says. They went to one side of the room, where Mrs. Short sat in a chair, and Harry pulled up another one and sat facing her, his back to the others, blocking their view of Mrs. Short."

She had been telling the detectives she objected to the newspaper stories, and was disappointed that the *Examiner* reporters—who had been so helpful at first—were saying that Betty seemed to be "not a very nice person."

The stories and the inferences and slurs the reporters were creating were a kind of blindfold, Hansen told her, that could work both ways. The police *knew* the truth, he said, and the public didn't. Only by knowing the truth would the police have success in apprehending the person that killed Phoebe's daughter.

Hansen was notified by a deputy coroner, and he told Phoebe it was time for her to make the identification—it had to be done for the record. He escorted Phoebe to a waist-high window where venetian blinds were pulled up. The sheet-covered body was on a gurney directly behind the glass.

Ginnie and her husband joined Phoebe at the glass as the attendant behind the window pulled down the sheet, revealing the face.

Phoebe and Ginnie stared at the face, which in death was

still puffed and battered. Ginnie said, "I can't tell, Mama. I don't know. . . ." She turned to Hansen and asked if they could lower the sheet a little beneath the left shoulder.

"She has a beauty mark there," Phoebe said. Her voice was distant. The shoulder was bared and Ginnie made a sound. It was Betty.

The family members were then escorted upstairs to a hearing room on the first floor of the Hall of Justice. Phoebe testified during the inquest, along with Hansen, Red Manley, and Jess Haskins. She was excused after giving her testimony and, avoiding the reporters, began the trip back to Berkeley. The body was released to Pierce Brothers, to be delivered to the Oakland funeral directors.

Three days later the six family members, dressed in black, sat huddled near the edge of the hillside grave in Oakland's Mountain View Cemetery. It was a gray day and the mourners were outnumbered by police and reporters standing at a respectable distance. The officers had wondered if someone "suspicious," as they put it, might chance to make an appearance. But there were no onlookers, no curiosity-seekers. The graveside service was over with quickly.

The pink marble stone chosen to mark the grave read simply: DAUGHTER, ELIZABETH SHORT, July 29, 1924 — January 15, 1947.

As soon as it appeared that the case had fallen from page one, a mysterious package wrapped in brown paper, addressed "To the Los Angeles Examiner and Other Papers," was picked up from a mailbox near the Biltmore Hotel.

The lettering had been cut out from newspapers and pasted on to form the words: "Here is Dahlia's Belongings," and "Letter to Follow."

The small package was passed to the postal inspector because one end of it had been opened. The inspector called the *Examiner*'s night editor, informing him that the package would have to be examined under postal regulations, and the next morning detectives and newsmen were summoned to the federal building. There the contents of the package were removed and examined: an address book with Mark Hansen's name and the year 1937 stamped in gold on the cover, business cards, Beth's birth certificate, her social security card, several photographs of her with different servicemen, and claim checks or stubs for the suitcases she'd checked at the Greyhound depot. The address book was filled with a mass of names and numbers, but several pages had been removed.

"Everything had been soaked in gasoline to remove any trace of latent prints," Willis says. "Though it was dry by then, you could smell it. The address book was so full of names it meant mountains of work to track down each and every person in the hopes of making *some* connection to the murder. . . . It meant being completely swamped all over again.

"A couple of prints on the outside of the envelope were badly smudged from the gas and couldn't be used for comparison. It was a big scoop for the *Examiner* and some of us wondered about that. But more important, if the package wasn't a trick, then it had to be a real communiqué from the actual killer. If it was a hoax, the question was which one of us had taken that address book and things before they'd been booked in evidence. There was no reference to the items in the log, so it would be a serious tampering of evidence."

One detective says, "*Examiner*'s Jimmy Shambra had met with his brother, Detective Al Shambra, two days earlier, following the discovery of the Dahlia's suitcases at the Greyhound bus depot. . . . Al was razzed a lot because Jimmy was a reporter and Sid Hughes and his pals had a sheepish look about the package. Just when things were falling off, their newspaper gets a skyrocket boost that erupts like a volcano—Hollywood names, a mysterious doctor on South Lake Street—hints of all kinds of stuff, and the newspaper article about the war hero's death and the bride he was going to meet and marry in Medford, but the words 'and marry' were scratched out."

Sergeant Floyd Phillips of robbery homicide had worked the Dahlia operation for two weeks. "After the newspaper hoopla to do with that telephone book of hers," says Phillips, "with Mark Hansen's name on it, the investigation got complicated beyond hope. Of course, mum was the word. A slip of the lip sinks a ship and all that sort of shit. . . . We're on a merry-go-round trying to get a concrete lead on a killer. The address book was suspicious to me because a whole lot of pages were torn out, very recently, and probably just before the book was brought to anyone's attention.

"Then there was a bunch of business cards all stuffed in it, and these had been hand-washed with gas to take away prints..

"I didn't personally get a look at the claim checks for the girl's suitcases. Those two things were the only bit of proof that the items *had* been sent by someone who last saw her. I didn't know whether what we had were the actual *claim checks* or the *stubs* taken off the suitcases after they were found. Only the girl would have had the claim checks since she checked the *bags* herself—alone, while Red drove around the block waiting for her. I did not know whether they were what she received upon checking the bags, or if they'd been the stubs on the bags themselves. If they were the latter, it was a pretty sorry stunt being played and only could've been played by some of our people in cahoots with someone at the *Examiner*."

As long as they had a piece of evidence with Mark Hansen's name stamped on it in gold, Harry Hansen and Donahoe thought it would be a good idea to see how far they could push him. While a pair of detectives began to shadow the nightclub owner, other detectives traced and interviewed the individuals whose cards were found in the address book.

Martin Lewis was one of them, and believed that someone had tipped the police about his lunches and coffee breaks with Beth at the cafeteria. "Those detectives were ruthless in their attitude toward her. . . ." Martin says. "I was practically down on my hands and knees with them, pleading with them. Several times they came back with photographs of her, and photographs of other ones. The detectives seemed to believe nothing I said.

"I'd tell them again and again, yes, yes, she bought shoes. How the devil did *I* know where she got the money? I was managing a retail shoe store. What did I care where my customers got the money to buy shoes? But they didn't believe me, and I didn't blame them. I admitted that I ran into her at the cafeteria on Selma—or outside of it, and she joined me for a snack or coffee—no, I didn't know where she was going or who she knew. We sat at a table. I should eat standing up? I shouldn't join an attractive customer who is congenial and friendly? She was a *customer* for shoes. They wanted to know if I had a record of sales to her. I had no way to determine such an accounting.

"I was able to prove that my wife and I were in Portland during the middle of January. My father-in-law was seriously ill with kidney problems, and my wife and I were in Portland at the time that the girl was murdered. So, thank God, I have a fool-proof alibi that is supported by my in-laws, by the staff at the hospital in Portland—the children had remained in the Valley, with my mother who I called several times. I had the dates—the records of the calls."

The police wanted to know why Lewis was so worried, since they were only asking questions. "But you see," he says, "that is not what they were doing, and if it had not been for a good friend with the Hollywood *Citizen-News* who was very close with the Hollywood chief of police, they may have continued to badger me. It was necessary to ask my attorney to call the detectives' superiors downtown. It was a very difficult situation, and I quickly discovered through my newspaper friend that a number of people—well-meaning and some rather influential people— were being badgered in a similar manner. But the detectives made it seem innocuous, in that they decided that anyone that was not connected in some material way to the girl's death should not be afraid to divulge as much information as possible to help them get to the bottom of a difficult case. But we could quickly see that it was a form of trapping someone and it was extremely uncomfortable, and irritating, and for me, I was very guilty about it—I was lying to the police in a murder investigation, but if I told them the truth I'd either be fried on the coals or some greasy man would pay me or my family a visit at some least-expected time.

"We were *not* volunteering to have our names published in the newspapers. My attorney made that clear. There were a number of people who were questioned—I learned this from the detectives—who were very concerned about undue publicity that could harm them.

"I could have gone to jail, maybe even prison, if a D.A. had wanted to be nasty about it. I thought of my children. I did not chase around after women like many people I knew. I had three children. For some time there had been some problems between my wife and myself. It was not an excuse I made for my actions. It was a weakness on my part and I am responsible for what I did, being unfaithful to my wife, and other things that were not right. But what I am excusing—in myself, that is—is that I concealed my unfaithfulness from the police for the purposes of not harming my family, and to avoid publicity that might have been very embarrassing, and very harmful for me as a businessman."

For days addresses and notes and names were checked, rechecked, cross-checked, and logged into the expanding files of detailed information and clues still leading nowhere.

In contrast to the skepticism of most of the detectives, Brown believed the package had actually been sent by the killer. "The thing that convinced me it was his genuine work," he says, "was the same manner in which he cleaned everything so carefully with gasoline. It was the same kind of psychopathic cleanliness he'd used in the handling of the corpse."

But if it had been a hoax drummed up by the press, Brown felt, it would only have added to the rotten confusion the reporters created from the start. Some detectives' hatred of the press was only seconded by their dislike, mistrust, and suspicions of one another.

14

What about that bathtub murder a couple of years ago?" Aggie asked Detective Fremont. She wanted to talk to Donahoe about a possible connection to the Hollywood Canteen and one of the Sheriff's unsolved cases.

Fremont said he knew Donahoe would refuse to give priority to a sheriff's old case. "And Hansen's liable to start yelling if he thinks someone's trying to give this baby to the county."

"Nobody's *giving* anything to the *sheriff*," Aggie said. "Nobody's getting into a pissing contest either! We're talking about dead girls and empty jails."

The Georgette Bauerdorf murder had been just plain poison, says City Editor Louis Young of the *Herald-Express*. "When the murder broke, we jumped and played it big. All the Hearst papers did. It was that kind of case—glamorous socialite, young and pretty, and the grisly bathtub death. We were close to the end of it, and planning on different angles since the sheriff wasn't getting anywhere."

Young then received a memo from Hearst. "It was one of those imperative memos. You had to drop whatever it was you were doing and follow instructions. I had another line waiting, and my conversation with Hearst kept going on—I wasn't sure what he was driving at. He said, 'Nobody's going to miss one no-good goddamn sonofabitch when he's hanged. But some *good* people will have scars all their lives that their children's children will inherit along with their family name that's *seven generations* good as of now.'

"I said I certainly understood, and I was told to get off the line and put the senior editor on. But I *didn't* know what he was talking about. The senior editor then said to me, 'Kill the damned Bauerdorf story.' I said, 'Why?' He said because the boss just told you to kill it. I said, 'Oh, so that's what he's talking about."

Follow-up stories were pulled at the *Herald*, and at the *Examiner*, and any other Hearst publication that might've had a reason to run something else on the case.

"If you cheated to make a good story, it was okay," Young said. "If you lied it was okay. So there were lies at the Herald to offset the lies at the *Examiner*. I suppose Hearst thought it was just a little competition between relatives—little family rough-housing.

"But Hearst would get peculiar once in a while over certain things, like they were little personal crusades and he'd lay down new laws affecting anyone in contact with these issues."

Aggie Underwood was not only friends with Captain Gordon Bowers of sheriff's homicide, but also with Lieutenant Garner Brown, supposedly still working the Bauerdorf case. Earlier Garner had convinced Aggie there was a connection between Georgette's murder and the Short girl. But whatever it was she had received from Garner, he was now reluctant to discuss for fear, Aggie said, of "repercussions from high sources."

"The county's sitting on the Bauerdorf investigation," Aggie said. "It's not being acted upon. You got prints. You got enough to make a case?"

The lieutenant said, "Not good enough to get a warrant."

Aggie said, "What do *you* say, Garner?"

The detective said he couldn't say.

"Well, for God's sake," she said, "*why* can't you say?"

He said he couldn't comment on why he couldn't say. "The case has no leads and is dead."

"The only thing dead about it is the victim," Aggie said. But she knew someone else who could comment: Frank Esquival, a young detective, recently assigned to Central. Esquival would tell her what no one else seemed able to say.

Booked into sheriff's property, along with the piece of towel removed from Georgette's throat, was a diary in which Georgette described her meetings with servicemen and celebrities at the Hollywood Canteen. She made notes about her dates, friends, and acquaintances—like "Beth" during the summer of 1944 and again in September. Arthur Lake had referred to "the other one" when he saw Beth and called Georgette "cutie-pie," confusing the two girls. He'd blushed, too, Georgette told her friend, and he said, "You kind of look alike."

Someone in the sheriff's office made a connection between the Bauerdorf murder and the Dahlia case. The suspect Aggie had been told about might be "one and the same—if anyone can figure out who he was."

LAPD received the lead on the Canteen and three detectives were assigned to follow it through: Marty Baughm, J. Wass, and Frank Esquival. They told Aggie, "If there is a link, it's the only one we've made. It's not our case and it'll have to go upstairs. The Canteen is L.A., but the murder was in the county, so it's the sheriff's unsolved. . . ."

It was not clear if Short *had* acted as a hostess at the Canteen, though the detectives had been told by Brown that she'd met several guys there, including Gordan Fickling.

While records were checked with the Canteen sponsors, Esquival interviewed a former hostess who remembered that Arthur Lake once talked to both of the murdered girls.

Lake was immediately contacted and met with the detectives. He said he wouldn't be able to help them, and if they insisted on asking him questions that might be adverse to his past "patriotic activities," then he thought it necessary for his attorney to be present.

Baughm said he didn't think that was necessary, since the questions had nothing to do with Lake personally. They only wanted to check out some information about Elizabeth Short and her association, if any, with Georgette Bauerdorf.

Esquival says, "Dagwood looked at us straight in the face from one to the other, and said he wanted us to understand that his wife, Patricia, was the niece of Marion Davies, a close friend of William Randolph Hearst; and George Bauerdorf, the murdered girl's father, knew Mr. Hearst; and Mr. Hearst's position was that he did not want any 'muckraking' to do with George Bauerdorf's daughter. The situation of the poor girl's tragic death in itself was more than the family could bear."

The detective assured Lake that any murder was a tragic situation; but as lawmen they were committed to bringing the cases to a close as soon as possible, in hopes of preventing further tragic situations.

"Reluctantly, *very* reluctantly," says Esquival, "Dagwood admitted that he may have talked to Elizabeth Short *and* Georgette Bauerdorf in the Canteen. There'd been more than 135 girls in the Canteen. He believed it was at a benefit. He was given a gigantic Dagwood sandwich, and he made a joke about the two girls in front of him looking more or less alike, 'dressed almost alike as though it was a kind of uniform.' He believed one was Georgette, and somebody told him the other one was a bit player in the movies."

Lake was shown photographs of Elizabeth Short. "I've seen these in the newspapers," he said. "Maybe that's the other girl." He then said he couldn't recall anything else and anything further would have to be addressed through his attorney.

"We had no bone to pick with Lake for the moment," Esquival says, "and we thanked him. But the feeling was—well, you had this movie actor and this gorgeous bit player . . . that sort of idea, though it was not pursued."

The Canteen sponsors dug out some papers and photographs and suggested Esquival talk to some of the gals that had been friends with Bauerdorf the summer and fall of 1944.

"Since this was the sheriff's case," Esquival says, "we were out of our jurisdiction, but I tried to contact one of the homicide inspectors I'd met on occasion. Ray Hopkinson had actively worked on the case and said, while the case was officially open, there was no further active investigation. If LAPD had any leads for them, he'd take note of them. But, he said, they'd had a lot of static with unnecessary publicity, and this, he believed, had caused the investigation to be closed down. What I wanted to confirm or check out, he said, had to go around into the back door."

Al Hutchinson, who had responded to the dead body call at Bauerdorf's apartment, indicated to Esquival that a gag had been put on the case. His "personal view," based on what "floated around," included the idea of a possible suspect— "a soldier, about 6'4"," that the victim dated until she thought he was a bad egg. Hutchinson said, "The guy would've been tall enough to easily unscrew the bulb in the victim's foyer without a ladder or stool, which nobody found."

The deputy said one key print was lifted off the bulb by expert John Shiffling, and Hopkinson thought comparison was made with prints from the apartment and abandoned car.

"That print was the clue we needed," Hutchinson told the detectives, "the *incontrovertible* evidence of the guy's premeditation.

"From what I understand, the victim kept this diary and wrote about another GI, who was friends with the bad egg." Hopkinson had been led to believe that the sheriff's inspectors had been unsuccessful in identifying the tall soldier mentioned in her diary. He never got a clarification on the prints.

Esquival learned that Gordon Bowers and Garner Brown had concentrated on a search through the neighborhoods in the twenties and thirties blocks around San Pedro and Trinity, with the assistance of LAPD officers.

The week after Georgette's murder, Aggie Underwood got a tip that a tall, thin young man had been noticed walking away from 25th and San Pedro where Georgette's car was found. The person, who appeared to be a soldier, looked "darkly complected, but was not a Negro," Aggie was told. He was not wearing an army jacket, just the shirt and trousers of what seemed to be an army uniform. The person, it was noted, appeared "to proceed in a halting gait."

She thought the tall soldier might be someone impersonating a serviceman in order to get to the girls in the Canteen. The friend of Georgette who had recalled the tall, thin soldier was no longer available to interview.

Short's killer, Aggie believed, either worked or lived near San

Pedro and 25th Streets, "a beeline from 39th and Norton where the girl's body was found."

Following his meeting with Hopkinson, Esquival met with Aggie, who said she'd try to arrange a confidential talk with Bowers. "Pressure's being applied to keep the Bauerdorf case quiet," Aggie said. Esquival wasn't sure what he was developing or looking at. What surprised him was Aggie's confidence that both murders had been committed by the same person.

If it was impossible to get the fingerprint sheets and photostats of pages from Georgette's diary, Esquival still felt that a connection could be made between the cases and a unified investigation undertaken between the LAPD and the sheriff's department.

Both murders apparently involved the body being in a tub of water, or in the case of Short, the tub was used in some manner to bisect the body or to drain the blood and scrub away whatever evidence might have remained.

There appeared to be strangulation or partial strangulation in both cases—something inserted into the throat of Georgette, ligature marks on Short's neck—but apparently without damage to the interior of her throat. While it was reported in the newspapers that Elizabeth Short strangled on her own blood from lacerations to the mouth, there was no blood found in her throat or larynx. Georgette had a wedge of material jammed into her mouth with such force that it caused tears at the corners of her mouth. It was very possible, Aggie suggested to Esquival, that something like a gag or some material had been inserted into Elizabeth Short's mouth which had prevented the blood from entering her throat, while at the same time causing suffocation.

While Aggie and Esquival were speculating on the unusual and similar details of the murders, the city editor, without warning or explanation, took Aggie off the case, benching her. He said, "Do nothing; just sit."

"I was taken off the Black Dahlia case," she says. "No reason given. Later I realized it was Hearst—he was making up his mind—would I or wouldn't I mind my p's and q's.

"Question was—would I go to the *Times*? Would the boss make up his mind—figure out what to do with me. Fact was, I was trying to figure out why I was benched—but I had the feeling I knew damn well. So I sat in the hall embroidering. The rest of the gang got a kick out of that, laughing their boots off. Next thing, the assistant city editor says a decision has been made, and I could go back on the case. The decision was made overnight."

Aggie went directly back to Bowers, but the captain said he would not meet with Esquival. In confidence he told Aggie, "We were handed other assignments and those came down the command. We closed the investigation on the Bauerdorf case. That's all I can tell you and what I've said is absolutely off the record."

Aggie was ready to make her "beeline" to Donahoe's office with Esquival's information, but again she was stopped by the city editor. He told her she was off the case again, but this time she was in for a surprise.

"I wasn't being benched," she says, "I was being kicked up the ladder—to city editor! It made my head spin. I said to Lou Young, 'What about the Bauerdorf case?' He put his finger to his lips and said, 'That is a word dat's *verboten*. We will not recognize that name anymore at the *Herald*.'

"Then it began to come clear—I could dish out whatever I wanted on the Dahlia case, but the connection I'd been trying to make with Georgette's murder had pushed me off the crime beat to keep me too busy running the desk to write any more stories.

"But did I want to be city editor at the *Herald*, or did I want to be a reporter with my thumb on a doorbell? I wanted to be a city editor at the *Herald*. That's all I'd ever say about the Bauerdorf case—but I'd lay awake many a night wondering if I did the right thing."

Esquival found himself cornered in Donahoe's office with Baughm and another detective. "Baughm looked bad," Esquival recalls. "The captain was standing up when I went in and he told me to sit down, but he stayed on his feet and said the sheriff's office was responsible for its own cases, and in the long time that had elapsed since that homicide you're inquiring into, he said, they haven't hit a single lead with a payoff, and it's no concern to the department. He said that Baughm and I were to hand in all reports, and I was to return to Hollenbeck. He thanked me for my assistance on the Short case.

"Outside Donahoe's office, Baughm told me he thought he was being shipped over to Highland Park. He said if I didn't watch *my* neck, I'd be pounding tortillas on a rock."

After that meeting, Esquival immediately called Aggie at the *Herald* to tell her he'd been taken off the case and was being returned to his old division. She told him she had a call into some other sources—long-time friends. "They made a lot of horse sense," she said, "This is a pretty complicated situation."

"Whatever it is," Esquival said, "regrettably they've got to do it without me." He was low man on the totem pole, with five years on the force and four small mouths at home that needed "a lot of tortillas," he said. But he would make sure she got whatever information he could pry loose—though he wouldn't be working any of it officially.

And for God's sake, as Aggie would say, every bit of it was confidential and off the record.

15

Stamped "open and unsolved," the Black Dahlia case was running out of steam. The new team member, Detective Sergeant Stephen Bailey, had transferred from robbery and resented his assignment—as had other officers before him—a kind of caretaker duty, dealing with crazies and chasing leads going nowhere. "Hansen and Henry Hudson were puttering around with the Dahlia case," Bailey says, "keeping themselves busy by putting together a file on Mark Hansen as a suspect, as though they didn't have anything else to do. Harry claimed he was actually going to go for an indictment against the guy.

"The problem was that Mark had friends, one being Tommy Devlin, who had a way of pulling up dirt on anyone. Without getting into specific names, say there was someone in the D.A.'s office that, if a cork was pulled, they'd have a pretty messy time. . . . This was a stumbling block in Harry and Donahoe's plans to fry Mark for the murder of one of his own girls. But Short had taken off from his place a couple of times and maybe never was one of his girls in the fine line of it.

"Mark didn't have a good time of things," Bailey says, "and

they leaned on him for a while. They wanted an indictment even though there wasn't the evidence—just that she had lived at his house along with some other dolls—and the Dahlia had his address book, one with his name on it.

"But Devlin, as I understand the situation, had the D.A.'s office pull back from prosecuting Mark, and Donahoe had to try different angles. Had to get another goose to cook. The problem was that no advancement had been made in the case, no leads paid off; only schemes to keep bouncing away from answering *why* there'd been no progress made.

"As a result of failing to set up Mark, a lot of pressure came down to do something about a whole string of murdered women—all pretty much the same sort of lust murders—and the department had nobody in jail. Dr. Paul de River, of the so-called Sex Offense Bureau for the City of Los Angeles, was spending a great deal of time in conference with Harry and Donahoe while the city was saying, 'What the hell's the police department *doing*?'"

Councilman Debs was raising questions about the doctor, saying there was "nothing in de River's employment file to indicate that he should render professional, scientific, technical, or expert services of an exceptional character, exempt from civil services provisions. . . . There is nothing to show that he is a psychiatrist. De River's statements that he had trained at several prominent schools are denied by the schools themselves."

Despite his lack of qualifications, the doctor had managed to enter the police department on salary, without the obligation of taking a civil service examination.

"Whenever we had a homicide that wasn't a killing for profit," says Bailey, "or that was committed during a robbery, de River moved in, interviewing suspects extensively, taping confessions if there were confessions—or if there weren't confessions, it was hoped he could coax one out of the accused."

"De River put together files on sex criminals and had these cross-referenced with every known type of sex crime or offense—from peeping Toms to rape-murderers. He had his own offices and whatever he needed was made available to him upon requisition to the chief's office.

"There were some people critical of him because they couldn't see what his purpose was, but Chief Horrall treated him like a lap dog."

By late 1948 it was believed that the doctor was not only a quack but that he was operating a scam with kickbacks to judges, right out of the department. "De River wrote up papers and books on the sex killers," says Bailey, "and had a deal going with the superior court that involved psychiatry cases—ones put on probation—and these would be referred to de River for treatment for a fee. When the fee wasn't paid, the judge would infer to the 'patient' that unless it was paid, probation might be terminated."

The public and press were up in arms about police apathy and the inability to protect the public from killers and gangsters. "A whole *lot* of criticism was torpedoed right at specific individuals," says Bailey. "On top of this was Chief Horrall, and then it filtered down through homicide and robbery and the chief's gangster squad.

"With no developments or satisfaction, not only in the Dahlia case but in other bad, brutal murders of women—all unsolved—no leads, no suspects, no nothing—we had to make a big showing and it seemed de River had found a way to regain the public's confidence. He came into the chief's office and said he'd found the means to that end. He'd landed a lead in the Dahlia case, and he believed it could be 'worked' into a 'fairly decent suspect,' as the doctor put it. Right away the chief assigned Lieutenant William Burns and a team of other detectives out of his own offices. Hansen and Brown were to coordinate with de River in 'getting results.'"

In October 1948 27-year-old Leslie Dillon, a Miami bellhop and aspiring writer, wrote a letter to Paul de River. The bellhop had read an article about the Black Dahlia case in a detective magazine in which "police psychiatrist" de River was quoted.

Dillon mentioned that he'd worked in San Francisco where he talked to an acquaintance, Jeff Connors, about the case. He said Connors told him that he had known Elizabeth Short just before she was murdered. Dillon said he intended the letter as a "possible lead," and Connors might have other information helpful to the investigation.

De River responded to the letter by telephoning Dillon in Miami, where the bellhop lived with his wife and baby. Dillon was surprised and impressed that the doctor was calling. "He said he'd be very interested in talking to me," Dillon says. "I had told him I was interested in the subject matter, that I'd researched sex psychology, and on the phone I told him I had some ideas for a book on the subject. De River said that he, too, was working on such a book, and that it might be conceivable that I could assist him in some way."

Dillon had another conversation later in the week with de River, and then an airplane ticket was sent to Dillon in de River's own name. "I would fly to Las Vegas where he would meet me," Dillon says, "and we could share ideas on the subject."

Dillon was undergoing money problems, and de River suggested the possibility that Dillon could be hired on as de River's secretary. "That way I would be paid by him," Dillon says. "I flew to Las Vegas where he was waiting at the airport." Another man with de River was introduced as the doctor's chauffeur.

Recalling the "cause and effect of circumstances," as Detective Bailey puts it, "from the time de River was first contacted by Dillon, and then personally talked to him, we were getting more and more flak about the unsolved killings. . . . Some showing had to be put on to get us out of the red.

"When de River knew he had the chief's approval, he got the plane ticket for Dillon. He wanted time with the suspect, and because Dillon had mentioned a San Francisco connection, de River figured there'd be room to jockey him around. It would be cordial, getting the guy into the situation the doctor wanted. Everything that went on was to be noted and recorded in secret. The chauffeur for de River was Detective John J. O'Mara, out of Chief Horrall's office."

The conversations in the doctor's "chauffeured" car concerned Dillon's past. De River was most interested in Dillon's time in Los Angeles since the fall of 1946, and especially curious about Dillon having lived in a trailer on South Crenshaw Boulevard when he worked as a bellhop in a Santa Monica hotel.

He had then worked in San Francisco and lived on Sacramento Street with his wife Georgia, whom he'd met the year before in Oklahoma.

"I told the doctor I'd used the name Jack Sands sometimes when I was writing," Dillon says, "and he said it was an interesting alias. I said it wasn't an 'alias' but a pen name. . . . He asked me if 'Jeff Connors' was also a pen name. I told him 'no,' it was the guy in San Francisco. He then asked me about spending time in the Navy, which I'd only mentioned to him during our phone conversation. I'd said I'd been discharged irregularly. I'd told him since I'd been married I was trying to make some changes in my life. . . ." The doctor seemed to have personal information about Dillon—about his few minor scrapes with the law. It was apparent that de River had "run a make" on Dillon, who became increasingly uncomfortable as de River's interest intensified.

"He was very interested in that I was trying to change my life," Dillon says, "and he pointed out that I'd been married less than a year when Elizabeth Short was murdered. I'd been in Los Angeles at the time, he said. I said that was right, but I didn't see what he meant until he started to get into the subject of mental instabilities that could occur in a young man early in his marriage—like during the first year when perhaps things weren't as they seemed. . . . He wanted my thoughts on that, since I'd experienced those things, and that my information could be of great benefit to him. The conversation right away became more and more psychological on his part, and when we got to the town of Banning and stopped in a motel, the doctor told me out of a clear sky that he believed I had murdered Elizabeth Short."

Dillon was shocked. He denied the accusation and said de River was all wrong. The doctor immediately told Dillon he was the most intelligent man de River had met in a long time, and that he knew more about "sex psychopathia" than many psychiatrists. As that was being said the chauffeur put handcuffs on Dillon.

"They kept me in the motel room until three or four other men arrived," Dillon says, "and then they began to question me. In the middle of it de River insisted that I was too smart to be fooling myself. I had no idea what he meant, and he said I was 'too knowledgeable' and 'too intelligent' to conceal the truth from myself.

"I said I didn't know what I'd be concealing from myself, and he said 'facts too painful to remember.' Then he began to ask me intimate details about the mutilations and the things that had been done to the Dahlia. The only thing I knew about them was what I'd read in the papers and from the detective magazine. But de River would ask me a question and then put the answer right in my mouth."

De River and the detectives questioned Dillon about the person he had mentioned—Jeff Connors. Dillon told them what he knew of Connors and what Connors had said about meeting the Dahlia shortly before her murder.

"Will you take truth serum or a lie detector test?" the doctor asked. "Which will it be?" Dillon said he'd take either one, but if they were intending to hold him prisoner he begged them to allow a call to his wife and a lawyer.

"But they wouldn't let me make any kind of calls," Dillon says. "I couldn't talk to anybody, only the doctor and the detectives . . . or both sometimes, and maybe only one of them again, or then three or four of them. Then suddenly handcuffs were put on my wrists again, and we were driving to San Francisco."

Dillon was secured in the car, accompanied by de River and two detectives, while more followed in a separate car. In a cooperative effort with a select group of San Francisco detectives, a day-long search for Jeff Connors was undertaken. When Connors could not be found, de River became convinced that Connors was a figment of Dillon's imagination or "an aberration after the fact."

The caravan carrying Dillon turned south the next morning. It was now the end of the first week in January 1949, and the grilling of Dillon continued. "I still couldn't talk to anyone," Dillon says. "I couldn't make a call to my wife or try to find a lawyer or anyone to help me. We were at Paso Robles in some other motel, and they kept questioning me. They wouldn't stop. They made me take off all my clothes and took photographs of me stripped naked. While they had me handcuffed to a radiator, they kept on with the questioning.

"They really got nasty. They said they had traced me for two years, and they could blast all my stories and alibis. I told them and kept telling them it was the truth. De River would send the detectives out and then he'd work on me alone. He said, 'What you tell me is in confidence. We'll treat you like a sick boy, not a criminal.' He wanted me to confess I'd killed the Dahlia, and I couldn't. I hadn't done it and I couldn't confess to it."

De River told Dillon that in his "drastic illness" he had committed a crime so horrendous that his conscious mind rejected any references to the deed. "It was as though some other being lurked inside of me," Dillon says, "that de River wanted me to look at—not as a criminal, but as a drastically ill human being.

"I tried, but I couldn't find the drastically ill person he wanted me to believe I was."

The caravan again was on the move—now to Los Angeles. Dillon was brought to a room in the Strand Hotel on Figueroa where he was held incommunicado while three additional two-man teams of detectives joined in the interrogations.

For the week that Dillon was questioned and held a secret prisoner, de River continued his attempts to convince him that he was "a psychologically disturbed boy" and that he had forced the real facts from his conscious mind.

"They had me just about convinced that I was crazy or something," Dillon says, "that maybe I *did* kill the Dahlia—and then just forgot about it."

Despite his desperation and fear, Dillon managed to scribble a postcard which he secretly dropped on the street when the detectives took him to dinner. The postcard was addressed to well-known Los Angeles criminal attorney Jerry Giesler. It read: "I am being held in room 219-21 Strand Hotel . . . in connection with the Black Dahlia murder, by Dr. Paul de River as far as I can tell. I would like legal counsel. . ." The card was signed by Leslie Dillon.

The following morning Dillon was transported to the police department and brought into Chief Horrall's office by Detectives Burns and O'Meara and Lieutenant James Ahearne, followed by Hansen. Horrall questioned Dillon personally, and then while Dillon was detained in another room, de River and

Burns discussed their findings with Horrall.

The chief immediately recommended turning the case over to the top men in the prosecutor's crime branch to successfully prosecute Dillon. Horrall then called the newspapers and told reporters, "There is no doubt in my mind that Dillon is the hottest suspect there has ever been in this case."

Meanwhile Dillon underwent further interrogation by two assistant district attorneys. It went on for about ten hours," Dillon says. "I was losing track of what was happening. I kept insisting I hadn't killed her, but the doctor tried again and again to convince me that I was blocking out the truth and that it was necessary for me to *confess* the truth and be free of the troubles I was facing."

Dillon was officially booked during the night and charged with suspicion of murder. His handcuffs were removed briefly and he was allowed to be photographed by the press as the "hottest suspect," but newsmen were not allowed to ask him any questions. The handcuffs were snapped back on and he was led away under a five-man guard with no word of where he was being taken.

"We're not going to let anybody talk to him, except ourselves, until we've got a closed case," the D.A.'s spokesman told the reporters. De River confided to the newsmen that Dillon knew "more about the Dahlia murder than the police did, and more about abnormal sex psychopathia than most psychiatrists."

District Attorney Barnes voiced his own opinion by telling the press that only the killer himself or a man directly connected with the crime could know the things Dillon knew. He said, "I'm convinced and support the police assertions that Dillon is the hottest suspect ever."

By the end of the next day Dillon's postcard had reached an attorney, and Dillon's mother had been contacted in Oklahoma. She retained the L.A. attorney, who then immediately filed a writ of habeus corpus.

San Francisco and L.A. detectives had found Jeff Connors in the town of Gilroy, south of the Bay Area. He was staying at the home of a girlfriend when he was arrested and returned to San Francisco, to be held for questioning by L.A.'s assistant chief of police, Joseph Reed, who flew to San Francisco with two members of Horrall's special detail. Questioned in San Francisco, Connors was not booked on a specific charge but was taken into technical custody "en route" to L.A. for further interrogation.

The story Connors gave Assistant Chief Reed was almost the same as Dillon's account. Forty-year-old Connors described himself as a "freelance writer and actor," and said he'd met Dillon while both worked as busboys in a San Francisco cafeteria. "I was working there to gather atmosphere for a book I was going to write, and Dillon said he was also a writer and we got to talking about it."

Denying any part in the Black Dahlia murder, Connors could account for his exact whereabouts when Elizabeth Short was murdered. "I am absolutely innocent." he said. "I never told Dillon anything about the Black Dahlia murder case or that I knew Elizabeth Short. All I mentioned was that at one time someone had pointed her out in a Hollywood bar. . . . And then she was found murdered sometime later. I volunteered this information to the police at the time of her murder, but they ignored it and said it wasn't important."

As soon as Connors, Assistant Chief Reed, and the detectives reached L.A., Connors was requisitioned by Deputy Chief Bradley, Captain Francis of homicide, and Hansen and Brown.

By mid-morning the D.A.'s office held a special meeting and issued a statement that the police had developed insufficient evidence to justify a complaint against Leslie Dillon. The assistant D.A. told the chief of detectives, "We can't go to trial with this case. . . . I was ordered by the district attorney to sit in on police conferences which have been conducted behind closed doors, and based upon my presentation to our offices, we will be unable to prosecute in this matter."

Shortly afterward the chief of detectives ordered Hansen and Brown to release Dillon, and at the same time to "book Jeff Connors on suspicion of murder in order to complete our investigation." The chief said that, as soon as Connors was booked for murder, he would be released and exonerated.

"None of Horrall's special detail detectives were available for comment," says Bailey. "They all seemed occupied with other duties. This left the mop-up mess to Hansen and Brown. . . . Let Dillon out of jail, but most important, make sure he was sincerely and genuinely apologized to—otherwise the department's neck was on the line."

De River was the first to reach Dillon's cell, where he attempted to explain the reasoning behind the special procedures he had employed, and the "importance" of certain investigations attempting to uncover the truth before it could be exploited in the newspapers. Certainly Dillon, as "such an intelligent person," would understand and appreciate the "official point of view, and the necessity to ask psychological questions."

Hansen and Brown went to Dillon and led him from the jail. "A free man," said Brown. Dillon spoke briefly with the reporters, who asked him if he had stated that Connors was the man responsible for the Dahlia slaying.

"I never made such a statement," Dillon snapped back at them. "I said I only thought that he knew Elizabeth Short. I can't understand why the police tried to blame me for the murder. I just can't understand why they didn't believe me."

Then, like a kind of pint-sized Samson, Leslie Dillon saw himself pushing down the pillars of a rotten adversary by promptly filing a $100,000 damage claim against the city of Los Angeles.

16

Although the push by Dillon failed to topple the structure, it turned the city council's scrutiny on Chief Horrall's "high-handed bungling and illegal methods employed in the reopened Black Dahlia investigation," according to Councilman Ernest Debs.

Horrall's public announcement that Dillon was "the hottest suspect we've ever had in the Dahlia case" had backfired. A grand jury impaneled to investigate police corruption focused on the Dahlia case and other unsolved homicides, vice bribes, payoffs, inter-departmental jealousies, and squabbles. At the same time, Councilman Debs was demanding an open hearing into the qualifications of Paul de River.

The officers from Horrall's special detail that had handled the "Dillon catastrophe" were called before the grand jury, including Harry Hansen. The final report signed by the foreman stated as follows:

> The 1949 Grand Jury probed into the murder of Elizabeth Short, who is known as the "Black

> Dahlia." This is but one of a number of unsolved brutal murders which have taken place in Los Angeles during the past six or seven years. . . .
>
> Testimony given by certain investigating officers . . . showed apparent evasiveness. . . . This record reveals, in the opinion of the 1949 Grand Jury, conditions that are appalling and fearsome.
>
> Criminals are using varied techniques in writing a record of crime that includes murders, mysterious disappearances of persons and loathsome sex crimes. The criminals in many cases have gone unpunished. . . .
>
> Because of the character of these murders and sex crimes, women and children are constantly placed in jeopardy and are not safe from attack. . . .
>
> From its study of the evidence placed in its hands pertaining to the wave of crime that has swept over Los Angeles County during the past few years, the 1949 Grand Jury has come to the conclusion that something is radically wrong with the present system for apprehending the guilty.
>
> The alarming increase in the number of unsolved murders and other major crimes reflects ineffectiveness in law enforcement agencies and the Courts, that should not be tolerated . . . in some cases jurisdictional disputes and jealousies among law enforcement agencies . . . where one or more departments were involved, there seems to have manifested a lack of cooperation in presenting evidence . . . and a reluctance to investigate or prosecute.

A shake-up of the police department followed the release of the 1949 Grand Jury Report—wholesale police transfers and the "retirement" of Police Chief Horall.

By only a secondary involvement in the Dillon and Connors

fiasco, and because he acted as ordered by Chief Horrall, Finis Brown did not cast a shadow on his brother's position; and Thad Brown took over command of the detective bureau. It had been Horrall, in his hunger for notoriety and publicity, that had usurped the detectives in charge of the case by placing his own "special details of higher-ranking detectives" to lead the renewed investigation, "with de River playing the coach for the team," Brown would confide.

The fact that Hansen had played an active role in what the grand jury was calling "an underhanded inter-squad wrangling and rivalry," and his eagerness "to seek a confession from *somebody*—by any means," as Bailey puts it, threw a damper on Hansen's attitude toward Black Dahlia suspects. The homicide team adopted a posture of "show me" or "prove it to me" in its further inquiries, which became less and less intensified.

"It became protective and guarded," says Bailey. "Before Horall took a hike, you had *crooks* from the chief's office, through the gang squad and right down to the guys walking the beat, *on* the take. So from then on you had to do your job—because the job never ends—with eyes in the back of your head, as every move you're making is watched by commissioners."

While Brown was still assigned to the Dahlia case, and working that almost exclusive of other homicides, the rift widened with Hansen. Thad Brown had steadfastly requested that his brother remain "a part of the primary investigation," which again, for all ostensible purposes, "shut itself down as far as any active search for a killer," says Bailey.

A month following the grand jury's convening, Brown was notified by Manley's wife that Red had suffered "a nervous breakdown" and was receiving electric shock treatments from private doctors. "Manley's wife," says Brown, "was pointing the finger at us for having rousted him so severely that he'd never be the same. . . . Not that I bought that, but it was just another snag in the whole case. Harry still thought Red knew a little more than he'd been saying, though he didn't believe Red was involved in the murder. He'd been cleared completely, but there was something about Red that had kept nagging at Harry, and of course this led me to wonder if maybe Red's conscience wasn't bothering him a little. And so I informed him of Red's nervous breakdown and Harry said, 'The sonofabitch was hiding something, Brownie; it's been eating at him and now he's footing the bill.' And Harry said it wouldn't be the last time we'd hear about Red."

Since the grand jury, Brown had developed a personal belief that Harry tended to go off the deep end from time to time, "You could only go so far with such a case and no further."

The mysterious trail of the Black Dahlia had been traced relentlessly by battalions of detectives, but still with no answers as to how or why or when—with each new possibility, each new finding, the trail seemed more and more a puzzling maze, the most mystifying in the city's history, complicated by rumors and baseless speculation.

"The grand jury had recommended continuing the investigation," Detective Bailey says, "but there was nowhere to go with it—except to keep going back over the same ground. What new leads came in were in left field, time-consuming, or just plain stupid."

While the press was blaming the police for secrecy, Brown was blaming them, in part, for homicide's failure to nail the Dahlia's killer. "I'd have had a better chance if not for the reporters. It's because of them that I had to waste a lot of time running things down that didn't tie in with the facts. . . . And what happened was so much coverage of the stuff that we had copycat crimes being encouraged. I had nine cases after that, all sex crimes, and I know that these guys—the killers when we got them in—had wanted to imitate the Black Dahlia murder. They told me that's what they'd done."

The Dahlia's path was traced back from Massachusetts to Chicago, to St. Louis and Indianapolis, and to Miami through Hollywood and the movie crowd, then to Long Beach again, and San Francisco, Texas, New Orleans, Santa Barbara, and back to Boston—an almost impenetrable, ever-eddying pool of mystery.

"No lead had any conclusion," Brown says. "Once we'd find something, it seemed to disappear in front of our eyes. Following any of those leads was like going down one-way streets with dead-ends."

"Another factor complicating the case was the obsession developed by men with the Black Dahlia in death—as many as had been obsessed with her in life. And some of these came into LAPD to confess to having murdered her."

The detectives had a series of questions, the key ones screened from the information Harry had sequestered from the general file. None of the "confessing Sams" had the right answers.

If there was ever the possibility of someone outside of homicide finding out some of the concealed information, Hansen would deny the facts as being inaccurate. "The chance of a crackpot obtaining something like this is too remote for consideration," Hansen said. "What we worried about is the press or someone getting wind of it, so we adopted the position that if anything comes close, we'd simply say it has no bearing on the case. The chance of them proving their point was equally as remote."

The detectives received a news tip at about the same time as Red Manley's first nervous breakdown. "It came from Chicago," Brown says, "about a doctor in Indiana who'd examined the girl late spring before her murder." Brown had been to Chicago and worked with police there when it had to do with Gordan Fickling, the first week of the investigation. But it seemed during her meeting with Fickling in Chicago she'd visited a doctor in Hammond, Indiana.

"Only because this physician had had some problems of his own, and a review of his female patients became necessary, did the girl's visit to him come to our attention through Chicago police." This was confirmed by Fickling in North Carolina. He knew she had visited a doctor in the Lake County region.

She had used the name "B. Fickel" and given her correct birthdate and her unusual blood type—AB. The Chicago detective advised Brown that the doctor's record revealed that the 21-year-old girl had consulted him about a possible colposcopy—but that the doctor had been unable to make any gynecological diagnosis since he believed the patient had "some sort of physical abnormality that made vaginal examination impossible. . . ." The Hammond doctor had described the condition as "morphologically related," referring the patient to urologist David Stine,

M.D., with the Cook County Hospital in Chicago.

For Hansen, having the Indiana doctor keep this confidential became an immediate priority, and his solution to the problems of "how to do it" were spur-of-the-moment and almost inspired.

Under the critical watch of the L.A. newspapers, Brown flew east for another "investigative" questioning, "off on another cross-country junket at the taxpayers' expense," the L.A. papers said. He flew to Boston, ostensibly in connection with an extradition, but again interviewed Marjorie Graham, who had returned to the Boston area, as well as a young man Beth Short had dated in Cambridge. On his return flight he arranged a layover in Chicago and drove with a Chicago detective across the Indiana line into Lake County, where the doctor was being questioned.

"The Hammond doctor was in hot water," Brown says, "and having a rough time in his own jurisdiction. Information in Chicago had been filed on him, but with no follow-up except his tie-in with a couple of Lake County lawmen. When I met with him, the doctor's lawyer was present, but I talked to the doctor alone, though the attorney was nervous. The doctor identified Short as the girl who had visited him that one time, but he could tell me nothing more than he'd told the Chicago detectives."

The necessity for keeping the information confidential until Los Angeles had their suspect behind bars was impressed upon the doctor. Brown told him L.A. could assist him in his troubles, if he stayed on the level—that maybe the charges against him were not right, but if he cooperated with L.A. they'd see what could be done to mitigate his problems. The doctor assured Brown he *was* on the level and the charges against him were wrong.

Brown later claimed that he "kept the story floating about another doctor because he wanted to steer the press away from the facts when the opportunity presented itself. I told a couple of newsmen that I personally believed she'd been killed by a guy who ran a Hollywood abortion clinic. I found out that the girls from the hotel where she lived were seeing this quack, and Harry had thought at first that the guy downtown was this guy, but that wasn't accurate. He was a weirdo—a nut and sex pervert—and he did a few things to some of the gals that made you think he ought to be put in a padded cell.

"We were starting to lean on him, and about a year after the murder of the Short girl this character killed himself—committed suicide. This was a bit of engineering, but I said I thought this guy was responsible for her murder—that she'd gone to see him about an abortion.

"It didn't hurt the quack who killed himself, and it did serve to steer those damned news assholes away from the fact that the girl couldn't have sex if she tried it standing on her head with the good fairy of the north giving her all the blessing of the world.

"I don't know how the press chewed on it, but what it did was give me a bit of satisfaction, and it didn't hurt Harry, nor any of us, and it did help to protect the case a little.

"Personally, I never thought he'd come walking in, not the real guy. He'd play his hand some other way. So what we did was screen the crackpots, nothing more than that. I knew we'd never see the guy—we'd never know who he was except by a fluke.

"Harry stayed on the Short case, fussing with these papers and records and making a science out of it. I said to hell with it. We weren't *investigating*—we were like pigeons and when something came in, we'd go out and check it out—sometimes—and a lot of times Harry said it wouldn't lead to anything and not be worth the follow-through. And it was always with a chip on his shoulder, with a defensive attitude *against* making any headway with it.

"I left the case a while after everyone's ass got in a sling over jurisdiction problems. I wasn't ready to get hauled up for a second grand jury. Everyone was fighting with Harry because he and Donahoe wouldn't cooperate on any crossover participation, not even with our own damn divisions."

He believed Harry in the beginning, Brown says. "He was a brilliant detective, a smart, smart man; but a loner and an odd bird. He wasn't liked—not that he was *dis*liked, he just wasn't liked. He was too removed and too above others in his own thinking and in his way of holding himself and his opinions about others and police work in general.

"He didn't know it then, maybe none of us did, but Harry'd met his challenge with the Dahlia case. He'd met his goddamned Waterloo."

The cross-indexed cards that Hansen had set up on the case were inherited by Sergeant Danny Galindo when Hansen retired. At the request of Thad Brown, Galindo took over the case. "It's not punishment, Danny," the chief of detectives said, smiling. "But you've been familiar with it from the start. There's no more police work on it right now, but there will be activity from time to time just because of the sensational stuff the press keeps pumping up. What it amounts to is a watchdog job."

Galindo's familiarity with the case was first-hand. He had interrogated—in Spanish—confessors and would-be suspects with little or no command of English. Galindo took over the case, as Bailey had, reluctantly. He checked the records and the files, going over the leads worked by other detectives—cross-checking and adding his name on the back when the lead was closed out. Galindo could see the struggles of previous detectives mirrored in the files, the near impossibility of the case, and the strange mystery that seemed only to become more complicated with the passage of time.

"You run every lead to its finish," Galindo says. "You have to sew up the holes. You go back and you go through it again. But when nothing pans out, you have to move on with other investigations.

"The murders in L.A. don't stop because you're stuck on one that doesn't have any answers. So the case stays open on file as *unsolved*, but the investigation closes.

"You don't know who he is. You know he knows who you are. Sometimes you have to wait for him to make the next move. . . ."

17

Information was received by the police department that a certain individual wanted to talk about the murder. He was being paid by an informant who brought a strange story to homicide. The "catch," according to the informant, was that the individual wanted it understood that the information was *not* based on *personal* knowledge, but came from a third party whose present whereabouts were not known. The information was therefore "hearsay" and "circumstantial."

Detective Marvin Enquist was the first in homicide to be in contact with the informant. "The individual we talked about," says Enquist, "is the only one that I know of in the long history of the case unwilling to make eyeball contact with the police."

Enquist listened to a nine-minute section of a tape recording the informant brought with him, which was garbled in places. The detective suggested a duplication could be made by the department that might "electronically" improve the quality of the recording. Did the informant have any objections to leaving the cassette with them? No, he said, he had transcribed what was on the tape. There were a number of details that were not recorded, which the informant then related to the detective, repeating how the body had been severed. This had taken place in a house on 31st Street near San Pedro. The individual who had told the informant these facts was using the name of Arnold Smith.

Enquist summoned John St. John and his partner, Kirk Mellecker, to hear the informant repeat the story. John St. John, one of L.A.'s most celebrated police officers, was the subject of a book and a television series, "Jigsaw John." During his record-breaking career, St. John worked many of the city's notorious murders and had been in charge of the Black Dahlia case about a year.

To the detectives, Smith's account of the murder was of great interest, though the story seemed confused one moment, then sharply in focus the next. Parts of it seemed vague or contradictory, as though fragments were cut from the story and set aside, creating lapses. It was obvious the information being presented was not the whole story, and that the gaps were areas that might directly implicate Smith with the victim in a situation no longer hearsay or circumstantial.

"We never could have considered the circumstantial evidence against this individual if it hadn't come in through the back door, in a manner of speaking," says St. John. "Probably from the very start, from years back, we'd never had enough to get a fix on a suspect. So often he's there, he's around, and you know he's there but you can't get him in your sights.

"Everything that works against an investigation had been present in the Black Dahlia case right from the start when the investigators first hit the streets to find the guy—long before I became involved."

St. John wanted to talk to Smith "very badly," he said. "Is he going to be willing to talk to us?" he asked the informant. "Would it be possible for you to bring him in to talk to us?"

"No, it wouldn't," the informant said. Smith had confided in him based on the idea that he'd remain out of the picture.

St. John said, "With this sort of information, I can understand why he wants to avoid the police. I don't suppose Arnold Smith is his real name?"

"He told me that was his name, though when I first met him, I think they called him something else."

The informant gave a detailed description of Smith, which Mellecker made notes of—very tall, over 6', very thin, with one leg shorter than the other. "So he walks with a limp?" St. John asked.

"That's correct," the informant said. He could offer little information on Smith's whereabouts.

"You were there when he talked about all this?" St. John asked. The informant said yes, and then St. John asked, "What else did this guy say he did to her?" The informant repeated the scenario Smith had detailed, and in several instances St. John said to Mellecker, "I want to find out where he is and talk to him as soon as possible." St. John wanted to know the history of the informant's relationship with Smith.

The informant said he'd met Smith "quite a few years earlier," at an apartment in the Silver Lake area occupied by a man named Eddie and a girl. "The garage was filled with stuff that was probably from burglaries—too many electronic things around the house, stereo and hi-fi equipment, medical stuff like microscopes, golf clubs, a lot of silverware . . . most of it handled by Eddie. Two other people were there that night, an Indian who worked for a steel plant and burglarized houses and apartments and had dealings with Eddie, and a tall, thin, sick-looking man who was introduced to me as Arnold Smith. Eddie didn't say what Smith was doing there or anything about the nature of their acquaintance. The group was drinking, talking, and listening to records the girl was playing. Some of the talk was about Los Angeles when the Hollywood Freeway was being built, when hundreds of old houses and tenement-like buildings were being demolished between Temple and Sunset Boulevard, and this was in the forties. The conversation came up about some murdered women downtown, and Eddie, who was older, asked Smith, "Wasn't that where the Black Dahlia was murdered?"

"Smith said that wasn't where the cops had been looking. Eddie told us that Smith had known the Black Dahlia and he'd seen a photograph of them together. . . . I asked him about it, but mostly Smith talked to me about some other guy, a female impersonator from Indianapolis.

"When the others were in the kitchen he told me how this guy he called Morrison used to pick up girls downtown. He'd get them in his car and take them to his hotel. Morrison would make like he was choking them, because he got a kick out of that. Smith said Morrison almost killed one once by doing that, and she started hollering and she stormed out, but nothing came of it. And then Smith said, this time was probably around 1945 or 1946, that Morrison described his idea about a waitress from an Italian restaurant on Figueroa. He told him she could be tied by the hands and feet like a pig, and could be fucked like that, bent over, and that she could be held a certain way, sort of backwards, as he described it, and choked or suffocated. I asked how he would do that and he said by putting something into her mouth. When something was put in the mouth a certain way it stopped one from getting air into the breathing passage through the nostrils."

Of the times the informant met with Smith, he said the man never referred to Elizabeth Short by name. "He did not call her Elizabeth, or the Short girl, or Beth. He would say *her*, or like he would say '*her*, who we're talking about,' if I didn't follow what he was saying and asked what he meant. When he told me what he claimed Morrison told him about knowing how she died, he did not talk about it with any feeling or regret, or that he was sad or cared one way or the other if she was dead or not. He did not use her name, just 'her,' as I said, and he never used the words, 'Black Dahlia."'

Smith said he had seen *her* in Al Greenberg's café on McCadden once or twice and that she was friends with a 'phony' writer's wife. The guy was Henry Hassau who lived on Sycamore up by Grauman's Chinese. Smith told the informant there had been a number of robberies that involved several men that hung around Greenberg's café, including Greenberg. At one point, while drinking at a downtown bar, Smith told the informant that he knew one of the gang members, Bobby Savarino, and that there had been trouble between them.

He said that because of the trouble with Savarino, he'd been worried that he would be pulled in and implicated in the robbery of a nightclub. This was around January 1947. He said that Hassau had been caught and Greenberg was arrested, and others were arrested for that robbery as well as other stickups.

"There was a blonde woman at the Roosevelt Hotel on 29th Street, and she was friends with a Chinese man who owned the old apartment flats where Smith claimed he stayed at times, though I think he had lived there on and off. At one time his mother lived there, but she went into a nursing home. Smith claimed he stayed in Hollywood during those particular days because he was afraid of being arrested for the robbery. Hassau's wife told the cops the tall kid, the skinny one who was drunk and had a crippled leg, was living in the south part of downtown. That was why Smith was worried. She knew the blonde, and said she remembered she'd been in movies and was also a hooker; and she managed the old flats on 31st where Smith had stayed."

During another meeting at the 555 Club on Main Street, Smith brought an old See's Candy box held together with rubber bands in which he had some newspaper clippings and personal things, photographs, hairpins, and a hankie that had belonged to Elizabeth Short. One photograph had been taken in the bar that was there before the 555 Club. It showed Smith when he was younger, Elizabeth Short, and a blonde girl. There was another young man in the photo who Smith said was Al Morrison. Smith did not want the informant to handle the photograph, and held it by the edges so that the informant could examine it without touching it. It was Morrison that Smith would claim was responsible for Elizabeth Short's murder. Morrison had a room in Hollywood at the Wilcox Hotel, and when he was not there, Smith would use the room to "sleep it off." On more than one occasion Smith shared a bottle with a clerk working nights at the hotel.

The informant said that Smith told him the room was a corner room, almost V-shaped, the foot of the bed opposite a window and the headboard across from the small bathroom doorway. The informant said, "He seems to remember those kinds of details." It would be to this room that Smith claimed he brought her one night "when she didn't have any other place to go to."

Morrison was in San Francisco at a "she-he" club, so Smith had said, and he brought her to the room following another drinking session with the clerk. He'd bought a bottle with money he had earned that day from "hawking" on the boulevard, getting bus customers on the daily tour of movie star homes, he told the informant.

In describing the scene to him, Smith related that she sat on the edge of the bed and Smith was on the chair next to the desk. Smith didn't recall them saying anything at first, except she was surprised when he said he was going to stay in the room also. He said there was something not quite "copacetic. . . ." Smith opened the half-pint, he said, and fetched a glass which he half-filled with water from the bathroom, and brought it to the desk. She said, no, thanks, she didn't want any.

He asked if she minded if he drank, and she said no. Smith remembers asking her if she wanted to use the bathroom. She said no. He told her he was going to take advantage of the shower nozzle. He excused himself and said that he was half-expecting she'd be gone by the time he finished in the bathroom.

With a towel wrapped around himself, he came back into the room for the bottle. She was still there, on the bed, but he saw that she had all of her clothes on. On top of that she had moved to one side of the bed, taking the bedspread with her, turning it over herself as she faced away from the center of the bed. That was how Smith described it to the informant.

Then Smith asked if she wanted to get more comfortable. She didn't answer, but she kicked off her shoes. He said he remembered there was a big hole in the foot of her stocking and he could see the red paint on her toenails showing through the stockings.

Smith got onto the bed, he said, but she didn't move. He told the informant he moved close to her and put his arm over her, or around her, and he gradually turned her over onto her back. It was not too easy because she seemed lifeless, like someone who had drunk themselves into a stupor. But he knew she was awake. She breathed in a real exasperated way when he moved his hand on her breasts, feeling them through her sweater.

Smith said he asked if she wanted to take her clothes off, but she didn't answer him. "It was more like she was clearing her throat, he told me. It seemed to him she was hardly breathing, not moving. He said he thought, hell's bells, who needs all the problems, and felt like he should reach between her legs, get it going. But there was such a cold shoulder attitude, if she wasn't sleeping."

Smith said that he put his mouth near the side of her face because she had it turned from him and she began to come over, rolling a little nearer to him, but looking upward while he unbuttoned her clothes. He loosened her skirt and raised the sweater she had on. Smith told the informant that he "screwed around with the clasp on her brassiere until she put her hands on his hands and said she didn't want him to do that. 'You're going to be disappointed anyway,' he said she said to him."

He said he told her he wouldn't do that if she didn't want him to. He said he saw nothing about her that would disappoint him and he put his mouth to her stomach instead where he had raised up the top part of what she had been wearing. "It was very awkward, he told me, "the rest of it, and that upper part of her, her head and her upper body barely moved. Maybe she didn't move at all—she just lay there probably looking up at the ceiling."

Days later, when Morrison came back to L.A., Smith said he met him in a cheap bar called the Ace-Hi. He had been staying in Morrison's hotel drinking. "He didn't know how many days," the informant says. "Then Morrison showed up unexpected, and he told Smith he was going back to San Francisco, but he supposed that Smith had guessed what had happened. Smith said that, by saying that, Morrison meant the killing."

According to police she had been missing from the evening of January 9th until her body was found in the vacant lot on January 15th, and though a number of leads came up— "Black Dahlia sightings," they were called—none were verified. On the night of January 13th, though, Smith told the informant, she had slept at Hassau's apartment on Sycamore. Hassau had been arrested, the informant said, "along with a couple of the other guys from Greenberg's place."

The following statement is from the Arnold Smith transcript in Los Angeles police and Los Angeles County sheriff's files:

> She'd told Morrison she slept on the couch downstairs in Hassau's after he spotted her walking to the corner of Hollywood across the street from the Roosevelt Hotel. So he says, "Hey, what the hell are you doing?" She got in the car and sat with him for awhile, and then she got out and was walking away from the car.
>
> She gets sad and gets back in the car, and he heads south on La Brea. She wanted to know where he was going and he headed down to Washington and then east as far as Flower. Then he drove down that way, going south from there toward San Pedro Street. They drove further south, to another hotel near 29th Street, also called the Roosevelt Hotel, but not connected to Hollywood's Roosevelt Hotel.
>
> He got the key there, that guy that knew the blonde—this is the one that shacks up with the Chinaman, and she had the key. Then he drove her to the Chinaman's house on 31st, but he couldn't get into the place.
>
> There was something wrong with the key, as I remember the situation, as it had been described to me. Morrison had to drive to a small factory on the corner, around on 33rd Street and Trinity, to straighten out the problem with the key. She was complaining about having to get back because of Henry's wife. Later on, I asked him, "You think she was trying to get back to see me?" He turned red when I said that. You see, the first thing is you couldn't fuck her at all. He said he'd screwed her and I said he was a liar. See, she made my dick hard every time I looked at her mouth. But I swear to God, I never put it in her, and I knew he was a lying sonofabitch.
>
> There was a red bottle, had a glass stopper you use for putting fancy perfume in. And he could've taken her eyes out with that. But you understand, that's what he said. Because his mind was gone. You know, half those

hoods had their mind eaten away because of syphilis. I know his mind was gone to have done what he did to her, and knowing he did it all along, but knowing it was just that he had to do it, you see what I'm saying, so there was an excuse in part of this.

I remember being told something about pulling the car into the dirt driveway and to the back by the incinerator. The car was parked there so that it was close to the building. There was just so much room, so you get out and go around front to the building, since the back door's locked.

This is the Chinaman's house in the 200 block on East 31st Street by San Pedro Street and Trinity. . . . This is an older two-story brown wood-frame building that rented rooms and units.

You go up to the place by these steps right in front that're wood and you go in the hall. Right there is the stairs going up. So what we're talking about, he goes up behind her to the second floor. This place smelled bad. You get the idea to go there and it smells so bad like it's been closed up for a long time. Right away he opened the beer and sat on the couch, but he didn't pull that goddamn drape back. That's the problem, there, because she says she can't breathe because it is so dusty, but he doesn't say anything—he is just waiting there.

He has to tell her to be quiet, again. But she says she has to make a call and when she starts to use the phone there he says, "You can't." He put it back down. She said something like she is a prisoner and he says, "That's right. You're a prisoner." She says she is going to make a call from the market. . . . She means the market where they just were. She gets her handbag up, and he says, "No, you're not going." But she was starting out, just starts out of the room. He came out of the hall up there and goes to the head of the stairs where she is standing, and he says, "You better come back inside of here. You better not go outside now."

She didn't say anything and he said okay. And he

went to her and grabbed her arm like this, and started to pull her back but she hauled off and let him have it with the purse. Just swung it out and caught him across the side of the face. He slugged her once and her knees got weak. He pulls her back into the room, and he leans her against the door while he locks the door with the key. She just stayed there as though she was unsure exactly what would follow or admit it. He said he then grabbed her and pushed her and she fell down like it was against or on the couch. Then off that and is on the floor with her dress up on her body. He said he stood over her and said something about he was going to screw her ass.

She started to yell so he bent down and slugged her again. He said he put his hand on her neck and holds her head still while he hit her a couple of times. She didn't move. Now he didn't know what he was going to do, except he went out of the room, through the door he had locked and went downstairs to the rear of the first floor to the kitchen. . . . He knew what was going to happen.

When he got outside he heard the funniest sounds he'd heard. He couldn't tell whether it was people making noises inside the joint or whether hearing people over the fences in those crummy houses. He wasn't sure. He could almost hear voices like they were talking, you understand? Anyway, he checked the gas in the car and checked under the seat in the car. He had to get north. He went back upstairs and through the back door, through that back part, there was this concrete. They were cementing a walk for the back part there, and he had to step way over it or sink his shoe in the dirt, the mud there. He remembered a hose that was going. It was leaking and the water was running down the back, just leaking and going back by the incinerator.

It was in his mind all the time. Everything that was going to happen. He said he didn't have to think about anything, because it was laid out in front of him.

He got a small knife or he got the knife on the back porch, like a paring knife, and on the back porch was a rope, this clothesline hunk of rope. This is what he had in mind for the waitress. Then he said there was a larger knife, like a long butcher knife that was two inches, the width of the blade near the handle. He said he thought that such a knife could be used to dismember her body. He said he didn't know what he was going to do with the knife, except to scare her or keep her back up in the room. He went upstairs but she hadn't gotten up off the floor, but up on an elbow or an arm and was looking around.

She was on the edge of the couch, I think maybe he had her arm—up here at this part of her arm—and had brought her up on the couch, but this wasn't a couch like you think; it was a studio bed on a metal frame, only it was littler than a regular bed you'd consider for that, and he said, "You had enough trouble?" She said she had, so he opened this bottle. . . . This is what he said, oh, and had this opened from the sink place downstairs, the washtub just before you went out the back door. She kept saying, "What are you going to do?"

Drinking that, and she said her mouth hurt. She was scared of the knife and got up and was moving but he ran to her and hit her again, but it didn't put her out and didn't seem to stop her. So it was necessary at that point to indicate that he was going to hurt her with the knife.

He tore at the clothes, not tearing but cutting at the clothing. I don't know what . . . I didn't know he said something and I can remember him scared or his face was white and his eyes didn't even look anywhere near like it was real eyes. Like they were glass and they were shining and he was cold but he was sweating and he turned the light away. . . . This light, like a desk light, and it was bright, as bright as this is. It was like when you see flashes of light when you get hit on the head. But he put a rag in her mouth. He used her underpants and he knocked her out a few times. She was all tied up to that couch and she'd been stripped of all the clothes and cut up bad.

I couldn't even tell you how bad it was. I mean, this is from the information I have that I know about. I knew it had to be some other Chinese. They'd cut her mouth across it and there was blood on the couch. He knew he'd get stuck with it and had to get rid of it.

She was naked, only he'd tied her hands and these were up over her head like this, and he stabbed her with a knife a lot, not deep, not enough that would kill you, but jabbing and sticking her a lot and then slitting around one tit, and then he'd cut her face across it. Across the mouth. After that, she was dead.

Her legs weren't tied at this particular point, but it was plain that they had been tied by the rope—this hunk that had been tied was cut, but it was still anchored at the frame, and there was the piece of it that was there.

The knife was on the floor next to where the rope pieces were, a small knife, a paring knife that had been used to stick her with. I think it was seeing that rope down in the back, and that wire stuff, like a gauge heavier. I don't mean the wire part of the hanger but like you got on the other kind of hanger, that's the hook on the top part of it, going over the clothes pole, but it wasn't like that, it was soft and around the frame part. That's what stands out in one's mind.

There was the matter of getting rid of her, and what probably was the first thing was the incinerator out back. Burn the clothes and things and the knife. He got the knife idea from the situation that someone had put the rope around her neck, and held her down on the couch. Now these underpants or these ladies pants, they were all clotted with her blood, like a wad of some blood that was hard to see right off since the material was black, but blood does show on black, and there were these other particles of material that probably did not belong to her and the problem that these had to be burned as well. So, it is easier to try to think what he told me about all this situation, though you look at it like a movie, you see what I'm saying.

There is a larger knife that can be used, but he had to go back down and outside and get these boards they were using for forms. Maybe there were three of these boards, or maybe there were four of them back upstairs, and went through the room she was in and into the bathroom which is off this one room, but there is a short hall. It's not a hall in that sort of sense except with—well, this window and you can see the roof of the car and the trunk of the car if you look out. And on the other side, the opposite side is the alcove, not a closet because there is no door, but it is arranged with a clothes pole going across, and some curtain material that is a bathtub shower curtain, there is one of these in front of where the clothes pole is across. But in the bathroom these boards are put across the tub, straight across it—set out that way. She was brought into the bathroom first, if I recall exactly what the information is. So, partly brought into the bathroom. I think dragged the rest of the way, and looking down at her, is the way I understand it. He had fooled around with her stomach, too, using the knife on her, the decorations in that manner. He had done a few other things to the body, figured she'd still been alive, and seeing how she could take it.

As much as possible, you understand, well . . . There was a purpose to this in such a way though a person undergoes so much and it's possible that this person has to be, what you would call—anesthesia. It's a word in a crossword puzzle. . . .

There was this other muscle portion or the part of the jaw, during the time she was dying. But this had been taken care of, and she had to be laid across the tub, on top of the boards. Then he tied the arms and tied the hands to the faucet handles and the shower, the pipe. And then put a leg, the one that was nearest hanging over the side of the tub. Her leg was put up on the tub, on the boards, the board that was arranged for that part of the leg. She was laying across one board just underneath the back part, and the other one was underneath the hips here, under the ass—see, a rope around each leg and pulled them downwards, pulling them so that you then tied these ropes around the bottom of the can—the toilet bowl, but there is the pipe. There is not the wall section of the water storage, the tank. It is that vacuum housing part there and the water pipe, so he had her drawn and fixed down, because there wasn't a particular way of getting into the tub with that kind of knife. That particular knife.

The idea was first cutting off the legs at the top of her thighs but then this would have to be done twice, so the decision to separate, to cut this in half, that way to move the two parts easily, and get her there was the way to transport. . . .

Burning of the body in the incinerator was not the actual plan, but that the body could be separated for disposal purposes so there was this commencing with a different approach. The body was on the planks over the bathtub. Her middle was over the tub and the boards were width-wise so she was open, at the waist and back, and so the cut was across the middle, pulled tight like she was, as it could go clean through and have her body opened.

The knife was the larger knife. I would say it was approximately ten inches long, the length of the blade, and there was two inches at the handle part, not the handle of it but just at the end of the blade. It went further than figured with this knife and went all the way across and down through her body. The drain was into the tub below. But blood did come out and onto the boards and some even jumped out of her, came out and upwards in such a way, but it was clean through, and then there was some trouble to do with going through her backbone of the bone's part there. The important thing is that the starting of it has to be finished. If one would intend to make the separation as to what we're talking about.

When the board was removed from underneath the rear part, that low section went down into the tub, but hanging at an angle, and drained in this manner. The same with the top half which hung down into the tub and there were marks made on the body's back, the upper part. Both sections of the body drained in this way, leaning, you could say laying down at the incline into the bathtub, but the bottom section, the hips and these parts of the legs was leaning against the slope of that part of the tub, but the upper part was straight down, not as straight as the back of a chair, but straight more down than the lower section. She stayed in the tub and the boards were taken down and out back. The boards and stuff went into the incinerator.

The broom was where the mop was and the mop and the rags were used, and then these things went down and were put in the incinerator and lighted on fire.

The covers and the mattress padding—it wasn't a padding, but it was like thick felt, like a heavy material. It was covered with shit. It was messed so bad, and these were bundled, put into a bundle. They were not put on top of her, but the water was in the tub. It had run before. The tub had been filled with the water. So it was put up around where the hands were, up around where the faucets were and this way it was not in the tub. The blood was thinned out by the water. It was on the chain, a stopper, down in the drain, but it was plugged in first and then the water made the body rise, and it came up as the water filled in the tub.

There was some worry about the rope areas, and these were then cut. He said he was sitting on the toilet and he cut the rope, the part that went around the base of the bowl and the pipe behind the bowl and these then were taken off of the places of the body where they were tied around. It was in the water but this was drained and it was filled again and the body was in the water at this time. The body tended to stay higher with the surface as it came up. There was movement in the bathtub with the body when the tub was filled with water. And whatever skin contact there was, this was removed when there was the draining.

And it was removed by cleaning it off. There was this idea that she was not dead because her eyes were open and they had a look in them that she was not dead. This, I think, what it was, that he was scared and getting more scared and knowing that they had to be gotten rid of. I think it was that the water drained and ran in and around the open parts of the body. . . . It was not excitement or that sort of a feeling, but because of the jaw that I said earlier, it made it so that it was necessary to take care of the rest of it.

The skin contact had been taken care of, and then back downstairs was the oilskin tablecloth off the kitchen table. But this wasn't enough, so there were these curtains and the shower curtain from the hall there, by the pipe. She was wrapped over in the curtains, both parts in the two curtains, and what was it. . . . It was used to pull on the tablecloth or I think it was the shower curtain to take the sections downstairs. The bag was on the floor of the trunk. This was the cement bag from the rear of the house.

She was put into the trunk of the car, and then drove until the place was reached that he could put the body—put her out of the car. The top section was carried by the arms held up and put down on the ground and the bottom section was on the bag and put down that way. The body was put down in the manner that the bottom was put down and moved this way, moved by the one leg this way, more away from the sidewalk, and then the top part was picked up again and put in order.

The cement sack was left where it was when he took hold of the ankle and put away from the sidewalk. The shower curtain and the tablecloth were in the trunk of the car. There was nothing of the clothes that was not cut, except the shoes and her purse. The pocketbook was on the floorboard. It was put into a storm drain. All of this was put into a storm drain.

18

Tell me again how he placed the body on the bathtub . . ." said St. John. He and the other detectives listened intently as the informant repeated the details told to him by Smith.

"You were present when this Smith said these things?" St. John asked. The informant said he was—Smith had told him that what he was saying had been relayed to him by Al Morrison.

St. John said, "As much as I'd like to talk to this person, you can understand our position—without knowing who he is or where to find him—there's no way we can go out into the city and look for him. If there is any possibility that you might be able to talk him into coming in and seeing us, or if you can get a fix on where to find him, then I'll be able to do something with this. If we can get a lead on this character, then we'll be able to act upon this information."

The informant had only an idea where Smith might be—in the area of the Cromwell Hotel off 7th Street. The informant explained to St. John that contacts with Smith were difficult.

Smith would call or leave messages at a Chinese café on 7th. Sometimes he'd call from a pay phone and have the informant return the call to another pay phone. "That's how it had become," the informant said. "It hadn't been that way earlier when we were drinking by the Cromwell or in a couple of bars we'd go to."

St. John asked the informant again about the boards—how far apart had they been placed. St. John seemed especially interested in the details about how the body sections had been placed in the inclined positions in the bathtub for a certain passage of time. The informant again related the details as they had been described to him by Smith.

While in steady contact with the informant, St. John conferred with other detectives, examining the information from the informant along with police files. St. John again met with the informant and said he now believed that Smith was using "this Al Morrison character as a smoke-screen." Smith was "throwing Morrison out as a live decoy," St. John said. "His references to the other party are in the form of this other guy supposedly telling Smith these things, which Smith is telling you. It's the old story of 'let me tell you about what happened to this pal of mine,' when it's actually yourself you're talking about.

"What Smith is doing," St. John said, "is airing what he possibly knows of the murder first-hand, while putting the words in someone else's mouth, an as-told-to story, if you get my drift."

The detective believed that Smith was present or in some way took part in the murder, and that he knew the reasons why the body had been left where it was. He knew details that no one else would know—except the detectives or the coroner.

In time St. John accumulated over 88 pages of transcripts and one key tape recording. After careful examination of the material, St. John began attempting to corroborate Smith's statements from the confidential police files, and through a woman who had known Elizabeth Short personally. This woman was able to verify most of the intimate details about the victim that Smith seemed to know as a matter of course. Many pieces of the puzzle were fitting together.

But Smith had structured the retelling of the murder to the

informant so that it *was* hearsay. "Even though," St. John said, "he might be the one we've been waiting for all these years, and I'd give anything to solve it—how am I going to pin a crime on a man I can't find?"

A suggestion came down from the captain to set Smith up. St. John's younger partner, Mellecker, could go undercover and arrange to be at a bar when the informant next met with Smith. Mellecker could engage the informant in a conversation which would prompt another round of drinks. The informant cautioned that it would have to be done on short notice, as he never knew exactly when Smith would contact him—except if he needed money.

The following week, while the cat and mouse game continued, St. John was told that Smith was beginning to run scared. St. John said, "What we're going to do is have you try to pin him down. I want to bust this guy so bad it's killing me." A meeting with Smith was set at Harold's 555 Club for the end of January, and the informant notified St. John and Mellecker.

Detective Enquist said, "I am glad they're going to get the sonofabitch."

Los Angeles County Sheriff's Detective Joel Lesnick would soon pull the same suspect closer to the Georgette Bauerdorf murder. He would become aware that Arnold Smith was only one of a dozen aliases for Jack Anderson Wilson, a 6'4" alcoholic, emaciated individual with one crippled leg and an intense though fearful compulsion to talk about some long buried secrets.

Detective Lesnick had been a sergeant first class in the tank corps during the Korean "police action." After the service he joined the department, worked uniform patrol, the Los Angeles County jail, covered the Firestone Station, Watts, Willowbrook, and Carson areas before working undercover with the Detective Division.

"I made several arrests in Harold's 555 Club on Main Street that had to do with dope deals. We worked any type of case in any incorporated city within L.A. County. As a police matter we advised LAPD narco control of this case prior to going into L.A. city.

"A number of investigations crossed over between LAPD and the sheriff's unsolved homicides. The Mocambo 211—the robbery which was our case, the sheriff's, and the McCadden gang—which was fresh information to me. One of the bandits was 6'4" and very thin, with a scarred-over face.

"There seemed to be a possible link with the murder—almost neat and simple. The psychology of the players in all of this became vitally important—linking them together.

"If Smith was involved in the Mocambo 211 and skated while the others were busted, it could have been the real reason he snuffed Elizabeth Short, according to the sheriff's point of view, because she, through her association with Smith, might have known of the holdup. And as it was to turn out, not just a simple 211, but with a long string to some pretty powerful people involved with organized crime.

"Elizabeth Short was on a hard road, couldn't seem to land a job and having to mooch off friends. . . . She wasn't following through with long-range plans, I believe, and bounced from situation to situation; hence the number of apartments and rented rooms she was in. Was she a true friend to the drunks and downtrodden, or was it part of an act?

"This brought her in time to Smith, who had already killed once, as far as we believe—in a rape-murder. He was the *outsider* of the Mocambo gang. He hated the Black Dahlia for traits he might have shared with her, but he thought he was much smarter and saw through her. She apparently knew of the crime and with his loathing for these traits in her, which he operated on in a way that no one else knew, it became what he was to call, the 'crime of confusion'—which was the best reason for killing her.

"Smith was not very remorseful about doing her in," Lesnick says. "He was primarily fearful about getting caught for both the 211 *and* murder, and was amazed when he slipped through the cracks. So why wouldn't someone living under this pressure become a violent full-time drunk—what's he got to lose?"

Based on the transcripts that would become confidential sheriff's records, Smith, aka Jack Anderson Wilson, is described as the "possible and probable suspect in not only the Georgette

Bauerdorf murder, but in the murder of Elizabeth Short."

"As the years went on," Lesnick says, "Smith's ego drew him closer, not to confessing, but wanting to tell someone in a roundabout way what he got away with primarily through luck, and if he could make a few bucks, all the better."

Even with Smith's long, violent record on file, he remained an enigma for the detectives. His criminal record showed sex offenses and arrests for sodomy, yet he said he never knew the "queers" Morrison palled around with or those in the "she-he" joints.

Lesnick says the suspect was born under what appears to be unusual circumstances. "His father refused to give the child a name, and the birth certificate for the 5th day of August in 1920 was left blank where it calls for the child's full name." Opposite the mother's name, Minnie Buchanan, the father's name, Alex F. Wilson, was written in and then crossed out. Sometime later the name Grover Loving is inserted as father and the child is named Grover Loving, Jr.—though "Wilson," in parentheses, was written in following the mother's last name.

Physician Atlee R. Olmstead, Lesnick says, delivered the baby at eight in the morning in a house on southwest Francis Street in the southern section of Canton, Ohio. With those corrections on the birth certificate, the "no" for legitimate was crossed out, but a second "no" was scribbled onto the document. Information that was to surface was sketchy at best. His parents—if in fact they *were* married—were from Newland, North Carolina. In Ohio his father was a machinist, if in fact Alex Wilson *was* his father, and worked for the Timken Roller Bearing Company plant in Canton.

"Grover Loving, Jr. was raised in a somewhat rundown neighborhood near Canton's industrial plants. There were no numbers on the houses in this section of town—no paved streets and no electric lighting.

"His father remained with the Timken Company, while Grover Loving, Jr.'s mother, Minnie, stayed home as a housewife. She was twenty-three when the child was born, and Alex was twenty-six.

"It appeared that the mother of either Alex Wilson or Minnie Buchanan came to Canton from the Newland region in

North Carolina and lived in that house when Wilson and Minnie relocated to southern California, leaving the boy behind. Apparently he remained in Canton with the relative from Newland. Though it appears he was shuttled back and forth between Canton and North Carolina, most of his early years were spent growing up in Ohio."

Lesnick was able to obtain documentation that Wilson (aka Smith), while incarcerated during the fall of 1958 in Oakland city prison, California, told an inmate a story about a "queer's" head he'd seen in a glass box in Cleveland. He'd said this was at the same time he saw Johnny Weismuller as Tarzan. "It would seem to tie in," Lesnick says, "with Wilson saying Elliot Ness had been outsmarted by a Cleveland killer that was never caught."

Forensic Psychologist Paul Cassinelli pointed out what Wilson said about seeing Sally Rand, the striptease artist: that he had "jacked off" in his pants while watching her dance in Cleveland. Sally Rand was featured at *The 1936 Great Lakes Expo* held in Cleveland. Esther Williams appeared in an aquacade with Johnny Weismuller, and the city of Cleveland had a police exhibit dealing with the Cleveland Butcher, which included a replica of one of the victim's heads contained in a glass box.

Although Wilson talked about the decapitated head as that of a homosexual, and spoke derogatorily about homosexuals in general, his rap sheet showed arrests for "crimes against nature"—sodomy—and he seemed to prefer the skid row homosexual bars and juke joints.

"Wilson seemed to prefer the company of low-lifes," Lesnick says, "the moochers, and apparently second-rate female impersonators. He referred to one being connected with a murder in Indianapolis, and he mentions this person working in a bar called the Pair of Jacks, and another joint, Jud Logan's Bar, in the same area. He alludes to that room in the 7000 block of West 10th Street, downtown; and all of this having some peculiar skid-row feeling of activity to it, and these talks about rape and murder that are in those transcripts—the methods mentioned by Wilson coming peculiarly close to actual conditions to do with the bathtub murder of Georgette Bauerdorf. Of course this became of great interest to the unsolved homicide division of the sheriff's department."

Consulted regarding Jack Wilson and the murders, Jonathan Pincus, M.D., Chairman of the Neurology Department, Georgetown University School of Medicine, pointed to Wilson's severe alcohol problem and history of violence mirrored in the personality of "the repeatedly violent individual" who may commit a first murder while in his twenties, but who would, in prior years, have been involved in aggravated assault. "The difference between aggravated assault and murder is just a matter of chance, very often," says Dr. Pincus.

"Alcohol is the primary drug that precipitates or worsens episodes of violence in individuals with a past history of violent behavior. The state of pathologic intoxication is not synonymous with ordinary drunkenness; it is a state in which the individual engages in a violent act after drinking." According to Pincus, drug or alcohol use by the killer would be suspected when the victim is "overkilled," such as in the Elizabeth Short and Georgette Bauerdorf murders.

"From the documentation," Lesnick says, "it appears that Smith, as Grover Loving, Jr., surfaced in Los Angeles in the late 1930s, then did not reappear there until 1942 as Jack Anderson Wilson. He had obtained an affidavit allegedly signed by his mother, stating that the birth certificate of Grover Loving, Jr. was inaccurate. His legal name was Jack Anderson Wilson, and Alex Wilson (dead for several years) was his real father. It's possible that Jack Wilson's mother and father were legally married in the hospital just before Alex Wilson passed away.

"With his 'rightful name' documented, Wilson now shows up in L.A., working as a sign hanger for Coger Brothers on Bixel Street. He gets picked up by the police for a selective service violation, then leaves the sign hanging job and drifts back to Indianapolis. He seems to hang out again with the female impersonator and turns twenty-four years old that August. He is bumming around the city until a young female, a WAC, is murdered in a downtown hotel. And it seems that immediately Wilson leaves

Indianapolis and turns up back in Los Angeles."

According to what the officials could piece together, Wilson next lived with his mother, Minnie, on 31st Street near San Pedro. There was a brief, questionable period of time in 1944 when he may have enlisted in the army, but served less than a year. And it was this year in particular that has been of significance to the sheriff's department.

Referring to the photograph he would not allow the informant to handle, Lesnick says, "It was possible that there was some writing on the back of the photograph, plus it might have been taken by a photographer, like the kind who took pictures in night spots and restaurants, quickly developed them, and sold them to the parties. They also put their name or company and phone number on the back in case you wanted to order copies. If Wilson had paid for the photograph, it was possible that copies existed."

The sheriff's department obtained mug shots of Jack Wilson from the Medford, Oregon, police—one of Wilson's many arrests. He had been a cook at the Veterans' Administration hospital when he was arrested for public drunkenness. Detective Louis Danoff, working on the unsolved murders in the homicide bureau, compiled reports, transcripts, and documents on the suspect. The sheriff's record states "Jack Anderson Wilson is a possible plausible suspect for the Bauerdorf murder and the murder of Victim Short (The Black Dahlia Case) . . . to make or clear Wilson as a suspect requires that his prints be compared to the latent prints . . . obtained.

"The information obtained through an informant indicated that Victim Bauerdorf and Victim Short knew each other; worked at the same USO canteen; and that Victim Bauerdorf mentioned Victim Short, by name, in her diary . . . both victims were very attractive young women, with similar looks.

"The Bauerdorf case has been very hard to investigate due to the fact that the Bauerdorf family was very influential, and did everything it could to play the murder down. . . . A possible suspect was identified as a 6'4" soldier who walked with a limp, whom the victim was said to have expressed she was afraid of him."

Sheriff's files identify the soldier as:

> JACK A. WILSON, MW, DOB: 8/5/20 OTHER: 8/5/24
> AKAs: Jack Anderson Wilson; Jack Olsen; Hanns Anderson Von Cannon; Jack A. Taylor; John D. Ryan; Eugene Deavilen; Jack McCurry; Jack H. Wilson; Grover Loving; Grover Loving Wilson; Jack Anderson McGray; Jack Smith; Arnold Smith. . . .

When the informant talked to Smith about getting together at the 555 Club the last of January, he also asked him about a couple of little things that St. John had been interested in—some articles of clothing and a washcloth.

Did Smith have any recollection of items like that? "Yes. Some things were stuffed in a storm drain a couple of miles south on San Pedro. There was blood on the clothes—his clothes," Smith said. "He'd wiped all the makeup off her face with a washcloth. He threw that away with the clothes."

The informant told Smith that he had some extra money for *him*. "Not *extra*," he said, joking around a little. "But I got some bills here in my pocket for you, so we'll get a couple of drinks at Harold's, okay?"

Smith said that was agreeable to him. Then he said, "You know, I'll tell you something . . . If you look at the map of the city, and see where she was put, where the body was placed, it is the only section of the city that is shaped like a woman's pussy."

19

The Los Angeles Police Department was being handed the most perfect murder suspect for the Black Dahlia case," Joel Lesnick says, "and this guy wasn't going anywhere *near* the cops. He'd touched all three bases with that weird confession—if you want to call it that—and made it home free. . . ."

Lack of corroborating evidence can be sidestepped with the least amount of reasonable corroboration. In retrospect, suspect Smith knew this very well. "While he wanted the truth to be told," Lesnick says, "he wasn't willing to hang himself for it, so just as St. John figured, Smith pawned the murder off on a decoy."

Louise Sheffield, a former deputy sheriff, had been a criminal investigator for the state of California. She later was recruited by the Monterey Park Police Department, and as a detective worked a number of undercover assignments in connection with the LAPD narcotics division.

After conducting an undercover investigation into marriage counseling frauds for the California state legislature, she worked as investigator for IRS intelligence undercover operations investigating organized crime, and was contracted by then-Attorney General Robert Kennedy, to conduct undercover investigations into organized crime elsewhere in the United States.

"I was employed on a contract basis for Attorney General Robert Kennedy," Sheffield says, "because at that time there was no provision for female agents in the U.S. Government."

Shortly after her career as a criminal investigator for the state of California, Sheffield was contacted by William Herrmann, formerly with LAPD metro division homicide, to investigate the possible criminal associations connected with the "subject known at the time to use the alias of Arnold Smith. . . ."

"I did not recognize him as anyone I had come in contact with in the past," says Sheffield, "and I was unable to find or uncover any lead concerning the existence of an Al Morrison, a female impersonator."

Sheffield, as undercover agent, participated in a meeting with Smith just previous to the arrangements made for Smith's meeting with St. John. "This was ostensibly to discuss Mickey Cohen and the Al Morrison connection with Cohen, as described by Smith. He was a tall, gaunt, older man coming to see the person I was with, who was the LAPD informant. Smith seemed nervous and uncomfortable; and seemed to have a negative response toward me, just toward my presence. He said his name was Arnold Smith, and that he was here to talk to the other party. He spoke briefly about Al Morrison, and that Morrison had a record with San Francisco and Oakland police. He did not mention the name Elizabeth Short.

"He appeared to be in his 60s, and I received a highly unfavorable impression of him. In fact I remember stating, after he left, something to the effect that the man appeared to be crippled, as he walked with a noticeable limp. He left almost immediately, although encouraged to stay by the party I was with.

"Through William Herrmann I was able to connect the man I had met as being the one Herrmann believed was linked to the Black Dahlia murder, though naming Al Morrison as the suspect. The individual I had met was later identified as Jack Anderson Wilson, but I was unable to make connections with any organized crime members and the individual I'd met."

According to Detective Herrmann and the undercover agent, it appeared that Al Morrison did not exist. Everything that could be traced or revealed about Morrison was looked into—his Indianapolis background, his connection with female impersonator clubs, underworld or "street" contacts, and the records division of the San Francisco Police Department. Nothing could be found.

To Forensic Psychologist Paul Cassinelli, and to Dr. Walter Finkbeiner, chief of autopsy services at the University of California Medical Center in San Francisco, an interesting aspect of Smith's observations was his cryptic references to the 39th and Norton area. "In a sense," Cassinelli says, "you could compare such a siting to the very condition Ms. Short presumably had, an undeveloped vagina; a 'blank' place. And then carrying this somewhat further, you have this same area developed and resembling the genitals of a female—as pointed out by the suspect who makes the statement that 'the place where she was left is in the shape of a woman's pussy.'

"Without interviewing Smith, one cannot presume to explain his reasons or to attempt a logical conclusion since it is a completely subjective thing."

He knew the area—knew the city and the maps of the city during his sign-hanging days, and while working there he lived on 31st Street. When Coger Brothers moved to Exposition Boulevard, it was a "beeline" as Aggie Underwood called it, and exactly midway between Smith's place of residence and where the body of Elizabeth Short had finally been deposited.

"In some way," says Cassinelli, "Smith discovered that Elizabeth Short was 'imperfect.' When Smith discussed a night in a hotel in some of his interview, it was as though he had staged what was to come—a preview that she would be dead and he would be with the body, or the part of the body that he selected to be with, previous to some form of 'separation' as he called it, or possibly *following* such a procedure."

She had a condition that kept her from fulfilling a normal relationship with a man, the psychologist said. "But she liked men, enjoyed their company, partied with men, was a fun companion and always out for a good time, without having sexual relations—specifically intercourse. She sided with underdogs, 'wallflowers,' because, despite her vivaciousness and natural beauty, she was a wallflower herself."

"Smith knew about Short's problem. He said, 'She couldn't be fucked,' and that there was 'nothing there.' His clue was in selecting the location to place the body in full view, suggesting that he had fixed the situation.

"What he called the decorations on the body—the crisscross cuts in the rather hairless pubic area, done after death, represented deliberate decorating in the manner of a grid.

"The lacerations on the abdomen, the four-inch incision, might well have served some sexual purpose for him, unrelated to the markings in the pubic area. It would be too peculiar a coincidence," Cassinelli says, "that Short had the problem she did—and the place where her body was left had the shape of the female genitalia, and had been missing that same shape previously. He *had* cut an opening in her body above the pubic area, 'correcting the problem,' as it were, and possibly using this alteration for sexual purposes. Though due to the excessive cleansing of the body, there were no traces of spermatozoa."

Dr. Walter Finkbeiner examined areas of the Short autopsy report and compared facts with the transcripts of Wilson. He then reported, "The descriptions of the murder contained in the transcripts were consistent with the information provided in the pathologist's testimony."

The slight curvature of the spine, as noted, would appear consistent with the manner described in which the upper body was lowered into a tub, from an angle of support or partial support beneath a region higher than the shoulder blades but below the shoulder, consistent with the upper torso having been in a reclining position; while the lower section indicated the body had been semi-recumbent.

Shortly before Lesnick began piecing together the puzzle of the Bauerdorf murder, Dr. John Money, director of the psychohormonal research unit at Johns Hopkins University School of Medicine, had received copies of the Smith transcripts with great interest.

To Dr. Money, Smith fit the profile of the lust murderer, one quite likely to have spent a period of time getting socially acquainted with his victim and not having stalked a stranger. According to Dr. Money the relationship can initially appear indistinguishable from ordinary affectionate dating. The bond of affection may have been consummated in sexual intercourse or other genitoerotic activity on several occasions prior to the fateful encounter, which culminated in lust murder.

Dr. Money read the Smith transcripts and the coroner's documents while flying to Berlin for a conference. Nine days later, upon returning to Baltimore, he wrote: "There is insufficient information in the documents for me to arrive at any conclusion regarding Ms. Short's genital status. If she did have the androgen-insensitivity syndrome, that would not necessarily have rendered her incapable of sexual penetration. For some patients have a blind vagina, although short, that is progressively lengthened over a period of time, as a sequel to repeated penile penetration, with the penis acting as a dilator.

"Despite the incoherence of parts of the interview, the overall content is consistent with the possibility that Ms. Short met her death as the victim of a lust murderer. Its Greek name is erotophonophilia. . . .

"If a lust murderer commits multiple lust murders, as is sometimes the case, then all of them are usually carried out in the same way.

"I think it is very likely that Arnold Smith was himself the murderer of Ms. Short."

Following Dr. Money's examination of the subject, Joel Lesnick compared the Short murder with the Bauerdorf homicide that was being handled by Detective Sergeant Louis Danoff, in charge of unsolved murders for the sheriff's department. Danoff's file on the Bauerdorf case includes Jack Wilson's fingerprint classification, mug shot, and arrest record and statements relating to Wilson.

Both murders involved the body being in a tub of water, and strangulation or partial strangulation by the insertion of something into the mouth or throat, as opposed to pressure on the surface of the neck. Although in the case of Short, ligature marks on the neck existed, but without damage to the interior.

In reports on Bauerdorf, the material wedged in her throat was torn at the teeth, clenched shut in death. In the Short case, the black underpants were removed from the mouth when the victim was unconscious. No blood was found in the throat or larynx from the hemorrhage that the coroner claimed was due to lacerations of the face.

In fact, the most startling and significant piece of information in the Short case was in clear contradiction to the cause of death as ruled by the coroner. The lack of blood in the victim's throat would have been consistent with Smith's claim of material being inserted into Short's mouth to serve as a gag. Smith describes the amount of blood absorbed by this material. The gag would have caused unconsciousness from suffocation or strangulation, as in the Bauerdorf case, though from the autopsy it appears that Short had not met death by suffocation.

"Death resulted at the time of the severing of the body, and this is supported by the *ecchymosis* discovered along the line of incision, and at the location described by Smith, where blood spurted out, as he put it," Lesnick says. "The blade severed an artery, and death was almost instantaneous due to the hemorrhage at *that* point. The rest of the sectioning of the body occurred quickly, almost simultaneously.

"Whether Smith believed she was dead or not, he indicates surprise that blood 'spurted' from the body. So hemorrhaging *was* the cause of death, but not due to lacerations of the face but during the torso being cut in half."

Their conclusion left no doubt that the two homicides bore similarities, though Lesnick believed that with Bauerdorf the murder had probably not been the suspect's initial intent, but came about during the assault. The beating Bauerdorf endured was very similar to the blows inflicted upon Short.

Although Smith was a strong suspect in the Bauerdorf murder, as could be proven by comparing his fingerprints to latent prints from the murder scene and from Bauerdorf's automobile, LAPD would find it difficult to gather physical evidence linking him to the Black Dahlia murder—apart from the circumstantial evidence. Lesnick says, "Smith seemed willing to divulge the most pertinent information to do with the Short murder—through using his decoy device—but only once did he mention the Hollywood Canteen."

LAPD detectives, while reluctant to combine any efforts with the sheriff's department, sought diligently to uncover any shred that might have been overlooked by Smith in his skillful erasure of *any link to the murder, except as hearsay*.

According to another detective, John St. John left "no stone unturned." His relentless, perceptive abilities at detection were riveted to the sketchy overview of the murder—like a muddy pond with a few sparkling shapes appearing and disappearing—those fragments that some detectives believed *only* the murderer could have known. St. John wanted anything— "a laundry list," he said to the informant, "a snapshot of them together—maybe a letter, *something* showing some concrete link between Short and Smith, and with that I can move ahead and work on some corroboration, but with*out* it, I'm stuck with the hearsay and circumstantial evidence. I don't mean to say that isn't good enough to solve this damn case, but before I can *do* that—and with this suspect I think I *can*—I need even a damn laundry list with her name or his and hers, and anything that makes a connection between the two. . . . If you had that photograph from the bar that he showed you, and that stuff in the box, that could do it; that could be the key I'd need to close the books on this one."

By now the *Herald-Express* and the *Examiner* had merged into the *Herald-Examiner*, but lost none of its flair for sensationalism. Searching through the rumors, and notified by police beat and sheriff's liaison, the newspaper managed to obtain a story based on the informant's information from Smith. The *Herald-Examiner* ran a front-page story. In the article, it mentioned that the "other person" referred to by Smith was operating a bar in Nevada.

St. John contacted the informant, concerned that such a "leak" might not only spook Smith but, if in fact he had possibly been involved with an accomplice in the murder, would make it almost impossible to track someone with such an "alert advantage."

"I'm not mad at you," St. John said to the informant, "but I am concerned. I want to keep a lid on this. The press will blow it up and this could jeopardize any serious work on the case—maybe making it impossible to get a real fix on this guy."

Smith wasn't returning any of the informant's calls that were made to the Chinese café. At the same time, the café was being staked out—an effort to zero in on Smith and track him to where he lived, in order to obtain the connecting evidence sought by St. John.

Following a late-night call to the informant from a Hill Street pay phone, Smith said he had to go to San Francisco and needed more money. A meeting was talked about for the following week, allowing Smith time to stay drunk in the 7th Street hotel room he had occupied for the past four years, a solitary, almost shadow-like individual. A few days after the call, Smith passed out on his bed, and within a short time was swallowed up in flames.

20

When the fire broke out, one resident of the Holland Hotel hurried the block and a half to the fire station to report the fire. Station 11 and nine other engine companies responded to the alarm. Only one room was involved in the raging fire, but it was a threat to the entire building.

When the engines arrived, it was apparent the fire had been in progress for some time. The room was fully involved and the glass panes of the two windows that overlooked 7th Street had burst outward from the blaze.

"The interior of the room was well burned," recalls the fire captain, "with the plaster-like wall surfaces and the underlying support structures burned away to expose the framing of all four of the walls and the ceiling. All of the furniture of the room was totally burned, including most of the bed mattress.

"The carpeting on the floor was somewhat protected by the heavy debris of wall plaster and the ceiling that had crumbled and fallen down."

The firemen found a body while fighting the fire. But since the flames were still very strong, it was not until approximately

35 minutes later, when they had extinguished the fire, that they were able to make a pronouncement.

The manager of the hotel told the officers that room number 202 had been rented by Jack Wilson, whom he said was very tall and thin, and walked with a limp. He told them Wilson had received a social security check in the mail, cashed it, and left the hotel. When he returned, he was carrying bottles in a paper sack. The manager said Wilson had lived at the hotel about four years, was a heavy drinker and smoker, and there had been four different minor fires in the room from Wilson's apparently careless smoking.

The body was lying to the left of the bed, which had collapsed on the floor. The head was back, and the legs were bent at the hips and the knees with the feet doubled backward. The right arm was bent into the "pugilistic position" at the shoulder, according to firemen, and the left arm was extended from the shoulder and covered with debris that had fallen. The superficial and deep skin surfaces were burned away to the muscle structure over all of the body and extremity surfaces, except for a small area of the left buttock. The posterior side of the left upper back and shoulder were somewhat protected from the effects of the fire.

He was described as a Caucasian, with a height of approximately 76 inches; the body appeared to be very slender, with one leg shorter than the other. There were apparent upper teeth, but the front teeth were badly damaged by the fire.

Everything in the room burned except two keys on a metal ring, a fob-like item, the burned remnant of a $1 bill, and fragments of red clothing that were found under the body in places where there had been some protection from the fire.

The charred corpse was sealed in a black plastic body bag and delivered to the new Los Angeles County morgue, where it was tagged "John Doe Number 51."

From the "Unidentified Person Report" to the "Examination at Forensic Science Center," and several "Confidential Interdepartmental Work Sheet" documents, a composite profile was compiled on John Doe Number 51, also listed as "probably Jack Anderson Wilson," also known as Arnold Smith. One work sheet presents the possibility that the death was "possibly other than accidental."

Douglas Stark of LAPD turned the matter over to Arson Investigator Thomas Derby, who examined the room for evidence of arson. But the investigator could find nothing indicating that possibility, "because everything was burned, and there was a history of Wilson having caused four previous fires; but the room was so completely involved in the fire that it would be impossible to determine if arson was involved."

Since the decedent was being considered a suspect in an unsolved murder, the matter was returned to homicide.

When St. John was informed that the death might not have been an accident, he said he didn't believe it. "If it *wasn't* accidental, then it's suicide, and maybe someone who drinks as much as this individual is purported to have drank, then it's a pretty close call anyway."

Disappointed with the news of the death, St. John believed he still had a chance of closing the book on the case, and continued to dig for evidence linking Wilson to Elizabeth Short.

Wilson's five-page arrest record ranged from burglary to assault with deadly weapons; to armed robbery, sodomy and sexual assault; to drunkenness and resisting arrest— "not uncommon for some serial killers," says psychologist Cassinelli.

He had been arrested in several states and used more than a dozen aliases and three different social security numbers. He had been collecting benefits on a North Carolina social security number—which ended. The checks stopped coming after the news of his death.

The deputy coroners at the morgue were attempting to trace dental charts and veteran's records, seeking concrete identification—always a difficult process with badly charred bodies.

The suspect came into the world with a question mark for a name, and was delivered to the morgue with a question mark. The room he had occupied in the Holland Hotel was scarcely bigger than a cell. The tub in the cramped bathroom was half-sized, less than two feet across, and had no shower.

St. John's attempts to link Wilson conclusively to the Black Dahlia murder would span the next eight months—the length of time Wilson's body was held at the morgue pending disposition.

Deputy Medical Examiner George E. Bolduc, M.D., performed the autopsy on Wilson's unembalmed corpse. Dr. Bolduc reported "extensive charring and burn loss of most of the skin of the head, neck, trunk, and extremities.

"However, there is preserved skin over the posterior left forearm including hairs and there is also skin over the lateral left thigh extending to the anterior surface. This also has preserved skin and there is also preserved skin extending from the left thigh down onto the lateral left leg. There is also a large portion of preserved skin over the posterior left back. There are contractions of the elbows bilaterally as well as the knees bilaterally and the fingers of the hands are clenched forming fists.

"There are heat fractures of the right and left elbows and of the tibia and fibula bilaterally, as well as of the right ankle. There is the stump of a penis present, and the testes are also present and bilaterally descended. There is heat contracture of the scrotum. There are numerous loops of small bowel extending through tears of the right and left abdomen. These show heat coagulation of their serosal surfaces. There is exposure of the anterior chest from charring away of the soft tissues of this area, with exposure of the underlying lungs bilaterally, through the exposed intercoastal spaces anteriorly.

"There is a large skull defect on the right due to burning away of the skull in this area with exposure of the contracted dura and brain from heat. There is a smaller defect in the skull on the left, also due to a fracture produced by heat. This also reveals the contracted underlying dura and brain from heat. Most of the soft tissues of the skull have been destroyed by heat, with associated charring of the outer surfaces of the skull."

Dr. Bolduc stated the cause of death as "acute smoke and carbon monoxide intoxication," with "extensive thermal injuries of the body including charring; smoke and carbon monoxide asphyxiation."

Joel Lesnick says, "It was like he was there—and then he was gone. . . . My feeling is that if he'd been arrested, he would have made a complete confession, filling in all the blanks—not only for the Bauerdorf murder, but for the Short killing as well."

In time the transcripts, documents, photographs, and CII report with an outline of Wilson's background from birth to death and a summary of the sheriff's records were examined by Deputy Chief of Police Ronald Frankle, by Assistant Chief of Police Robert Vernon, by Commander of Robbery-Homicide John White, and by Captain William O'Gartland of homicide.

Some time after Wilson's body was released for cremation by the county, the Los Angeles district attorney's office was presented with the file, following the review by the deputy chief of police, the assistant chief, and the commander of robbery-homicide. From the district attorney's office, a view on the case was expressed as follows:

> The case can not be officially closed due to the death of the individual considered a suspect. While the documentation appears to link this individual with the homicide of Elizabeth Short, his death, however, precludes the opportunity of an interview to obtain from him the corroboration. . . . Therefore, any conclusion as to his criminal involvement is circumstantial, and unfortunately, the suspect cannot be charged or tried, due to his demise. However, despite this inconclusiveness, the circumstantial evidence is of such a nature that were this suspect alive, an intensive inquiry would be recommended.
>
> And depending upon the outcome of such an inquiry . . . it is conceivable that Jack Wilson might have been charged as a suspect in the murder of Elizabeth Short—also known as the Black Dahlia.

She was walking down the boulevard in a black sheath dress covered with pink roses, a slight bounce to her stride. Then she was sitting in the café and her blue eyes were shining. There was something about her eyes that was disconcerting—puzzling. Not exactly an impersonal quality, not appraising, but not quite matching her smile—more a distance. She was looking off to one side, her back against a window. Behind her, through the glass, the yellow trolley moved down the street.

When she looked at you she was soft. Her eyes were soft. She had to go, she said. She smiled. She didn't know when she'd get back. In fact, she wasn't sure where she was going! She laughed a little.

She left the café, walking with that fluid motion of her body. For a second she looked around, glancing back, her head lowered slightly and her eyes looking to their corners as she raised one hand slightly.

AFTERWORD

AFTERWORD

by John Gilmore

A sweltering dusk in the midst of an L.A. heat wave a few days before Thanksgiving. Under a darkening, moonless night, the downtown buildings looked as flat as a movie set. I was on Main Street, going to meet the man who had known the Black Dahlia thirty-five years earlier. I'd been trying to get together with him again for a long time. Although he had often phoned, suggesting we meet in a seedy hotel lobby or some other joint, half the time he never showed up.

For two years it had been touch and go whether the meeting would take place. This time when he called, he wanted to talk about the murder. He said, "I've got some urgent information."

As with any of these wild goose chases, I had no way of knowing that this man would become the closest to a shoe-in for Elizabeth Short's killer than anyone before him, or anyone after him.

On the phone, he'd said that if he wasn't in the Anchor Café, where we'd met before—a dingy narrow hole among a string of dark bars—the Filipino would know where he was. The air along Main Street was choked with exhaust as I walked past the pawnshops, tattoo parlors, and stinking doorways.

Through the Anchor window I looked at the peeling walls and greasy counter, at the yellow flypaper, black with its catch, wavering in the breeze of an electric fan. The skinny Filipino sat hunched on a stool, one eye closed as if the upper lid were sewn against the jutting-up cheekbone. He didn't know Arnold Smith. The man he knew was Jack—Jack Arnold, he said, rasping and sucking on a cigarette. Jack Arnold was one of many aliases for the man I was hoping to meet once again.

The Filipino stared at me with his one seeing eye, then behind me, as if making sure I was alone. He smiled. Teeth were missing. He said, "Jack said you'd give me ten bucks." Okay, I agreed. I pulled out ten bucks. He reached for it with a skinny, twisted hand. His parched skin was stretched as tight as a drum skin against his skull. He took the ten and said Jack was at the 555 Club. I said okay, and his lips closed clam-like over the wet end of the butt.

Outside, a big bearded man, wearing a ragged black coat fastened with pins and dirty adhesive tape, was pressing his face against a brick wall. He was talking to "God," jerking his arms up and down.

In 1947 the south end of the building housing Harold's 555 club had been called the Majestic Malt Shop—a frequent hangout of the Black Dahlia. The 555 had the biggest neon, an orange and white and pink sputtering sprawl, except for the burnt-out sockets. The windows had been blackened from the inside with stove paint that had peeled in spots, through which the dim interior light leaked.

The barroom was cavern-like, with ceilings so high you couldn't see them in the dark. Out of this blackness emerged a maze of huge metal ducts and pipes. Plaintive music—almost the gasps of a drowning woman—filtered from speakers mounted above the bar that ran the length of the south wall. "You're My Thrill"—a song from the mid-1930s, popular again during World War II—played scratchy and gauze-like. Pink lights illuminated the bar and its rows upon rows of liquor bottles. Some men were bent over billiard tables and others slumped at the bar. Some laughed or talked as if in hushed tones—others stared into their drinks. A few shapes could be made out in the dark corners. Light from a toilet door cast a yellow box on the concrete floor.

For maybe half an hour I sat in a booth with two bottles of beer. And then Arnold Smith limped into the bar. He was at least six-foot-four but rake thin, his gaunt body stooped in an almost S-shape, head bent at an angle. The long, unshaven face seemed pushed in from the sides—his mouth was an almost lipless slit, tightened as if by a wire at the back of his head.

The dark hair was badly cut and mussed, he wore a blue shirt and baggy pants, and the shoes were worn down at the heels. He stood just inside the doorway for a long time, and when he finally came to the booth, he didn't say anything. Just sat and stared at me as though it was an effort to raise his glance higher than shoulder line. The dark, bloodshot eyes showed nothing. It was a face made of cardboard. I was surprised he'd showed up, and cautious—wary that I'd make a wrong move and send him limping back into the shadows.

I slid the beer across the table. Only then did I notice the rumpled brown bag held against his side, about a foot long and as wide as a cigar box. He kept it pressed to his side as he drank the beer. He looked like a corpse.

"Like I said to your ex-wife," he said, "I saw you on television about that Hinckley kid taking a shot at the President."

"That was a while back," I said.

"Didn't exactly hit the fuckin' target, did he?" Smith's dirty fingers were yellowed with nicotine. "Got that fat guy. Is he dead—that fat guy?"

"No," I said. "As far as I know, he's still alive. Attempted assassinations are a little rough going."

His mouth moved to laugh—a slight smirk or just a reflex before he stuck a cigarette between his lips. Even as he struck a match, he kept his right wrist leaning against the package. He asked if I'd been paid to talk about Hinckley on television. "No," I said. "It was the news."

"You got any money?" he asked. He poured beer into a glass, spilling foam on the table. He wiped at it with his cuff. His head bent back a little as he raised the glass and drank, but the eyes were lowered toward me. I nodded. I had some money. He lowered the glass and set the package on the table.

"There's a picture I want you to see," he said, unfolding the sack and reaching into it. He brought out an old See's candy box wrapped with rotten rubber bands. One snapped, shredding, as he tugged them off. "Get us a couple of shots," he said. He wanted whiskey, and more beer to chase it.

When I got back from the bar, he had lifted the lid off the candy box, which was placed on the seat next to him. Inside were old photographs, folded papers, cut-out newspaper articles, and some black material I couldn't make out in the dimness.

Like a flashlight beam, Elizabeth Short's face seemed to shine straight out of the photograph he took from the box. There she was—the Black Dahlia. She seemed to be the only one in the group shot whose face was directly in line with the lens.

I reached for the picture, but he said, "I'll show it to you." He held it by the edges; he didn't want me to handle it or see the back of the photo. The black-and-white emulsion was lined and cracked as though it had once been carried in a wallet. I put my beer down and leaned forward. "Where was it taken?" I asked.

"Right here," he said. He meant the room we were in. With a kind of smile, he said, "Just about where you're sitting," and, turning his head, stared at the floor. I followed his gaze, thinking he'd dropped something. He said there was a line on the floor where a wall had been removed. "See," he said, "the wall in this picture used to be right here. That's the can—the toilet in the bar. Now it doesn't have that sign and that light on it. Maybe '53—after the Korean War's when they took out the wall and made it one joint instead of two." He gazed up and said, "A couple years ago they took out the ceiling that'd been in here since back before Pearl Harbor. You can't see up there in this goddamn light, but we're sitting right about the same place this picture was taken."

I studied the photograph again. To the right, in half-profile, was a younger version of the gaunt face across the table from me. The girl on Short's right looked like Ann Toth, the bit player. "Yeah," he said. "She drove downtown that day instead of them taking the streetcar. She brought her down here. You don't recognize the other guy? Not the gob, but the one that looks like a faggot?" I said I couldn't tell.

He didn't say anything more but laid the picture face up in the lid of the candy box. He carefully unfolded the piece of black cloth—a lady's hankie, with a red lace border and a small American flag embroidered with the letter "E." He called my attention to the photo again. "Look at her shirt on the right side." I could make out something that looked like the same handkerchief, fastened to the blouse by a flower-shaped broach. He said, "This hankie was hers. It's the one in the picture."

"How did you come by it?" I asked.

"That's an easy one," he said. "It was in her purse the day she was murdered. . . ." The handkerchief had been given to him, he claimed, by the faceless figure he so often quoted, the one he said who knew all the facts about *her*.

How would this other silhouette person have known so much? Arnold Smith or Jack Arnold said, "Now you're asking the 64,000-dollar jackpot question." The answer, he said, was going to cost somebody something, which brought us to the circumstances of "this meeting right here."

The important thing, first, was to frame a scenario to keep whatever information he had from "turning back" on him, so that he would not be implicated by details that related to "this so-called open homicide."

What would be related to me would be, technically, hearsay evidence. "In other words, what I'm saying to you," he said, "is something that's been said to me. I'm passing it on." The same sort of situation, he said, existed in what I'd written about Charles Schmid—the boy who thrill-killed three girls and buried them in the desert. "His buddy rats on him," Smith said, "to kind of get himself removed from the situation of being implicated in Schmid's shenanigans. Hearsay evidence, you see. That's the guarantee so my rights won't be in any jeopardy—the Fifth Amendment rights."

When he closed up the candy box, another rubber band snapped. He picked up the pieces and dropped them into the empty beer glass. Again he offered what came close to a grin. He mentioned the Toro bar across the street, said it used to be called the Dugout.

"One time she was giving a blowjob to a sailor in a back booth, and nobody was paying any fucking attention," he said. Well . . . almost nobody." Someone, he said, saw it as a betrayal. "Going against what someone's got in their thinking," he said. Folding the sack around the deteriorating candy box, he said, "That's why she wasn't living any longer than she did."

Over a period of several weeks, this man who seemed to be several in one, at once devious and exact, laid before me a tale that was indeed too "urgent" to be ignored—especially by the police. He blamed someone else for the murder but recalled details only the killer could have known.

Smith's rendering of Elizabeth Short's murder, as detailed in the supposed second-party "confession" by the untraceable Al Morrison—the man the cops, sheriff's detectives, and feds failed to put a proper face to—presented a portrait of her death with such precise detail that LAPD's team handling the still-open homicide summoned all their immediate resources to nab Smith in their "circumstantial" net.

My sojourn with Detective John St. John, LAPD's "Badge No. 1," followed some last meetings with Arnold Smith. The diverse pieces of the puzzle surrounding Short's death were linking together in a somewhat startling manner. I had gone as far as possible in my personal investigation. Unless the cops could examine the findings and weigh them against what they knew, Smith would remain as ambiguous as he appeared: a man who maybe knew more than he should, a man who claimed to know the killer and was now handing him over. Presenting Smith's version of the Black Dahlia murder to John St. John offered the chance of corroboration, or at least the official documentation of it—which would prove most important in my own work. However, I had not anticipated "Jigsaw" St. John's reaction.

"*This* is the guy," St. John said, "that I've got to talk to!" Where did Smith get his information? "He's pulling your leg," the detective said, "with this story of another guy confessing to him these details nobody knows—the guy knows more than *I* do!"

St. John quickly decided that Smith was using the shadow figure of Al Morrison as a smoke screen, through which he could admit his own involvement in the murder. "I've got to talk to him. Where can we find him? Will he come in and talk to us? Can you bring him in?"

Impossible.

Arnold Smith seemed outspoken earlier, but now he became as cagey as a rat, buttressing his tale of Morrison, and his own "hearsay evidence" position, like a man thrusting up straws against a collapsing wall.

Again and again, St. John reviewed the story and the three tapes of Smith discussing Short and the murder. The detective was convinced that the information answered the question—once and for all—of "Who did this?" No throbbing, twisted ego could rest without being recognized for an act so devastating. But how to escape the consequences? That was Smith's dilemma.

"He's blaming somebody else for the homicide, but he's got details only the killer could know—or details only the killer could have told him," St. John said. "He either takes us to this other joker or takes the rap for it himself. . . . This is the break I've waited for. All I need is to make a connection between Smith and Short—linking them together at the same time. . . . The perfect piece of evidence is the photograph you saw. With that, we'll bring him in, and I'll close the book on this case. I'll retire after fifty years of working this shit by closing the door on this one."

It wasn't inspiration that focused my attention on the Black Dahlia case—although curiosity and fascination played their parts. It was a matter of financial necessity. It was '63—times were a little rough—and tough-guy actor Tom Neal wanted to produce and star in a movie based on the case. I was living in Hollywood, writing screenplays and stories, and trying to keep my head above water. The deal with Tom offered cash up front and a big carrot on the other end when he raised the financing "to get the cocksucker on a roll," as he put it.

Tom knew a retired cop who gave him information about my father, about his connections in LAPD and his past ties to

L.A.'s former mayor, Fletcher Bowron. I took the "inside" door into LAPD and forged my associations with officers and detectives in homicide. After numerous ups and downs, the project with Tom collapsed almost two years later, when he was convicted of murdering his own wife in Palm Springs and sent to prison.

Actor/director Jack Webb of *Dragnet* fame, closely associated with members of LAPD's homicide, encouraged my unwillingness to give up on the case and prodded me to "keep hammering at the facts."

I met Elizabeth Short in late '46 when I was 11 years old. She had visited my grandmother's house with two male movie extras, seeking information about the "Short" side of my family—my grandmother's sister. They arrived in a large old Studebaker sedan with big oval chrome headlights. Beth Short was dressed in black, including black gloves. Her face was patted over with a kind of white, almost Geisha-like powder, and her lipstick was blood red. She talked to me about magic—one of my childhood interests—and I shared with her my posters of famous magicians I had seen at L.A.'s Shrine Auditorium and elsewhere.

Within months she was found dead. My father, a policeman working out of the Rampart division, was assigned to canvas the areas, repeatedly asking if anyone heard "screams" the night of the murder. In his police briefcase he carried a stack of photographs of the victim—a rendering from the morgue shot. My grandmother made me keep the girl's visit a secret from my father. What I understood was that if the police department knew the girl had been to our house months before her murder, my father would be questioned. Perhaps our family's chance encounter with the girl would burn a bad mark on his record. It would be years before he learned of Elizabeth Short's visit to my grandmother's house.

By then I'd gone too far in my "hammering at the facts" to turn back. Many people linked in some way to the Black Dahlia were still alive. I wasn't a cop. They'd talk without fearing that whatever they said "might be used against them."

A year later in Arizona I was involved as a journalist in the

Charles Schmid case. My connection to the killer himself, Schmid, formed my association with attorney F. Lee Bailey. I was responsible for bringing Bailey into the Arizona case, and for him subsequently defending Schmid in a second murder trial—resulting in my first true-crime book, *The Tucson Murders*.

My publisher, Dial Press, was interested in my work on the Black Dahlia case, which is how the concept for this book got started. I could not have imagined it would take more than twenty years to see the many puzzling pieces begin to form a picture—a study in shadow. The real story existed on the dark side of the moon. That's where I'd have to go.

In the Black Dahlia case, events and people moved in the dark toward uncertain destinations. Motivations and individual psychologies, riddled with ambiguity, intersected—collided—clashed, and scattered as if rebounding off one another. Where did it all lead?

Jack Webb said, "Maybe you're going too far with it; you're going beyond the usability of it in an entertainment sense. Sure, hammer at fact, but turn around when you got a shape hammered out and sell the sonofabitch. Move on to something else. Don't let it become an obsession. If you take one thing too seriously, you'll find yourself in a quagmire that's liable to suck you down under."

But I was hooked. It became a peculiar juggling act of those odd shapes and strange chunks. I'd jumped into that quagmire—a lonely hole—and I was heading for the bottom, not knowing what I would find. All I knew was, I had to keep going. It was an obsession, as Webb said, because I was chasing something and I didn't know what. I only knew that it was out there.

The first time I met Jack Arnold (who later told me he changed his name to Arnold Smith) was at a small gathering of Hollywood losers. The host, Eddie, a fence for burglarized electronics, was suspected by the FBI of being involved in an earlier kidnapping. Agents were always sniffing after him, seeking evidence. Eddie introduced me to Jack Arnold: "This guy knew that Black Dahlia gal you're talking about. He knew a couple guys she hung out with."

Arnold was a gaunt man with one leg shorter than the other,

a reclusive alcoholic who had been in and out of jails on charges ranging from sodomy to attempted murder. About Elizabeth Short, he said, "She was a fucking cockteaser. She'd swallow a dick like nobody's business."

"She swallow yours?" I asked him.

"I never said she did," he said. "She knew people I knew. . . . You'd have to ask them."

I did. And I asked Arnold more—again and again. He didn't want to talk, and only when he was thoroughly oiled did he let leak some sobering facts. He'd never refer to her by name—never "Beth," or "Elizabeth," not even "Short" or the "Dahlia." He'd say "her." He'd say, "She—you know who," and our sporadic chats would end with his abrupt, staggering departure.

This scene was repeated when my name was in the news—after I had appeared on television or been involved journalistically in some other crime, like the Sharon Tate murder—the eleven killings by Charles Manson and what he called the "family."

Arnold would be quick to call. We'd talk about murder or have hit-and-miss meetings in skid-row bars and decaying lounges near Hollywood. Hobbling up and down faster the more soused he'd get, the talk would invariably get around to "her . . . you know who I mean." Looking back the more than twenty years since he had last seen her, Arnold sketched rapid but precise pictures, many reflecting facts never made public. The corroboration on these gems proved infallible. He knew what he was talking about and who he was talking about. He knew "her," and only once mentioned "—that other one," but never named her, only said that she'd been found in "a bathtub."

From far and wide came little pieces of a seemingly distant puzzle. These little pieces began to fit neatly into an otherwise obscure picture—offering close-up glimpses into the veiled world they inhabited. Sleazy bars, dirty rooming houses, movie extras, a parade of drunken servicemen moving through Hollywood and Long Beach and Florida and Chicago. Mornings when no one knew the names. Figures dancing in dim-lit bars—then gone, no one knows where. Mystery and shadow.

Then, more than a dozen years after first meeting him in

Eddie-the-kidnapper's dingy hillside flop in Silver Lake, Jack Arnold or Arnold Smith made that call and said, "It's probably time we got together and talked about the murder."

"What murder?" I asked.

He said, "*Her* murder. You know who I mean. . . ."

Yes. Beautiful, ravishing Elizabeth Short, with a kind of sad loveliness that aroused desire in everyone. Yet some sacred element kept her from ever indulging in vaginal sex. Paradoxically, she would be sacrificed to an evil serpent—a tall, thin man with a crooked limp. Horribly frustrated artist and dreamer that he was, he had devised the most horrendous picture to thrust back at an unappreciative world. But not without an obscure signature. To read it with a normal mind was difficult, if not impossible.

"How do you feel about entrapping this fucker?" John St. John asked me in the homicide division of Parker Center. I said I didn't have a problem with it except that the "suspect" was quickly getting hip to what was happening. "Can you still get to him? Can you talk him into meeting with you?" the detective asked. I said I wasn't sure. I'd have to call that drop, leave a message. I didn't know how else to contact him. I told St. John I had someone tracking Smith down.

"You've got to realize how important this is to both of us," St. John said. "I want to shut this case down—I want to close this more than I've ever wanted anything. I can fucking *taste* it. You want to write this book. There could be a hell of a lot in it for you—for both of us—if we play the cards right. If we play ball together, we can both get what we want out of this, but I got to have him right here. I got to have him right here in the hot seat. I know this fucker like I know myself. He's pulling both ways—he's talking to you, and the other side of him's telling him to clam up. But the ego won't clam up. You can't shut up once you've gone this far in the water. I get him in here and we win the game."

But just days before his pending arrest, as if by a card sharp's sleight of hand, the tailor-made suspect with all the right answers—the first to emerge in the decades since Beth Short's murder—burned to death. His body burst like a skewered animal, and with death's rush went the hopes of an official end to the Black Dahlia case.

Was it arson? An accident? Homicide? Suicide? What difference did it make?

"It was in my hands," St. John said. "I could feel it. . . . We had it, but we lost him. . . . A once-in-a-lifetime chance."

LAPD's top brass, the coroner, the arson squad, and the district attorney's office made decisions—information was muffled, silenced. There was no way to indict or try a dead man. The detectives delayed disposition of the charred corpse in the morgue far longer than it should have been held, trying to quickly forge enough links to shut the door on the case with circumstantial evidence.

Though unwilling to let go, St. John could only carry on his crusade against the machinery for so long. "Times have changed," he said. "It was only thirty years ago I'd stuff him in a deep freeze until we'd turn that lead on this character, and then I'd sink it and walk away smelling like a rose."

But soon the burned body burned again—cremated by the county—thus shutting the door on the investigation, but not with a bang. It simply swung in on old, tired hinges, and the lock slid into place almost silently.

John St. John's dream of being the cop to "officially" break the Dahlia case had gone up in smoke with Arnold Smith. After more than half a century on the force, and as perhaps the last of L.A.'s true divisional detectives—the ones portrayed in all the old movies—John St. John crammed on his felt hat with the curled brim and creased crown and walked out, smelling like a rose anyway. Calling it quits, he retired shortly before the fiftieth anniversary of Elizabeth Short's so-called "unsolved" murder.

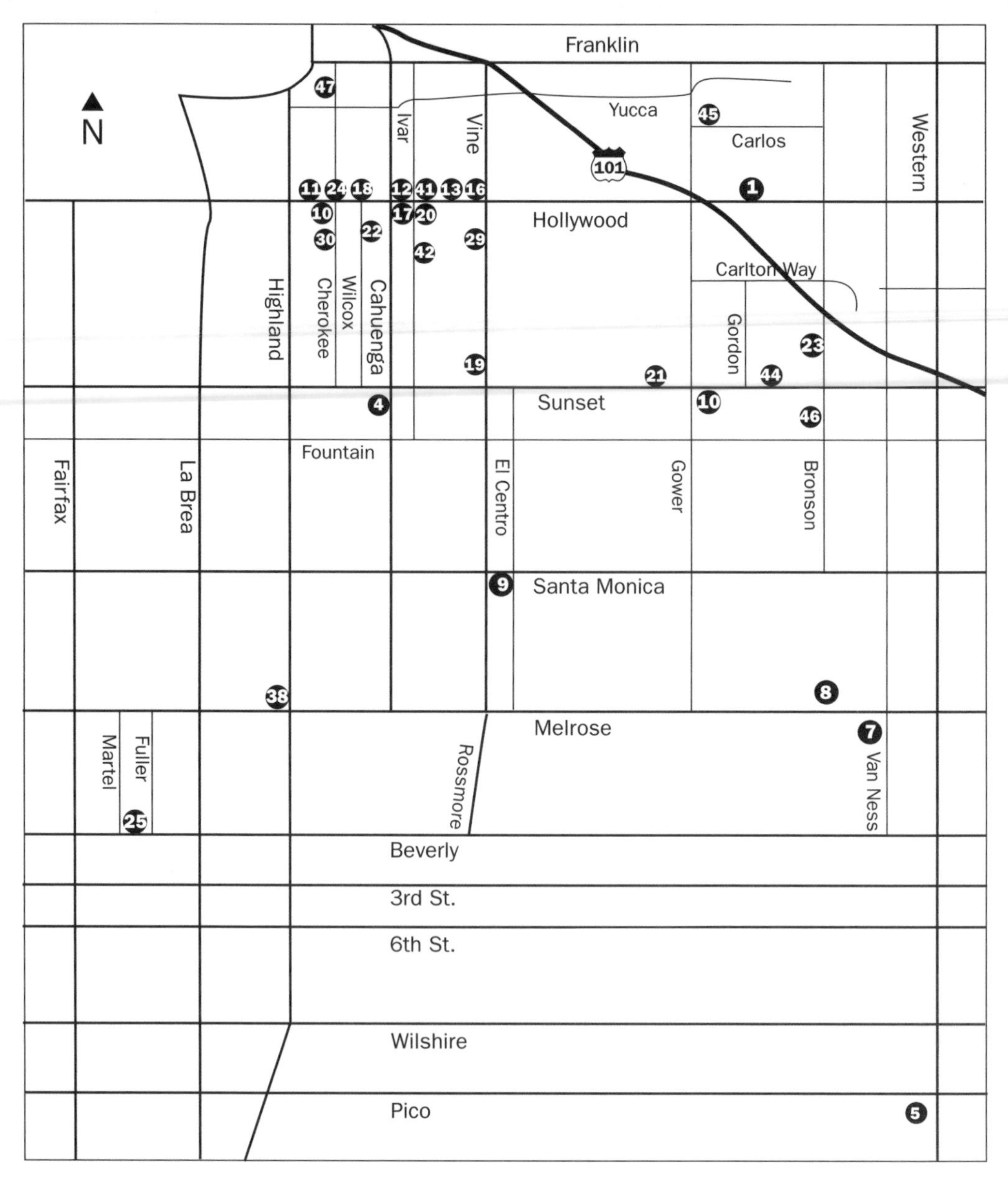

Places in Los Angeles frequented by Elizabeth Short

1. Florentine Gardens (Zanzibar Room), 5955 Hollywood Blvd.*
2. Roseland Roof, 833 S. Spring St.*
3. Pla-mar Ballroom, 937 W. 9th St.
4. Hollywood Canteen (USO club), 1451 Cahuenga Blvd.
5. Boogie Woogie Club, 1304 S. Western Ave.
6. Site of body discovery (inset)
7. Acorn Room, 5309 Melrose Ave.
8. Playboy, 5347 Melrose Ave.
9. Vagabond Isle, 6202 Santa Monica Blvd.
10. Pick Up Café, 6023 Sunset Blvd.
11. Streets of Paris, 6729 Hollywood Blvd.
12. Mayflower Coffee Shop, 6349 Hollywood Blvd.
13. Pig 'N Whistle, 6301 Hollywood Blvd.
14. Lime House, 708 New High St.
15. Club 49'er, 460 S. Main St.
16. Melody Lane, 6303 Hollywood Blvd.
17. Susie Q, 6700 Hollywood Blvd.
18. Stardust Café, 6445 Hollywood Blvd.
19. Tom Brenenman's Hollywood Night Club & Breakfast Café, 1552 N. Vine St.
20. Keystone Broadcasting System, 6331 Hollywood Blvd.
21. KNX Broadcasting, 6121 Sunset Blvd.*
22. Jack O'Brien Café, 1645 N. Wilcox Ave.

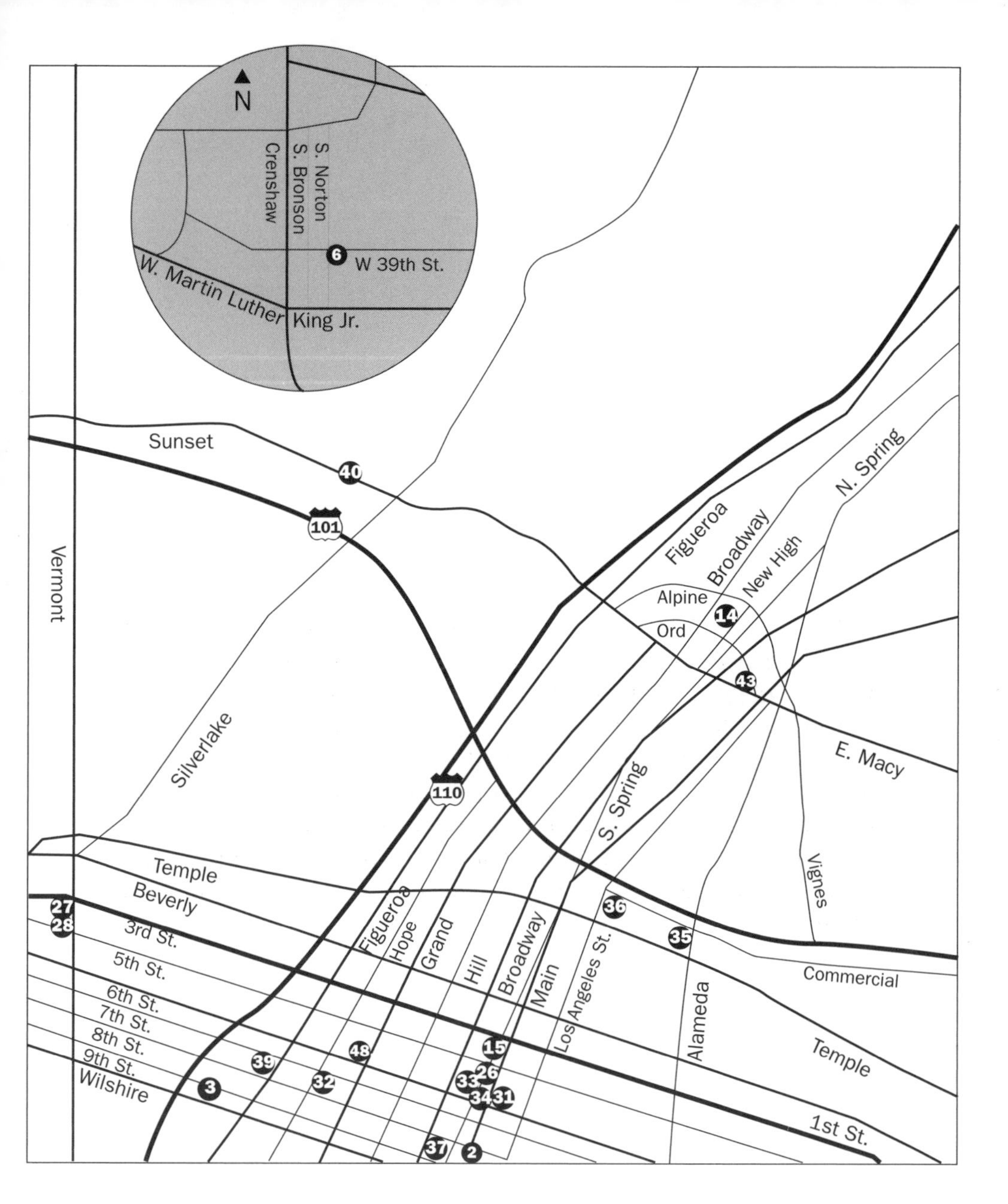

23. Oblath's Café, 723 N. Bronson Ave.
24. Snow White Waffle Shop, 6769 Hollywood Blvd.*
25. Spanish Kitchen, 7373 Beverly Blvd.
26. Rhapsody Club, 504 S. Main St.
27. Bimini Bowling Alley, 122 1/2 S. Vermont Ave.
28. Eduardo Cansino Dance Studio, 122 S. Vermont Ave.
29. 5-30 Grill, 1640 N. Vine St.
30. Steve Boardner's Bar, 1652 Cherokee Ave.*
31. Waldorf Cellar, 521 S. Main St.
32. Toto's Restaurant, Hope St. & 7th St.
33. Dugout, 506 S. Main St.
34. Majestic Malt Shop, 555 S. Main St.
35. Old Oriental Hotel, Alameda St. & Commercial St.
36. Italian Kitchen, Commercial St. & Los Angeles St.
37. Newsreel Theater, Broadway & 8th St.
38. Gaslights (& Under the Gaslights), 732 N. Highland Ave.
39. Zenda Ballroom Cafe, 936 W. 7th St.
40. Pucci Café, 3132 Sunset Blvd.
41. Radio Artists Agency, 6630 Hollywood Blvd.
42. Harout's Har-omar, 1605 N. Ivar Ave.
43. Green Dragon Café, Ord St.
44. KMPC Radio, 5939 Sunset Blvd.
45. Tamarind Apartments, 1756 Carlos Ave.
46. Bronson Arms Apts., 1417 N. Bronson Ave.
47. Residential Hotel, 1842 N. Cherokee Ave.*
48. Biltmore Hotel, 506 S. Grand Ave.*

* Still in existence

Born and raised in Hollywood, **John Gilmore** has traveled the road to Fame in many guises: child actor, stage and motion picture player, poet, screenwriter, low-budget film director, journalist, true-crime writer and novelist. He has headed the writing program at Antioch University, and has taught and lectured extensively; he currently divides his time between his native Los Angeles and an historic adobe in New Mexico. Having made an indelible mark in true-crime literature, Gilmore is now focusing on novels and a second book of memoirs.